VITAL STATISTICS
IN CORRECTIONS

Cover design and production by Capitol Communications, Inc., Crofton, Md.

ISBN 1-56991-073-1

This publication may be ordered from:
American Correctional Association
4380 Forbes Boulevard
Lanham, Maryland 20706-4322
1-800-222-5646

For information on publications and videos available from ACA, contact our worldwide web home page at:
http://www.corrections.com/aca.

FOREWORD

The American Correctional Association is pleased to present the latest edition of *Vital Statistics in Corrections*. This book compiles important statistical data on correctional systems throughout the United States and Canada. Detailed information about federal and state prison systems, jails and detention centers, probation and parole agencies, and juvenile departments is included, much of it in easy-to-read tables and charts. Their budgets and populations are included, as well as such specific information as the age and security classification of inmates.

In addition, *Vital Statistics in Corrections* provides useful information on compensation and benefits for correctional personnel, as well as information on unions and employee groups. Many topics in this edition have been added or expanded from previous editions including health care, the death penalty, computers, prison industries, and inmate fees. This book puts hard data at your fingertips, letting you know about a single jurisdiction and enabling you to compare that jurisdiction with others across the board. Using this book also is a good way to recognize emerging trends in corrections, providing valuable insight on where the profession is heading.

At the American Correctional Association, we take pride in the many publications and services that we provide, all of which are dedicated to the further improvement of corrections. If you would like more information about ACA membership and our publishing program, please contact us at 1-800-ACA-JOIN.

James A. Gondles, Jr., CAE
Executive Director
American Correctional Association

CONTENTS

MANAGEMENT ISSUES

PERSONNEL

CORRECTIONAL BUDGETS & EXPENDITURES

Operating and Capital Expenditures Budgets

Fiscal Year 1998

Fiscal information for adult and juvenile state departments of corrections

	ADULT CORRECTIONS		JUVENILE CORRECTIONS	
	Operating Budget	Capital Expenditures Budget	Operating Budget	Capital Expenditures Budget
AL	221,727,416	[1]	67,489,486	2,500,000
AK	153,710,004	32,293,012	25,570,100 *	7,000,000 *
AZ	535,257,200	11,459,000	40,008,700 †	674,215 †
AR	152,726,000	1,850,000,000	26,743,900	14,512,916
CA	4,024,313,000	273,627,000	375,207,000	24,945,000
CO	337,612,360 *	313,389,634 *	88,948,620 *	8,344,785 *
CT	413,466,479 [2]		32,444,050 *	—
DE	116,244,600 *	—	31,439,200 *	1,777,400 *
FL	1,654,465,125	78,510,365	332,129,487 †	53,382,379 †
GA	768,030,469	13,235,000	179,849,586 *	3,595,000 *
HI	117,336,029	17,165,000 [2]	15,541,818	—
ID	85,554,900	3,720,600		
IL	1,054,101,600	125,925,000	✦	
IN	409,700,000	209,305,590 [2]	✦	
IA	217,025,169	20,800,000	8,422,507 *	2,600,000 *
KS	203,875,834	15,165,409	68,500,000	1,400,000
KY	278,232,400	38,617,000 [2]	81,971,107	30,164,000 [2]
LA	516,378,702	79,205,000		
ME	82,192,808 *	—		
MD			135,882,134	45,300,526
MA	391,183,862	17,917,117	94,842,608 *	5,339,000 *
MI	1,441,935,000	15,000,000	80,034,200	37,200,000
MN	314,195,066	14,185,000		
MS	216,114,228	18,243,188	20,621,718	448,055
MO	416,223,234	199,980,585	46,169,325 *	—
MT	92,400,000	—	✦	
NE	85,259,906	31,815,383	15,888,990	—
NV	135,328,947 *	109,612,184 *		
NH	51,635,429 *	1,758,165 *	13,023,101	1,972,000 [2]
NJ	798,355,000	81,008,000		
NM	163,711,500 [3]	1,967,000	46,761,100	3,244,071
NY	1,891,138,562	429,062,000	357,536,000	74,463,000
NC	918,852,596	2,500,000	101,444,623	6,500,000
ND	25,602,100	7,809,500 [2]	6,733,700	2,185,200 [2]
OH	1,449,430,102	224,255,419 [2]	239,438,355	54,942,419
OK	385,601,641	—	67,498,378 †	—
OR	689,322,470 [1*]	12,134,402 [1*]	212,885,408 [2]	8,318,000 [2]
PA	951,004,759	525,437,204	82,272,000	—
RI	117,552,137	16,330,187	16,270,503 †	1,903,429 †
SC	313,558,599	43,482,177		
SD	45,590,509 *	—	✦	
TN	435,844,900	21,375,000	64,768,000	1,164,200
TX	2,084,338,005	39,300,000	233,054,702	13,483,909
UT	172,350,330	172,350,330	71,035,700	—
VT	45,202,137 *	6,200,000 *		
VA	661,968,500	6,665,103	180,389,671	13,576,839
WA	443,032,906	239,835,303	109,535,936	82,560,583 [2]
WV	53,300,000 *	67,693,337 *		
WI	700,464,800	157,000,000 [2]	100,814,500 *	—
WY	83,502,807	3,678,812 [2]	25,981,973 [2]	2,116,720 [2]
Total	26,915,950,127	5,549,013,006	3,697,148,186	505,613,646
FBP	2,865,733,000	433,917,000		
Cook	154,874,300	7,700,300		
NYC	786,126,000	83,057,000	95,542,799	11,342,000
PHL	140,963,704	101,790,000		
MB	59,878,900	—		
NS	39,430,000	—		
YK	8,726,000	—		
VI	14,943,440	24,000,000		

Notes:
† Data as of 3/30/97
* Data as of 3/30/98
✦ Combined Adult and Juvenile departments
1. Does not have capital expenditures budget
2. Biennial budget
3. Includes special appropriation

Major Operating Expenses

Fiscal Year 1998

Breakdown of operating budgets in preceding table.

	ADULT CORRECTIONS				JUVENILE CORRECTIONS			
	Salaries/ Benefits	Administration/ Operations	Maintenance/ Repair	Other	Salaries/ Benefits	Administration/ Operations	Maintenance/ Repair	Other
AL	137,414,339	70,658,690	2,738,786	10,915,601	27,547,123	16,361,857	928,170	22,652,336
AK	94,871,160	37,616,186	14,905,892	6,316,766	12,562,905*	12,536,600*	700,000*	469,900*
AZ	347,991,700	187,265,500	0	0	24,635,700†	14,854,500†	518,000†	—
AR	84,471,500	58,341,700	7,780,500	2,132,300	19,549,300	3,705,800		3,488,800
CA	2,618,075,000	1,065,346,000	—	340,892,000	318,798,000	51,282,000	5,127,000	—
CO	191,435,977*	143,472,038*	2,704,325*		38,339,341*	4,344,905*	—	46,009,459*
CT	270,450,041	54,710,331	7,125,017	81,181,086	16,750,457*	1,693,593*		14,000,000*
DE	74,283,700*	37,120,300*	4,840,605*	—	12,451,800*	17,124,700*	300,000*	1,862,400*
FL	1,099,986,694	532,807,563	21,760,868	—	93,718,324*	60,422,898*	509,559*	—
GA	526,392,481	212,919,384	1,987,624	26,730,980[1]	106,940,653*	71,273,656*	1,635,277*	—
HI	67,336,772	49,841,257	158,000		3,685,229	11,747,041	109,548	
ID	53,629,500	23,478,900	1,367,700	7,078,800[2]	9,050,100*	6,086,800*	—	11,006,300*
IL	745,400,800	299,931,000	2,691,200	6,078,600[3]	✦			
IN	293,676,510*	121,256,850*						
IA	170,025,169	45,480,153	1,441,602	—	7,773,284*	1,491,029*	169,198*	—
KS	106,327,421	73,201,998	2,477,694	21,898,721[4]	19,204,800	49,300,000	—	—
KY	139,562,400	38,089,100	—	100,580,900[5]	40,665,400	41,082,207	223,500	—
LA	230,654,663	62,863,879	2,797,953	220,062,207				
ME	50,727,393*	29,348,421*	618,151*	1,498,843*				
MD					61,594,573	74,287,561	—	—
MA	263,289,917	30,874,546	2,557,878	94,641,519	19,927,092†	6,587,092†	366,486†	44,975,029†
MI	997,294,400†	134,769,500†	—	215,631,300†	147,391,200	14,528,500	—	18,115,300
MN	175,280,882	136,258,177	2,656,007					
MS	111,026,835	57,918,610	1,200,000	45,998,783[6]	15,229,999	2,976,309	215,829	1,751,533
MO	221,072,960	193,898,776	1,251,500	—	28,136,969*	18,032,251*	—	—
MT	35,693,243*	44,229,571*	1,216,864*	1,510,455*	✦			
NE	58,649,420	21,751,865	4,118,621	740,000	8,250,568	7,638,422	—	—
NV	98,102,039*	33,264,792*	982,179*	2,979,937*				
NH					10,713,836	1,064,936	555,208	689,121
NJ	587,604,000	156,476,000	38,068,000	16,207,000	48,687,000*	7,993,000*	—	12,717,000*
NM	84,076,000	10,529,500	2,394,300	66,711,700	30,389,200	15,902,900	469,000	—
NY	1,561,083,000	330,055,500	—	—	—	—	—	—
NC	666,619,634	246,376,312	5,856,650	—	46,707,678	8,618,798	508,207	46,413,133
ND	13,576,200	10,845,100	605,200	575,600	4,549,200	1,891,000	230,500	63,000
OH	787,755,639	293,110,579	93,008,172	275,555,712[8]	111,022,478	69,569,290	1,972,823	56,873,764[9]
OK	197,322,300	179,542,015	8,737,326		29,825,327†	3,767,051†		
OR	296,100,626*	170,900,931*	4,844,928*	165,338,334*	105,541,651[10]	95,179,057[10]	1,427,692[10]	10,737,008[10]
PA	615,472,310	335,532,449	16,016,496	—	55,204,000	19,536,000	657,000	6,875,000[6]
RI	86,199,823	27,683,688	1,540,983	2,127,643	11,818,171†	1,704,225†	430,400†	2,317,707†
SC	223,311,815	87,729,303	2,517,481	—	46,877,192†	40,502,202†	—	150,000†
SD	27,512,038	21,711,417	—	—				
TN	179,751,100	252,389,100	3,704,700	—	41,016,200	23,331,800	420,000	
TX	1,038,370,896	1,017,036,274	28,930,835		140,119,370	87,594,747	1,525,828	3,814,757
UT	99,900,939	29,511,082			28,868,500	41,885,200	282,000	
VT	32,635,150*	12,002,007*	565,000*					
VA	466,681,199	181,988,816	13,298,485	—	88,429,566	91,960,105	—	—
WA	301,520,783	42,315,578	3,760,926	95,388,619	57,358,754	9,056,804	—	43,120,376
WV	31,877,000*	17,056,750*	450,000*	3,916,250*				
WI	349,395,400	—	2,900,400	348,169,000	50,585,300*	23,420,600*	505,605*	26,503,000*
WY	45,009,732[10]	32,370,735[10]	2,955,621[10]	3,056,719[10]	10,409,124	15,562,849	—	—
Total	16,955,208,500	7,251,978,223	317,379,464	2,163,915,375	1,850,324,364	1,045,895,376	19,786,825	374,604,923
FBP	1,925,026,000	940,707,000	—	—				
Cook	116,104,400	—	—	—				
DC	151,592,000†	23,137,000†	8,217,000†	31,122,000†	17,363,000*	18,933,000*	400,000*	1,195,000*
NYC	—	—	—	—	95,542,799	65,761,464	985,808	51,725,890
PHL	101,105,945	32,759,131	1,253,541	5,845,087				
CSC	593,483,000†	313,319,000†	12,202,000†	2,827,000†				
MB	—	—	—	—				
NS	30,441,900	8,563,500	424,600	—				
YK	6,712,000	—	2,014,000	—				
VI	10,288,207	4,423,233	232,000	—				

Notes:

  * Data as of 3/30/98
  † Data as of 3/30/97
  ✦ Combined adult and juvenile departments
  1. Subsidies to local jails
  2. Contract housing and services
  3. Capital reappropriation

4. Debt service interest, 3,940,000; state aid to local units of government, 17,928,721
5. Care and support for inmates, probationees and parolees
6. Private prison costs
7. Payments from NYC to NYS
8. Equipment, debt service, unassigned funds subsidies, inmate compensation
9. Equipment, 1,600,000; county subsidy, 5,500,000
10. Biennial

Capital Expenditures and Projects

Fiscal Year 1998

Breakdown of capital expenditure budgets in preceding table.

	ADULT CORRECTIONS						JUVENILE CORRECTIONS					
	EXPENDITURES			PROJECTS			EXPENDITURES			PROJECTS		
	New Building	Major Renovation	Maint/ Repair/Other	Maj New Proj	No Major Renov	New Beds	New Building	Major Renovation	Maint/ Repair/Other	Maj New Proj	No Major Renov	New Beds
AL	—	—	—	—	—	—	—	—	—	—	—	—
AK	23,264,891	7,399,262	1,628,859	1	13	216	7,000,000*	0	0	2	0	50
AZ	2,695,700	3,473,300	5,290,000	2	1	4,950	—	—	—	—	—	—
AR	0	0	800,000,000	0	0	0	13,915,300	577,616	20,000	4	—	—
CA	71,520,000	31,268,000	[1]	1	46	6,900	10,430,000	10,765,000	3,750,000	9	22	50
CO	227,762,893*	82,302,257*	1,912,319*	6*	9*	2,537*	7,907,585*	437,200*				
CT	—	—		0	47	0						
DE			128,000,000*				1,195,000*		582,400*	1*		10*
FL	47,716,592	17,524,744	13,539,029[2]	9	94	1,544						
GA		7,000,000	6,235,000	0	[4]	0	1,580,000*	2,015,000*		11*	25*	
HI	12,520,000[3]	4,223,000[3]	422,000[3]	4	3	2,752		638,000	—		1	—
ID	1,889,700	800,000	1,030,900	2	1	118		1,450,000*	120,000*	0	2*	0
IL	64,000,000	32,925,000	29,000,000[5]	2	35	1,488	✦					
IN	161,601,564[3]	23,546,250[3]	24,157,776[3]	11	68	1,750	✦					
IA	20,800,000	—	—	3	—	—	2,400,000*		200,000*	2*		24*
KS	2,156,547	—	13,008,862[6]	2[7]	—	213[7]		—	1,400,000	—	—	—
KY	31,138,000[3]	1,299,000[3]	6,240,000[3,8]	11	3	642	28,081,000[3]	783,000[3]	1,300,000[3]	6	2	120
ME							✦					
MD							43,516,000	1,305,000	479,526	2	1	216
MA	—	1,609,519	16,307,598	—	30	—	2,750,000*	903,000*	2,589,000*			
MI	12,000,000	0	3,000,000	—	—	—	37,200,000	—	—	1	0	0
MN	—	10,685,000	3,500,000	—	—	—						
MS	3,723,039	11,620,000	2,900,149	5	1	1,600	—	—	—	—	—	—
MO	169,624,130	12,056,025	18,300,430	6	7	3,640	16,490,688*			8*		
MT	—	—	—	—	—	—	✦					
NE	31,444,105	205,585	165,693	2	1	1,160	—	667,112*	—			
NV	96,160,550[3*]	8,547,477[3*]	4,904,157[3*]									
NH	497,800*	244,856*	265,509*	0	1*	0	0	1,000,000[3]	972,000[3]	0	1	25
NJ	9,526,000	65,855,000	5,627,000	0	61	0	14,800,000	13,106,000	2,602,000	3*	21*	228*
NM	98,000	1,929,000	—	0	4	0		3,244,071		1	—	50
NY	244,062,000	185,000,000	—	1	100	1,500	0	12,700,000	2,400,000	0	23	0
NC	—	—	—	2	0	400	6,500,000	—	—	7	3	256
ND	677,900[3]	4,897,500[3]	2,234,100[3]	1	2	240	—	1,400,000	785,200	0	1	0
OH	103,025,536	61,628,943	59,600,940[10]	9	38	2,250	97,456,779	7,577,184				
OK	18,000,000*			3*	0*	600*						
OR			12,134,402*				3,392,000[3]	576,000[3]	435,000[3]	1	1	50
PA	420,114,581	105,322,623	0	43	16	4,436						
RI	0	2,538,403	13,771,784[2]	0	4	86						
SC	35,375,000	6,120,512	1,986,665	3	12	2,524						
SD	—	—	—	—	—	—	✦					
TN	19,300,000	—	2,075,000	—	—	270	—	—	1,164,200	0	0	0
TX	—	33,300,000	6,000,000	—	—	—	0	8,008,794	5,475,118	0	8	0
UT	—	—	—	1	1	288	8,074,800	—	—	2	—	64
VT	5,700,000*		550,000*	1*	4*	116*						
VA	0	4,163,000	2,502,103	1	14	0	6,505,125	—	7,071,714	—	—	275
WA	186,297,795	34,366,844	19,013,937	4	1	256	55,694,841	20,265,842	6,600,000	10	17	180
WV	45,109,104*	22,584,233*		5*	4*	1,100*						
WI	—	20,000,000	—	2	23	1,600						
WY	3,420,812[3]	258,000[3]	—	2	2	96	—	2,116,720	—	0	4	0
Total	2,114,107,239	841,013,333	1,202,304,215	155	674	47,293	350,079,118	76,429,539	35,344,191	66	110	1,370
FBP	297,000,000	0	136,917,000	7	0	8,384[11]						
Cook	—	2,400,000*	2,100,000*	0*	1*	300*						
NYC	—	—	—	—	—	—	—	11,342,000	—	—	3	92
PHL	90,452,000	11,338,000	—	—	—	—						
CSC	86,052,000*	38,295,500*	46,100,000*	16*	13*	320*						
MB	1,400,000	1,500,000	—	—	—	—						
NS	—	—	—	—	—	—						
VI	24,000,000	—	—	—	—	320						
YK	—	227,000	—	—	—	—						

Notes:
† Data as of 3/30/97
* Data as of 3/30/98
✦ Combined adult and juvenile
1. Included in operating budget
2. Debt service
3. Biennial funding
4. Open—ended number
5. VOI/TIS federal grant
6. Maintenance, 6,203,761; debt service principle, 6,765,000; misc projects, 40,101
7. Reported in 1998 survey
8. New prison renovation, 63,440,000
9. Includes consultants, master plan study
10. Jails/CBCF/security/industrial equipment
11. Partial funding in FY 1999

Adult Correctional Budgets 1998–1999

Fiscal Year	Total DOC Budget	ALLOCATED COSTS PER BUDGET CATEGORY								
		Administrative	Custody and Security	Treatment Programs	Inmate Health Care	Operations/ Maintenance	Community Programs	Parole	Construction	Other
AL 10/98–9/99	$166,950,000	NA	NA	NA	$24,000,000 14.4%	NA	$1,500,000 9%	NA	NA	NA
AK 7/98–6/99	$158,210,800	$12,704,600 8%	$70,852,200 44.8%	$2,839,600 1.8%	$15,902,100 10.1%	$7,780,500 4.9%	$30,085,500 19% (includes probation)	$484,500 0.3%	NA	$17,562,300–1.1% Out-of-state contract facilities
AZ 7/98–6/99	$535,259,800	$22,395,000 4.2%	$423,938,700-combined 79.2%	NA	$67,357,300 12.6%	NA	$2,079,900 0.4%	$5,870,700 1.1%	NA	$13,618,200-2.5% Inspections; investigations; human resources
AR 7/98–6/99	$151,336,081	$3,854,621 2.5%	$114,499,810 75.6%	$6,155,940 4.1 %	$17,607,768 11.6%	$4,038,852 2.7%	$4,472,427 3%	$706,663 0.5%	$77,222,214 Percentage-NA	NA
CA 7/98–6/99	$4,114,265,000	$134,498,000 3.3%	$1,671,619,000 40.6%	$211,564,000 5.2%	$457,675,000 11.1%	$1,066,417,000 25.9%	$22,698,000 5.4%	$251,495,000 6.1%	$89,952,000 2.2%	$8,347,000-0.2% State-mandated community program
CO 7/98–6/99	$399,779,855	$40,924,606 10.2%	$217,810,568 54.5%	$20,999,494 5.3%	$31,196,109 7.8%	$12,942,999 3.2%	$7,667,267 1.9%	$8,099,863 2%	$132,884,693 Separate budget	$60,138,949-15% Support services; pardon board; correctional industries, canteen
CT 7/98–6/99	$414,417,475	$44,469,103 11 %	$238,145,355 57%	$31,528,989 8%	$50,636,145 12%	$34,753,958 8%	$14,883,925 4%	NA	-0-	-0-
DE 7/98–6/99	$141,163,600	$13,299,300 9%	$89,435,100 63%	$3,271,600 2%	$10,832,000 8%	$5,040,200 4%	$5,144,800 4%	$14,140,600 10% (includes probation)	NA	
DC 10/98–9/99	$250,733,000	$11,092,000 4%	$183,291,000 73%	$368,000 0%	$18,621,000 7%	$26,803,000 11%	$6,518,000 3%	NA	-0-	$3,410,000-2% Education/work programs
FL 7/98–6/99	$1,739,817,408	$31,400,743 1.8%	$941,035,949 54.1%	$59,546,118 3.4%	$231,275,468 13.3%	$74,101,778 4.3%	$72,531,331 4.2%	$208,441,582 12% (includes probation)	$82,403,215 4.7%	$39,081,224 2.3%
GA 7/98–6/99	$818,797,188	$68,419,895 8.4%	$430,319,404 52.6%	$44,178,200 5.4%	$109,323,734 13.4%	$72,948,551 8.9%	$64,642,219 7.9% (includes probation)	NA	$21,042,270 2.6%	$7,922,916-1% Fast Track/transitional units; security upgrades
HI 7/98–6/99	$127,212,273	$7,471,164 6%	$69,484,475 55%	$1,405,295 1%	$10,675,452 8%	$1,184,097 1%	$945,917 1%	$1,933,943 2%	$2,200,000 2%	$18,000,748-14% For mainland inmates
ID 7/98–6/99	$87,879,500	$7,414,200 8.4%	$33,029,600 3.8%	$4,509,400 5.1%	$7,617,800 8.7%	$15,605,200 17.8%	$14,022,200 15.9% (includes probation)	$949,200 1.1%	NA	$4,731,900-5.4% Education; transport; sex offender board; Americorps projects
IL 7/98–6/99	$810,145,200	Not available due to change in accounting system					$49,129,300—combined 6.1%		$7,928,100 1%	
IN 7/98–6/99	$445,100,000	$77,500,000 17.4%	$214,500,000 48.2%	$22,900,000 5.2%	$47,700,000 10.7%	$21,200,000 4.8%	$12,600,000 2.8%	$4,800,000 1.1%	$78,975,275 Percentage-NA	$43,900,000-9.9% Food is primary component

ALLOCATED COSTS PER BUDGET CATEGORY

Fiscal Year	Total DOC Budget	Administrative	Custody and Security	Treatment Programs	Inmate Health Care	Operations/Maintenance	Community Programs	Parole	Construction	Other
IA 7/98-6/99	$218,571,173	$18,141,407 8.3%	$79,023,228 3.3%	$16,611,409 7.6%	$12,013,106 5%	$43,737,634 2.3%	$49,044,389 22%	NA	NA	NA
KS 7/98-6/99	$217,035,260	$15,322,480 7.1%	$64,417,920 29.7%	$12,045,380 5.5%	$20,654,285 9.5%	$50,710,912 23.4%	$18,118,953 8.3%	$8,759,994 4%	$6,393,999 3%	$20,611,337-9.5% Debt service; correctional industries
KY 7/98-6/99	$268,262,400	$8,387,300 3.1%	$14,615,300 52.4%	$4,829,800 1.8%	$16,076,200 6%	NA	$56,970,700 21.2%	$19,518,100 7.3%	$15,686,200 5.9%	$6,178,800 2.3%
LA 7/98-6/99	$461,932,917	$17,665,788 3.8%	$175,565,796 38%	$1,379,086 0.3%	$26,119,716 5.7%	$11,706,638 2.5%	$2,871,249 0.6%	$32,136,173 7% (includes probation)	$75,620,000 16.4%	$118,868,471-25.7% Contract housing
ME 7/98-6/99	$55,664,096	$2,200,219 4%	NA	NA	$4,100,000 7.4%	NA	$1,785,136 3.2%	NA	$109,800,000 Percentage-NA	NA
MD 7/98-6/99	$476,961,647	$36,318,954 7.6%	$251,520,194 52.7%	$562,768 0.1%	$41,386,549 8.7%	$35,847,465 7.5%	$6,974,570 1.5%	-0-	-0-	$15,284,846-3.2% Payments to local jurisdictions
MA	$391,183,862[1]	NA	NA	NA	Not included	NA	Not included	Not included	Not included	Not included
MI 10/98-9/99	$1,441,935,000	$61,622,000 4.3%	$960,578,300 66.5%	$21,561,700 1.5%	$185,972,000 12.9%	$3,000,000 0.2%	$81,768,400 5.7%	$97,250,500 6.7%	NA	$33,182,100-2.3% Non-MH consent decrees; Prison industries
MN 7/98-6/99	$162,874,215	NA	NA	NA	Not included	NA	Not included	Not included	Not included	Not included
MS 7/98-6/99	$236,099,488	$19,951,210 8.5%	$115,926,152 49.2%	$2,198,872 0.9%	$20,946,581 8.9%	$1,000,000 0.4%	$12,701,587-combined 5.4%	5.2%	$12,271,412 Contract housing	$51,103,674-21.6%
MO 7/98-6/99	$510,506,279	$8,727,497 1.7%	$210,686,512 41.3%	$64,736,135 12.7%	$55,309,671 10.8%	$60,923,924 11.9%	$78,875,306 15.5% (includes probation)	$12,568,101 2.5%	$9,429,132 1.9%[2]	$9,250,001-1.8% Lease/bond payment for new construction
MT	$92,400,000[1]									
NE 7/98-6/99	$116,319,673	$19,816,997 17%	$33,365,590 29%	$5,165,614 4%	$8,360,167 7%	$12,979,119 11%	$3,880,180 3%	$1,307,643 1%	$31,444,363 27%	NA
NV 7/98-6/99	$259,151,610	$9,739,570 3%	$92,569,531 36%	$366,907 1%	$30,217,870 11%	$15,142,925 5%	$330,723 1%	NA	$109,636,503 42%	$1,147,473-1%
NH 7/98-6/99	$52,723,741 7.1%	$3,751,238 44.8%	$23,595,673 6.4%	$3,375,618 9.2%	$4,837,205 18.2%	$9,587,892 2.4%	$1,247,512	$5,355,603 10.2% (includes probation)	$973,000 1.9%	NA
NJ 7/98-6/99	$876,843,000	$51,514,000 5.9%	$379,987,000 43.3%	$44,922,000 5.1%	$77,499,000 8.8%	$116,646,000 13.3%	$43,593,000 5%	$35,064,000 4%	$11,824,000 1.4%	$115,794,000-13.2% Contract housing
NM 7/98-6/99	$164,105,700	$9,206,400 5.6%	$102,563,400 62.5%	NA	$19,623,200 12%	$2,381,900 1.4%	$4,227,400 2.6%	$14,528,200 8.9%	$3,400,000 Percentage-NA	$11,675,200-7% Prison industries; training academy; Education Bureau
NY 4/98-3/99	$2,250,567,900	$19,079,400 8%	$868,651,600 38.6%	$202,795,100 9%	$185,127,800 8.2%	$383,788,000 17.1%	Included in treatment	NA	$429,062,000 19.1%	$162,064,000-7.2% Industries; commissary; local assistance

ADULT CORRECTIONAL BUDGETS 1998–1999, continued

Fiscal Year	Total DOC Budget	ALLOCATED COSTS PER BUDGET CATEGORY								
		Administrative	Custody and Security	Treatment Programs	Inmate Health Care	Operations/Maintenance	Community Programs	Parole	Construction	Other
NC 7/98–6/99	$1,009,209,553	$34,900,706 3.5%	$477,567,412 47.3%	$16,550,414 1.6%	$123,055,681 12.2%	$6,335,395 0.6%	$11,184,505 1.1% (work release)	$109,001,249 10.8% (includes probation)	$1,979,698 0.2% (capital improvements)	$14,910,417-1.5% Welfare; federal grants
ND 7/98–6/99	$30,050,741	$2,993,087 10%	$6,869,157 23%	$2,047,355 7%	$1,684,558 5%	$5,783,174 19%	$2,273,680 8%	$282,856 1%	$3,132,023 10%	$4,984,851-17% Prison industries; victim services
OH 7/98–6/99	$1,360,432,077	$112,850,117 7.61%	$429,903,084 31.6%	$104,830,451 7.7%	$98,481,738 7.2%	$344,665,534 25.3%	$95,354,124 7%	$63,839,704 4.7%	$124,232,148 Percentage-NA	$110,507,325-8.1% Debt service
OK 7/98–6/99	$385,601,641	$39,893,406 10%	$144,733,420 38%	$23,559,896 6%	$22,964,179 6%	NA	$18,384,562 5%	$24,312,207 6%	-0-	$111,753,971-29% Private prisons; prison industries
OR 7/98–6/99	$537,861,432	$35,265,872 6.6%	$144,226,269 26.8%	$40,945,126 7.6%	$22,421,351 4.2%	$17,609,835 3.3%	$86,575,934 16.1%	NA	I $13,393,439 2.5%	$177,423,606-33% Debt service
PA 7/98–6/99	$1,013,598,572	$26,845,492 2.7%	$406,409,860 40.1%	$102,300,910 10.1%	$124,523,345 12.3%	$109,799,254 10.8%	$27,189,069-combined 2.7%		NA	$216,525,642-21.4%
RI 7/98–6/99	$129,384,126	$7,994,899 6%	$57,442,491 44%	$1,116,709 1%	$11,390,016 9%	$19,800,785 15%	$7,573,065 6%	$733,961 1%	NA	$23,332,200-18% Food service; support; commissary; case management
SC 7/98–6/99	$401,639,001	$17,454,865 4.3%	$225,970,179 56.3%	$6,444,072 1.6%	$43,991,189 11%	Est $8,500,000 2.1%	$3,500,000 0.9%	NA	$43,482,177 10.8%	$52,296,518-13% Prison industries; education; inmate services
SD 7/98–6/99	$33,527,779	$1,329,726 4%	$9,983,325 30%	-0-	$4,425,750 13%	$2,649,825 8%	$1,160,227 4%	$1,556,874 5%	NA	$12,422,052-37%
TN 7/98–6/99	$435,844,900	$41,592,300 10%	$206,703,000 47%	$19,702,500 5%	$39,332,300 9%	$75,261,500 17%	$31,226,200 7% (includes probation)	-0-	$22,027,100 5%	NA
TX 9/98–8/99	$2,084,338,005	$59,960,704 2.9%	$975,034,230 4.7%	$140,163,153 4.7%	$291,243,534 6.7%	$64,737,041 Percentage-NA	$200,354,172[3] 9.6%	$148,235,648 7.1%	$39,300,000 Percentage-NA	$269,346,564-12.9% Private prisons; state jail services
UT	$172,350,330[1]									
VT 7/98–6/99	$65,528,000	$1,906,634 2.9%	$29,769,511 45.4%	$2,212,000 3.4%	$5,887,000 9.1%	$8,194,700 12.5%	$12,809,000 19.5%	$217,155 0.3%	NA	$4,532,000 6.9%
VA 7/98–6199	$704,711,148									
WA 7/98–6/99	$578,711,172	$56,109,433 10%	$132,345,791 23%	$53,157,672 9%	$48,913,405 8%	$73,173,321 13%	$18,987,087 3%	$47,365,859 8% (includes probation)	$134,244,553 23%	$14,414,051-3% Includes interagency services
WV	$53,300,000[4]									
WI 7/98–6/99	$569,053,300	NA	NA	NA	$28,172,700 5%	$2,906,300 1%	$103,858,100 18%	NA	Percentage-NA; Included in biennial budget	$434,116,200-76%

ALLOCATED COSTS PER BUDGET CATEGORY

Fiscal Year	Total DOC Budget	Administrative	Custody and Security	Treatment Programs	Inmate Health Care	Operations/ Maintenance	Community Programs	Parole	Construction	Other
WY	$83,502,807[1]									
FBP	$2,865,733,000[1]									
BC 4/98-3/99	$187,653,870	$4,836,251 2.6%	$97,907,822 52.2%	$2,175,837 1.2%	$3,552,657 1.9%	$5,561,428 3%	$25,362,318 13.5%	$514,068 0.3%	-0-	$47,743,481-25.4%
MB 4/98-3/99	$47,400,000	$2,000,000 4%	$21,900,000 46%	$8,000,000 17%	$1,500,000 3.2%	$6,000,000 12.6%	$8,000,000 17% (probation services)	NA	NA	NA
NB 4/98-3/99	$17,632,091	$3,253,181 18.5%	$10,784,196 61.2%	$884,789 5%	$827,077 4.7%	$452,696 2.6%	$295,000 1.7%	NA	NA	NA
NS 4/98-3/99	$18,733,400	$2,263,800 12%	$16,033,700 86%	$435,900-combined 2%			NA	NA	NA	NA
SK 4/98-3/99	$44,051,000	$2,004,400 5%	$24,324,100 55%	$1,400,000 3%	$673,100 2%	$8,289,500 19%	$7,359,900 17%	-0-	NA	-0-
CSC 4/98-3/99	$1,180,987,000	$102,960,000 8.7%	$324,018,000 27.4%	$119,277,000 10.1%	$73,124,000 6.2%	$84,684,000 7.2%	$138,433,000-combined 11.7%		$158,527,000 13.4%	$179,964,000 15.3%

Notes:
1. Fiscal Year 1998
2. MISSOURI: FY99 is the off year of a two-year budget cycle for capital improvements.
3. TEXAS: Includes Texas Council for Offenders with Mental Impairments.
4. WEST VIRGINIA: Data as of 3/30/98

Budget Changes from 1997–1998 and Affected Programs

	Budget Increased or Decreased	NUMBERS RELATIVE TO INCREASES				Results of Decreases	Anticipated Changes for 1999–2000
		No. of Staff	No. of New Facilities	No. of New Beds	No. of New Programs		
AL	Increased	Lost staff	1	900			Current budget is considerably less; all costs will increase
AK	Increased (due to funds for contract facilities)	8	1	267	2 (halfway house and increase in beds at contracted facilities)		Increased alternatives to incarceration program
AZ	Increased	939	1	2,400	NA		Activation of state- and privately operated prison beds
AR	Increased	41	0	216 (added to existing CF)			None
CA	Increased	1,276.1	NA	3,857	NA		Population growth
CO	Increased	597.6 (est.)	3 (est.)	1 905 (est.)			1,528 new beds added for FY00
CT	Increased	None	1 (reopened existing)	500 - 750	None		Additional staff and annualization costs for reopened facility
DE	Increased	229	1	280	1		Additional security staff for new facilities
DC	Decreased (due to transformation from state/prison to county/jail)					Custody/security and operations/maintenance	Additional funding will be requested for institutions, halfway houses, and health services
FL	Increased	485	0	806	0		Population growth
GA	Increased	215	4	5,806	2 (expansion of existing facility)		Funding for 500 beds at 3 private prisons; 2 Probation Centers; 2 Transition Centers; 1 Fast Track Center
HI	Increased	18.75	0	0	0		$2,000,000 restriction
ID	Increased	47	0	84	4 (Life Skills, Detour program, substance abuse, sex offender classification board)		Reduction of staff at one facility; increase in appropriation
IL	Increased	783	2	2,756	0		Opening of delayed 500-bed institution; annualizing cost of other institution
IN	Increased	10	2	200 (Miami CF)	2		Funding for Miami CF and Pendleton Juvenile Facility; adding New Castle CF
IA	Increased	226	0	100	0		Budget will increase
KS	Increased	26	0	284	0		Nine additional parole officers authorized for 2000
KY	Increased	218	0	150	2 new, 3 expansions		Additional program expansions
LA	Increased	74	0	2,899	0		Transition costs; additional beds; women's dorm; 2 new juvenile facilities
ME	Increased	26.5	0	284	2		Budget increase
MD	Increased	155	0	284	0		
MA	No response						
MI	Increased	153	1	1,682	2		Addition of 5,000 new beds and associated staffing
MN	Increased	164.5	0	218	0		New facility at Rush City

	Budget Increased or Decreased	No. of Staff	No. of New Facilities	No. of New Beds	No. of New Programs	Results of Decreases	Anticipated Changes for 1999–2000
		NUMBERS RELATIVE TO INCREASES					
MS	Increased (due to opening of additional beds)	Minimal	4	1,600	0		Additional beds and security
MO	Decreased	1,383.65			1	Capital improvements	Will request additional funding for new prison, probation and parole staff and operational expenses
MT	No response						No significant changes
NE	Increased (due to salary increases and staffing for 2 new facilities)	13	0	0	0		
NV	Increased (due to population growth and expanded facility projects)	17	1 (expansion)	125			Addition of High Desert Prison, closure of Southern NV Correctional Center
NH	Decreased	32	0	0	0		Funding for new 500-bed prison
NJ	Increased (due to program expansions, drug court initiative new management information on system)	96	0	192 (expansion of existing)	2 (Roving Drug Interdiction Unit and Parole Day Reporting Program)		Enhanced MH services; responsibility of housing of civilly committed "sexual predators"
NM	Increased	6	2 private facilities	1,800	NA		Expansion of contract to house female inmates due to closure of state-operated women's facility
NY	Increased (due to population increase and capacity expansion)	688	1	800	0		Addition of 1 facility
NC	Increased	155					Increased funding for community treatment programs
ND	Increased¹						Increases needed to maintain full-year funding for new programs and continuation of existing
OH	Increased	843	1 (Richland Correctional)	1,855	No major programs		Additional personnel; more contracted bed space; increased health services
OK	Increased	218	0	1,101 (940 private, 161 state-operated)	1		Additional funds for new beds and population growth; additional funding for COP's for construction
OR	Increased	16	NA	707			Additional positions to open SCI Pine Grove
PA	Increased	507	1 (SCI Chester)	2,208			Additional positions to open SCI Pine Grove
RI	Increased	70	0	12 (budgeted)	1		Population adjustments; Y2K compliance funding; salary adjustments; health benefit cost increases
SC	Increased (to provide care, housing and security)	188	4 (additions to existing)	1,024	0		Operation of 256 bed housing units et existing institutions
SD	Increased						Population growth
TN	Increased	267	1	1,536			Start-up funding and partial year operational funding for approximately 700 new beds
TX	Increased	516	19	7	NA		Addition of four high security units
UT	No response						Will increase by $15,000,000
VT	Increased		0	350			
VA	Increased		2	2,499			
WA	Increased (due to population growth)	162	0	40	0		Budget increase due to population growth

BUDGET CHANGES FROM 1997–1998 AND AFFECTED PROGRAMS, *continued*

		NUMBERS RELATIVE TO INCREASES				
	Budget Increased or Decreased	No. of Staff	No. of New Facilities	No. of New Beds	No. of New Programs	Results of Decreases	Anticipated Changes for 1999–2000
WV	No response						
WI	Increased	158	0		2		Additional funding for contract beds and opening of Supermax CF
WY	No response						
FBP	No response						
BC	Decreased	NA	NA	NA	NA	Change in billing format	Need to make reductions to remain within allocation
MB	Increased (slightly)						Large increase with opening of two new high and medium security units
NB	Increased (due to first full year of Youth facility)		1 (NB Youth Center)				
NS	Increased (due to salary increases)	0	0	0			Increase in wages
SK	Increased	5.2	0	0			Funds for salary increases; population growth
CSC	Increased (due to programs and measures)	273					Reintegration of offenders in society; additional correctional officers

Notes:
1. NORTH DAKOTA: Based on biennial budget. In addition to staff, beds and facilities reported in the 1997-98 survey, grants for crime victims have increased.

1998–1999 Budgets—Specific Programs

	Community Programs	New Programs	Considered Alternatives to Incarceration	Juvenile Budget (Additional to DOC Adult Facility Allocations)
AL	Work release, community corrections		Community corrections	No
AK	Community residential centers (halfway houses), contract sites, community jails	Electronic monitoring, rural substance abuse treatment, house arrest/confinement	Electronic monitoring, house arrest/confinement	No
AZ	Home arrest, adult parole/work furlough	NA	NA	No
AR	Work release	None	No	No
CA	Work furlough, mother/infant, community correctional facilities	NA	NA	No
CO	Residential and nonresidential community corrections, youth offender aftercare program[1], community ISP		Community residential, community ISP, boot camp	No
CT	Community service offices[2]	NA		No
DE	Work release, home confinement, supervised custody	Kent Work Release Center	House arrest	No
DC	Halfway houses	None	Halfway houses	No
FL	Electronic monitoring, intensive day treatment, outpatient drug treatment, transition contracts, probation and restitution centers, PIE program	Photo imaging of probationers via cameras and PCs for local law enforcement	Pretrial intervention electronic monitoring, boot camp, jail beds	No
GA	Work release at diversion and transitional centers, street probation supervision	Education program expansion, substance abuse program expansion	Probation supervision, boot camps and diversion centers, detention centers	No
HI	Residential work release, community beds, Maui electronic monitoring program	None	Supervised release program, electronic monitoring	No
ID	Community work centers, electronic monitoring, parole transition program	Sex offender classification board, Detour program		No
IL	Work release, residential treatment facilities, substance abuse, electronic monitoring, local sentencing	Expanded Intensive Supervision Program	Electronic monitoring, boot camp, institutional treatment centers, community release centers, residential treatment facilities, local sentencing	No
IN	Community corrections, including work release, residential, home detention, new work components	NA	NA	Yes, $37,500,000
IA	Probation, parole, work release, residential, OWI, pretrial	No new programs	Probation, pretrial jail alternative, OWI, violator program	No
KS	State-operated work release, community corrections	Privatized conservation camps for females (opens 1/00)	County-operated conservation camps for males (opens 1/00)	No
KY	Inmate and parole beds in halfway houses	Community confinement program	Community confinement program	No
LA	Halfway houses		Work release, intensive motivational program of alternative correction treatment (IMPACT)	Yes, $91,161,060
ME	Prerelease centers, work release	Supervised community confinement	Supervised community confinement	Yes, $22,902,139
MD	Work release, home detention, contracted prerelease		Home detention, boot camp	No
MA	No response			

1998–1999 BUDGETS—SPECIFIC PROGRAMS, *continued*

	Community Programs	New Programs	Considered Alternatives to Incarceration	Juvenile Budget (Additional to DOC Adult Facility Allocations)
MI	Electronic tether monitoring, community residential centers, community corrections programs	Pilot in-prison drug treatment programs, pilot technical violator drug treatment program	Technical rule violator centers, boot camp, community corrections	Yes, $5,938,400
MN	None	None	Challenge incarceration (boot cams)	Yes, $16,972,986
MS	House arrest		House arrest, restitution centers, earned release	No
MO	Community correctional centers, women and children's center, day reporting	None	Electronic detention, boot camp	Yes, $95,945,400
MT	No response			
NE	Work release, office of community justice	Staffing for work ethic camp (opens FY00)	Office of community justice, work ethic camp	No but does include services for juveniles adjudicated as adults
NV	Restitution centers, residential confinement	Therapeutic community program for drug offenders	House arrest following completion of certain programs, boot camp	No
NH	AHC, electronic monitoring, work release, residential substance abuse, academy program	NA	Academy program includes strict probation and substance abuse counseling	No
NJ	Community-based contracted residential and secure treatment facilities, electronic monitoring/ home confinement	Revolving drug interdiction program, parole day reporting programs	Alternative parole sanction programs, drug court intervention program, parole day reporting programs, halfway houses	No
NM	Work release, electronic monitoring, residential drug treatment, domestic violence and therapeutic community program	NA	Residential drug treatment, intensive supervision program, community corrections	No
NY	Work release, day reporting, residential community housing	NA	NA	No
NC	NA	NA	NA	NA
ND	Work release, house arrest/home detention, electronic monitoring, community placement	Revocation center	House arrest/home detention, electronic monitoring, comlmunity placement	Yes, $8,618,000
OH	Adult parole authority, transitional control, fugitive section, offender services network, adult detention, halfway houses, victim services, recovery services, community corrections, community justice		Community corrections acts programs, community-based correctional facilities, some halfway house placement	No
OK	Community sentencing	Youth offenders education program	Electronic monitoring, halfway houses	No
OR	None	None	None	No
PA	Community corrections, group homes, work release, community work program	Emphasis on education and drug/alcohol programs	Community corrections, group homes, Quehanna boot camp	No
RI	Community confinement, parole and probation	Some funding for Project POST	Community confinement	No
SC	Work release, labor crews, work crews	Emphasis placed on substance abuse and youthful offenders		No
SD	Work release, community service		No	Yes, $15,551,342
TN	Supervision and counseling for probationers, community corrections	None	Community corrections	No

	Community Programs	New Programs	Considered Alternatives to Incarceration	Juvenile Budget (Additional to DOC Adult Facility Allocations)
TX	Probation, community supervision and corrections, pretrial services, sex offender treatment, substance abuse treatment, education and employment services	NA	Community justice assistance division programs	No
UT	No response			
VT	Probation, parole, intensive sanctions	Community development	Yes	No
VA	Detention/diversion centers, home electronic monitoring, boot camp, day reporting, residential facilities	Drug courts	Detention/diversion centers, home electronic monitoring, boot camp, day reporting residential facilities	No
WA	Day reporting centers, work release		Day reporting centers, sex/ drug treatment, community service	Yes, for juveniles adjudicated as adults, $4,677,125
WV	No response			
WI	Work release, intensive sanctions, halfway houses and transitional living placements	Enhanced community supervision projects, absconder locator unit	Division of Community Corrections - intensive sanctions	Yes, $179,403,100
WY	No response			
FBP	No response			
BC	Electronic monitoring, community service orders, cognitive skills, residential programs, substance abuse, anger management, sex offender program, spousal abuse	NA	Community services orders diversion services, electronic monitoring	No
MB	Work release for weekend sentenced offenders		Contract for supervision of prison-diverted offenders	Yes, $11,000,000
NB	TAS, house arrest		Alternative measures programs	Yes, $10,211,235
NS	Work TA, intermittence, YWCA program			Yes, $12,660,100
SK	Electronic monitoring/home confinement, halfway houses	None	Fine option, bail verification, electronic monitoring	No
CSC				No

Note:
1. COLORADO: Phases 1 and 2 programs for youths sentenced as adults and reintegrating into the community.
2. CONNECTICUT: Oversees residential and nonresidential services, including halfway houses and various client services for assistance and counseling.

Incarceration Costs Paid by Inmates

as of June 1998

	COST TO INCARCERATE ONE INMATE FOR ONE YEAR			Do Inmates Pay for Room and Board	Are Fees Assessed on Ability-to-pay Basis	Do Inmates Continue To Pay Costs Of Incarceration After Release	Does DOC Have Problem Collecting Fees	Are Any Collections Kept by the DOC/other
	Max	Med	Min					
AL	8,896 Composite			No, except for work release	No; flat 32.5% of wages for work release	No	No	DOC, in a special fund which requires legislative approval for expenditures
AK	No Response							
AZ	No Response							
AR	20,174	13,593	10,151	No, except for work release	No; flat rate of $13 for work release	No (as related to work release)	No	DOC for operation of workrelease facilities
CA	10,721 Composite			No	No	N/A	N/A	N/A
CO	30,361	20,661	18,325	No	Yes, but indigent pay nothing	No	No, except for medical	N/A
CT	25,926 (11 Mos Avg)	19,681 (11 Mos Avg)	18,133 (11 Mos Avg)	Yes, only if participating in Correction Industries Private Industries Program	Yes, on available account balance	No	No	State General Fund
DE	19,319 Composite			Yes, work release center inmates and some minimum-wage state agency jobs	No	No	No	State General Fund
DC	Unavailable							
FL	Unable to respond at this time							
GA	No Response							
HI	27,375 Composite			No	No	No	No	No
ID	Unavailable			No	No	N/A	N/A	N/A
IL	22,692	14,305	17,993	Yes; community correctional center or electronic detention inmates pay a pro-rated maintenance fee	Yes	Yes	No	Medical co-pay fees kept by the DOC; fees for lost Ids are returned to the State General Fund
IN	17,232 Composite			No	No	No	No	No
IA	17,500 Composite			Yes, $5/month	Yes	No	No	Yes, DOC
KS	No Response							
KY	17m766	14,724	12m892	No	No	Yes; may be assessed fees while on parole	Yes	State General Fund

| | COST TO INCARCERATE ONE INMATE FOR ONE YEAR | | | Do Inmates Pay for Room and Board | Are Fees Assessed on Ability-to-pay Basis | Do Inmates Continue To Pay Costs Of Incarceration After Release | Does DOC Have Problem Collecting Fees | Are Any Collections Kept by the DOC/other |
	Max	Med	Min					
LA	14,655	13,932	11,027	No, in state facilities; 50% of daily wage or $20, (whichever is less) if in community rehabilitation centers or sheriff's work release program	No	No; must pay supervision fees if on parole	N/A	N/A
ME	27,908 Composite			No; exception, $10 if on work release	No	No	No	Work release fees to State General Fund
MD	No Response							
MA	Unavailable			Yes, if on work release	Yes; generally 15% of gross wages	No	No, by statute wages are submitted to the institution and the 15% is then deducted from the check	State General Fund
MI	Level IV- 34,033; Level V/VI- 35,069	Level II- 20,648; Level III- 20,966	Level I- 16,191	Yes, if they fall under Prison Reimbursement Act, under certain circumstances	Yes; Prison Reimbursement Act allows recovery of 10% of costs for care or 10% of costs for two years (whichever is less); not to exceed 90% of assets	Yes, if court ordered; the state may continue to collect on that order until it is fully paid, even after discharge	Unavailable; however, 786,550 collected under the Act in fiscal 1997	State Fund, in most cases
MN	31,116 Composite			Yes, if on P.I.E. program; percentage of wages, depending on court-ordered obligations	No	Yes; work release participants pay a portion of halfway house costs ($7/day)	No	DOC
MS	21,601	17,002	15,790	No	No	No	No	No
MO	11,074	10,914	12,136	Yes; those in Community Release Centers, if they are employed	No	Yes; probation and parole officers attempt to collect	Yes, from halfway houses and those on electronic monitoring, especially	DOC
MT	16,600 Composite, excluding outside medical			No	Yes	Yes; $10 room and board; medical treatment, if able to pay	Yes, if they are revoked or lose their job	Pre-release center
NE	19,202 Composite			Yes; $10/day on community corrections work release; $1.50 for each hour paid if on Private Venture	No	No, but encouraged to do so if from work release; if re-incarcerated, past debt owing will be collected	No; relative to hobby areas or music equipment, inmates prohibited from participating if unable to pay	By the DOC and used for hobby/music equipment
NV	16,220	13,868	5,887	Yes, by a percentage of Prison Industry or Division of Forestry wages	Yes	No	No	DOC

INCARCERATION COSTS PAID BY INMATES, *continued*

	COST TO INCARCERATE ONE INMATE FOR ONE YEAR			Do Inmates Pay for Room and Board	Are Fees Assessed on Ability-to-pay Basis	Do Inmates Continue To Pay Costs Of Incarceration After Release	Does DOC Have Problem Collecting Fees	Are Any Collections Kept by the DOC/other
	Max	Med	Min					
NH	19,056 Composite			No	No	No	N/A	N/A
NJ	28,487	24,681 Composite		No; halfway house or work release participants assessed maintenance fee	Yes, based on percentage of wages earned while in halfway house or work release	No	N/A	Work Release fees by DOC; Halfway House maintenance fees by provider
NM	27,600 Composite			Yes; minimums on work release	No	Yes; $15-$85/month, unless otherwise determined by the Court	No	DOC; to Probation/Parole Intensive Supervision Program, if applicable
NY	31,293	28,395	23,538	Yes, when in Temporary Release	Yes, sliding scale based on wages	No	No	State General Fund
NC	29,185	24,765	19,575	Yes; $12.50/day on work release	No	No	No	Unavailable
ND	18,250 Composite			No	N/A	N/A	N/A	N/A
OH	17,195 Composite			No	No, but accrued and paid if and when inmate receives money in account	No	Yes	DOC
OK	15,126	13,315	13,812	Yes; program support on work release or private prison industry; lesser of $10/day or 50% of wages	No, but outstanding medical co-payments or legal photocopy fees are written off after one year	No	Yes; from inmates who receive little/no money from outside sources and are not employed in prison industry	DOC revolving fund for operations
OR	22,390 Composite			No, except those working on PIE program	No	No	No	DOC
PA	23,477 Composite			Yes, if in community correction center; usually 15% of wages	No	Yes	Yes	DOC
RI	Male-40,534	Male-31,078; 11-51,774; Female-45,663	Male-27,186; Female-45,663	No	No	No	N/A	N/A
SC	14,426 For 11 months	14,306	12,174	No, except for small percent working in Private Sector initiatives or on work release	No, except in Private Sector initiatives or work release, a fee is charged as a percent of salary up to a maximum	No	No	DOC
SD	8,848 Composite			Yes, including work release and Prison Industry	No for work release and Prison Industry (wages considered competitive); yes for other inmates	Yes; parole supervisory fees of $10-$15/month	No	Parole supervisory fees to the State General Fund; balance retained by the DOC

| | COST TO INCARCERATE ONE INMATE FOR ONE YEAR | | | Do Inmates Pay for Room and Board | Are Fees Assessed on Ability-to-pay Basis | Do Inmates Continue To Pay Costs Of Incarceration After Release | Does DOC Have Problem Collecting Fees | Are Any Collections Kept by the DOC/other |
	Max	Med	Min					
TN	20,248 Composite			Yes, on work release or in TRICOR Industry P.I.E. program	No, but sliding fee scale if on work release; half monthly wages if on P.I.E. program	Yes, if placed in halfway house; Parole Board can mandate fees as part of conditions of parole	No	DOC
TX	14,421 Composite			No	N/A	No	N/A	N/A
UT	No Response							
VT	24,138 Composite			No	No	No	No	N/A
VA	No Response							
WA	33,708	24,846	21,420	Yes; a percept depending on the type of work and generally considered "cost of correction"; $12.50/day for work release participants	No	Yes	Yes, attributed to lesser pay than charges on work release	State General Fund which largely funds the DOC; work release funds directly offset room and board costs
WV	18,500	16,500	14,000	Yes, if on work release	Yes	Yes; parolees pay $20/month for supervision	No	DOC
WI	Unavailable			Unavailable	Unavailable	Unavailable	Unavailable	Unavailable
WY	19,848 Composite			No	No	Yes; $10/month after first 21 days/subsistence in a Community Alternative facility	No	No

Wages Earned by Inmates and Garnishments

as of June 1998

	Date of Data	Number in Work Programs	Percentage of Overall Population	AVERAGE HOURLY WAGES EARNED PER DAY		Are Inmate Wages Controlled	Are Inmate Wages Garnisheed
				Inside	Outside		
AL	7-2-98	3,415 in work release; 300 approx. in Prison Industries	16.5	5¢-25¢	Unknown	A predetermined dollar amount per week is maximum allowable for purchasing from the canteen	Fees and fines; also, if needed, expenses for free-world clothing for work release participants are advanced and must be repaid
AK	No Response						
AZ	No Response						
AR	FY 1997	635	4	N/A	$8	Yes; Warden, based on unit policy statutes related to dependents' needs and/or victim compensation	Yes; court-ordered child support
CA	5-1-98	88,000 approx.	60	18¢ for support services; 55¢ for Prison Industries	No tracked	Yes; rules of the Director and of the penal code	Yes; restitution when court ordered; 22% for administrative costs; 10% fee on sales of prison industry commodities or services; $3 filing fee for civil actions
CO	6-98	Unavailable	90	$1/day	N/A	No, except for participants in the P.I.E. federal program	N/A
CT	1-1-98	11,548	74	$1.50	N/A	Yes; $50 weekly commissary spending limit	Yes; encumbered for testing fee for positive drug tests
DE	6-30-97	954	12.3	25¢ - $1.32	Min. Wage	Yes; subject to inmate's pay scale	Yes; restitution, child support, court mandate
DC	6-30-98	208	90	$21/month (based on 2-3 hours/day)	Unavailable	No	No
FL	Unable to respond at this time						
GA	No Response						
HI	FY 1997	2,130	49.8	25¢-63¢ for farm and work line; $5.25-$7.50 prison industry	Unavailable	Yes; facility business officers based on departmental rules and regulations	Yes; by law for child care support and restitution; photocopying; damage to state property
ID	6-23-98	870	23	68¢	$6.68	No	Yes; 25% in community work centers to defray operational costs
IL	1-1-98	44,703 + 2,934 (Ohio Penal Industries)	93.5 + 6 (Ohio Penal Industries)	$12-$22/month	$1.25-$2.82 (Ohio Penal Industries)	Yes; controlled by facility cashier in institution account, regulated by policy and procedure	Yes; outstanding fees, fines or reimbursements for lost or damaged property
IN	6-29-98	9,693	Unavailable	65¢-4.20	$6.50	Yes; if court ordered to reimburse for destruction of state property	Yes; child support and court costs
IA	6-18-98	5,409 FT	73	40¢	Unavailable	Yes; for payment of fees	Yes

	Date of Data	Number in Work Programs	Percentage of Overall Population	AVERAGE HOURLY WAGES EARNED PER DAY		Are Inmate Wages Controlled	Are Inmate Wages Garnisheed
				Inside	Outside		
KS	No Response						
KY	5-98	12,320	88	$1.30	N/A	Yes	Yes; reimbursement for destruction to state property, etc.
LA	6-30-98	17,105	96	7¢	Minimum Wage	Yes; based on standard operating procedures	No
ME	6-15-98	150 Approx.	10 Approx.	50¢-$1.00	$6.00	Yes	Yes; room and board on work release, savings accounts, fines, restitution, child support; a maximum amount that can be withdrawn is pre-determined
MD	No Response						
MA	6-25-98	384 (pre-release level)	82, pre-release; 91, minimum level; 42, secure	$2.00/day	$6.30	Yes; by department policy and monitored by institutional superintendents	Yes; child support if court ordered; court fines, restitution, etc., based on available funds
MI	Unavailable	23,104	50	$7.05/day, prison industries; $2.50/day, Public Works; 84¢ unskilled; $1.54, skilled	Virtually no work release at present	Yes	Yes; victim restitution ordered by the court
MN	1-1-98	3,170	60	25¢-$1, non-industry; 50¢-$2, industry	Unknown	Yes; based on the inmate's pay scale	Yes; court-mandated fees for victim restitution and child support and into a fund for crime victims
MS	7-1-98	Unavailable	Unavailable	20¢	Minimum wage	Yes; for the inmate's trust fund account	Yes; in certain situations, such as damage to department property
MO	6-98	18,670 FT	75	8.1¢	N/A	Yes; by Inmate Finance office	No; however, any funds in an inmate account (which may be from sources other than wages) above the $7.50 base pay may be used to pay outstanding debts or victim's compensation
MT	1-1-98	998	70	21¢-60¢	Work release not offered	Yes; through the Accounting office	Yes; restitution
NE	5-98	3,023	90	$56.45/month	$7.50 (Private Venture); work release, unknown)	Yes; as defined in Inmate Rules and Regulations and Administrative Regulations	No
NV	5-98	4,612	50	13.77¢; $3.86, if in Prison Industry	$7.27	Yes; pay scale set by wardens; statutes and policy control Prison Industry and Division of Forestry	No; but revised state statutes allow department to withdraw funds from inmate accounts for specified reasons
NH	6-19-98	600	40	40¢	$4.00	Yes; by community corrections centers if on work release	No

WAGES EARNED BY INMATES AND GARNISHMENTS, *continued*

	Date of Data	Number in Work Programs	Percentage of Overall Population	AVERAGE HOURLY WAGES EARNED PER DAY		Are Inmate Wages Controlled	Are Inmate Wages Garnisheed
				Inside	Outside		
NJ	6-26-98	22,618 approx.	100, unless in the infirmary	30¢-$1.25 (including those in administrative segregation paid for cell sanitation only)	$5.50	Yes; based on departmental and institutional policies and standards	Yes; fines and halfway house or work release maintenance fees
NM	6-24-98	Unavailable	90	10¢-80¢	$6.20	Yes; budget driven by shop manager and controlled by associate wardens	Yes; court-ordered fees and damages to state property ($300 for "Gate Money" must be maintained)
NY	7-1-98	2,775	3	30¢	$4.25	Yes; pursuant to state law requiring wages to be deposited by the superintendent into inmate's account	No; however, the Commissioner of Corrections may authorize superintendents to disburse inmate's funds for reasonable work release costs, support of dependents, court imposed fines and/or restitution
NC	6-29-98	16,587	52.2	70¢	$5.50	Yes; based on fiscal policy and procedures and Division of Prisons policy	Yes
ND	6-30-98	163	17.7	$2.50/day	$7/day	Yes; 50% toward restitution, court costs, fines and fees; 25% for own medical services and family needs; 25% for RA account	Yes; social services fees, if required
OH	12-31-97	22,773	56	Unavailable	Unavailable	Yes; department rules and administrative directives	Yes; restitution, if required
OK	6-30-98	1,874	12.6	32¢; $5.25 in Private Prison Industry	$6.40	Yes; deposited into inmate trust fund, with disbursements as approved by staff	Yes; medical co-payments, legal photocopies, fines
OR	6-1-98	5,746	71	N/A	N/A	No	No
PA	5-31-98	23,914 (not including community corrections	68.4 (not including community corrections	19¢-42¢	50¢ (not including community corrections)	Yes; departmental policy and corrections employment coordinator	Yes; destruction of state property, fines, court costs, restitution, medical co-pay and (in the future) for misconduct hearings if found guilty
RI	6-30-98	126	3.53	$1-$3/day	Varies	Yes; legislatively, work release supervisor identifies control by computer	Yes; 30% room/board; 15%, fines; restitution; $35 living expenses; attorney fees; bills
SC	3-1-97	876	4-5	N/A	$5.75	Yes, by agency policy	Yes, room and board, victim programs, and court-ordered restitution for work release and Private Sector participants

	Date of Data	Number in Work Programs	Percentage of Overall Population	AVERAGE HOURLY WAGES EARNED PER DAY		Are Inmate Wages Controlled	Are Inmate Wages Garnisheed
				Inside	Outside		
SD	FY 1997	504	24	25¢	At least minimum wage	Yes; (see "garnishments")	Yes; (if in private sector prison industries) federal, state, local taxes; reasonable incarceration costs; family support per state statute; court ordered fees; contributions to Victims Compensation Fund; but all not to exceed 80% of across wages
TN	4-30-98	11,201	79	17¢-59¢-TDOC; 25¢-$2.49-TRICOR; $5.15-PIE	$6.50	Yes; (see "garnishments")	Yes; room and board, first, followed by court ordered payments (but minimum balance must be maintained)
TX	6-98	206 (paid); 119,001 (unpaid)	83.39	Unavailable	$5.48 if working in a privately operated pre release facility overseen by the Parole Division	Unavailable	No
UT	No Response						
VT	Unavailable	Unavailable	Unavailable	25¢-$1.25 (on work details or inside industry)	No work release	Inmates are limited to specific amount and any balance is further distributed by the department to garnishments	Yes; restitution, fines, fees, contributions toward housing
VA	No Response						
WA	6-30-97	8,286	71	25¢ to that comparable to free labor	Unavailable	Yes, legal requirements and by court imposed rules	Yes; child support , court fines, restitution to victims
WV	6-98	1,000	33	Unavailable	At least minimum	Yes; by Inmate Benefit Fund	No
WI	6-6-98	475	3	82¢	At least minimum	No; BSI does not, but institution might	No; but institution might
WY	5-31-98	567	49	41¢	$6.90	Yes; by the Community Corrections facility	No

Specific Costs Paid by Inmates

as of June 1998

	Do Inmates Pay for Education Programs	Do Inmates Pay for Health-Related Programs	Do Inmates Pay for Any Other Programs or Services
AL	No, except for post secondary correspondence courses	Yes; $3 for non-emergency medical visits	No; however, repayments for destruction of property and discipline processes are being considered
AK	No Response		
AZ	No Response		
AR	No for GED or Voc Tech; yes for higher levels	No	No
CA	No	Yes; $5 co-pay for medical visits; however, fee is waived if there is no money in the inmate's trust fund	No
CO	No	Yes; $3 co-pay per visit	No
CT	Yes; $3 per elective vocational, post-GED, post high school, if begun after 1-1-98	Yes; $3 per inmate-requested sick call (no charge for staff-requested follow up); elective dental procedure; eyeglass prescriptions	Yes; $10 per extended family visit for eligible inmates; actual cost of test if use of drugs is confirmed
DE	Yes; post secondary only	Yes; co-pay for office visits and non-prescription drugs	No
DC	No	No	No
FL	Unable to respond at this time		
GA	No Response		
HI	No	Yes; new law passed by the Legislature for "non-emergency" costs currently is being evaluated for implementation procedures	No
OH	No	No	No
IL	No	Yes; Most medical visits initiated by an inmate require a $3 co-pay; indigent inmates receive care and the co-pay is accrued, to be paid later	No
IN	Yes; post secondary	Yes; $5 co-pay per visit; $5 co-pay per prescription	
IA	Yes; college level only	Yes; only if inmate on sick-call is deemed by medical staff not to be ill	No
KS	No Response		
KY	Yes; college correspondence courses	Yes; $2 for each sick call, based on ability to pay; also pay for elective surgery, if approved	No
LA	No	Yes; $3 for each self-initiated request for medical, dental or mental health services; $2 for each new prescription written; some local jail facilities also charge co-pay fees	Yes; postage for approved legal mail and two personal letters per week approved legal supplies; reasonable copies related to legal work; inmate padlocks; replacement of inmate ID cards
ME	Yes; post secondary college level classes	No	No
MD	No Response		
MA	No	(In pre-release institutions only) $5 co-pay for routine medical visits and prescriptions	Yes; (if not waived by the court at time of commitment) a Victim Assessment fee — generally a minimum of $50 for felonies and a flat $30 for misdemeanors; substance abuse tests that prove positive
MI	Yes; for college correspondence courses only	Yes; $3 co-pay, except for a work-related injury, an emergency, for mental health care, or for AIDS testing	Yes; $7.30 electronic monitoring fee; room and board in correction centers filing fees and costs for civil litigation (in state court, the fee is determined by the court)
MN	No, for general education; yes for higher education, with pay schedules varying by facility	Yes; $3 per visit	No

	Do Inmates Pay for Education Programs	Do Inmates Pay for Health-Related Programs	Do Inmates Pay for Any Other Programs or Services
MS	No	Yes; $3 per sick call	No
MO	No, for general education; yes for correspondence courses	No	No
MT	No	No; a co-pay proposal is pending for the next legislative session in January	No
NE	No	No	No
NV	Yes; for college programs only	Yes; co-payments for medical visits and pharmacy costs	Yes; profits from inmate store are used for many expenses, including medical, recreation, law libraries, etc. — this is an indirect inmate payment as they purchase store items
NH	No	Yes, $5 co-pay for requested medical services	No
NJ	No	Yes; $5 per visit for medical services and $1 co-pay for pharmaceutical prescriptions	Yes; postage, correspondence supplies, personal hygiene supplies, photocopies, telephone usage.
NM	Yes; except for some 100- and 200-series college courses and for correspondence courses	No; but may be considered	No
NY	No	No	Yes; Day Reporting program — $10/week if inmates report back to the facility for drug testing and counseling
NC	No	Yes	No
ND	No	No	No
OH	Yes; post secondary	Yes; $2 co-pay per visit for necessary but non-emergency dental or medical treatment from a non-Departmental facility	Yes; materials used in arts and crafts leisure time activity classes
OK	No for GED courses; yes for college courses	Yes; $2 co-pay for each medical visit and for certain prescriptions	Yes; legal photocopies
OR	No for ABE, ESL and GED (which are all mandated); yes for higher education	No	No
PA	Yes; post secondary only at $50 per course	Yes; co-pay began in June of this year	No
RI	No	No	No
SC	No	No; however, inmates in work release pay for care from outside providers	No
SD	No	Yes; $2 co-pay for sick calls, dental and eye doctor visits and any service initiated by the inmate; no for medical emergencies, prescriptions, infirmary care, admitting physical, dental or mental health screenings or for follow-up visits as required by medical staff	No
TN	No	Yes; $3 co-pay for self-initiated visits to the primary care clinics for medical and dental care	Yes, cost of drug screens if tested positive; disciplinary convictions on a sliding scale depending on the level of the disciplinary offense
TX	No for GED courses; yes for post secondary courses (fees are advanced by a State Revenue account and must be repaid as a condition of parole upon release); also for Industry Certification Courses		No
UT	No Response		
VT	No	No	No
VA	No Response		
WA	No	Yes; $3 co-pay per sick call visit when initiated by inmate	No
WV	No	No	No
WI	No for ABE, GED and vocational education; yes for post secondary college courses	Yes; $2.50 co-pay for any inmate initial visit with health care providers	No
WY	No	No	No

Jail and Detention Facility Operating Budgets

as of June 30, 1999

(Excludes States with Combined Jail/Prison Systems)

	Operations	Salaries
Alabama	$32,143,532	$19,048,669
Arizona	$25,762,921	$1,719,897
Arkansas	$9,577,480	$4,956,274
California	$999,552,281	$572,964,647
Colorado	$65,977,844	$39,986,777
Florida	$702,635,076	$442,785,415
Georgia	$186,047,303	$132,942,782
Idaho	$11,823,636	$8,525,185
Illinois	$88,298,187	$50,887,673
Indiana	$32,719,592	$13,209,556
Iowa	$21,830,375	$14,233,293
Kansas	$34,625,054	$18,748,650
Kentucky	$39,419,334	$20,023,958
Louisiana	$61,683,799	$43,244,247
Maine	$15,086,894	$12,186,986
Maryland	$97,377,316	$70,277,175
Massachusetts	$181,923,278	$114,939,749
Michigan	$112,675,799	$79,999,222
Minnesota	$72,724,942	$50,901,947
Mississippi	$13,036,945	$7,266,828
Missouri	$51,500,286	$36,099,961
Montana	$5,802,230	$2,874,351
Nebraska	$26,146,267	$16,126,405
Nevada	$97,865,296	$74,902,686
NewHampshire	$26,858,821	$19,035,350
NewJersey	$192,622,815	$140,085,419
NewMexico	$31,810,915	$20,567,104
NewYork	$1,090,214,991	$255,740,188
NorthCarolina	$73,492,601	$45,469,138
NorthDakota	$3,548,396	$3,322,293
Ohio	$151,085,981	$138,604,094
Oklahoma	$23,611,698	$16,054,593
Oregon	$69,532,205	$91,402,971
Pennsylvania	$368,620,093	$267,852,827
SouthCarolina	$80,195,305	$52,295,263
SouthDakota	$4,503,111	$3,629,572
Tennessee	$40,678,955	$22,570,109
Texas	$329,688,119	$1,077,127,482
Utah	$26,519,412	$11,110,644
Virginia	$222,676,992	$154,055,030
Washington	$178,493,265	$119,615,497
WestVirginia	$4,477,396	$1,176,444
Wisconsin	$113,003,906	$85,231,192
Wyoming	$9,935,844	$6,878,294
Total	$6,051,159,103	$4,385,918,437

CORRECTIONAL FACILITIES & POPULATIONS

Number of Facilities and Programs for Adults

as of June 30, 1998

	Institutions M/F(C)	Diagnostic Reception M/F(C)	L	Community Facilities M/F(C)	L	Prerelease Centers M/F(C)	L	Work Release Centers M/F(C)	L	Farms/Camps M/F(C)	L	Boot Camps M/F(C)	L	Medical Facilities M/F(C)	L	Vocational Training M/F(C)	L	Other Programs M/F(C)	L
AL																			
AK	(12)	(10)								1/								(21)	
AZ	40/4	1/1				/1												2/(1)	
AR	10/1	2/1	2		2			4/			5		1		10		3	20[1]	
CA	28/4(1)			15/1	0			20/5(3)				(1)		(1)					
CO																			
CT	18/			31/															
DE																			
FL	45/4	3/2		2/(8)				22/8		40/1		1/1		(1)	2			2/	8
GA	39/2(1)	1/	5	16/4				4/1		24/		2/	4	(1)	16	8/	3	36/1	5
HI	3/1(4)		2			/2			4						2				
ID	5/1							3/1				1/							
IL	23/1(2)		4					8/1(2)			9		3		2				3
IN	17/3		1			1/	1	2/1							1				
IA	7/1	(1)				9/1(11)													
KS																			
KY	14/1		1	1/(6)									1		1			(49)	
LA	10/1		3					6/2					1		4			1/	2
ME																			
MD																			
MA	11/1(1)	1/	1			2/	3			2/		(1)		2/	3			2/	
MI																			
MN	6/1											(1)							
MS	5/(1)		1	3/1		4/1		16/1				2/1			1			1/	3
MO	17/2(2)	1/1		(2)	1	7/					1		1	1/				3/	
MT	2/					7/						1/							
NE	5/2	1/						(2)							4				
NV																			
NH																			
NJ	11/1	2/	2	18/2(4)			1				8	2/(2)	1					4/3(26)[2]	6[3]
NM	8/2		2	3/4					5		1					(8)		(4)	
NY	47/4	1/	3					5/1	5	3/1	1	3/(1)	-	1/	3			2/1	7
NC	81/6		9	/1					47		3	2/1			3		47	9/1	14
ND	1/(2)																		
OH	22/1	2/	1			1/2					24		2	(2)					
OK	25/4			7/3(2)				14/1											
OR																			
PA	34/4(1)		2	12/2								(1)							
RI	5/2	1/																	1
SC	29/3		2			7/1					3		2		1		23		
SD	4/1																		
TN	8/1	2/(1)										1/		(1)					
TX	56/4	5/2				6/1					3		3	(3)				28/3(1)	2
UT																			
VT	6/(1)									1/									
VA	23/2		4	5/3					1	15/1	27	1/1[4]		1/	15		25	5[5]/1[5]	4
WA	6/1		1					4/2(10)		4/			1		1				
WV																			
WI	27/3	(1)				15/2		15/2		4/		1/		11/3		12/1		14[6]/1[6]	
WY	1/1		2	(4)						2/			1		2				1
FBP	68/3(16)									37/8[7]		2/1[8]		5/1					47
NYC	15/1	—	16	—	—	—	—	—	—	—	4	—	2	—	16	—	8	—	6
PHL	4/1(3)		2					1/							2		1	(2)	2
MB	2/1(4)									1/									
NS	9/1																		
VI	2/(2)		3						2		1				2		1		
YK	2/							1/											

Notes:

(C) Coed

L Located in other facilities

1. Regional maintenance
2. County jails
3. Other—Capital Sentence Unit—NJSP, male and female housed on same unit but kept separate
4. Females sentenced to boot camps are sent to Michigan and participate in their programs
5. Work centers
6. Out of state contracted facilities
7. Satellite Camps
8. Intensive confinement centers—includes ADX control at Florence and Carswell High Security

Number of Jails and Detention Centers

as of June 30, 1999
(Excludes States with Combined Jail/Prison Systems)

	Small 1–49	Medium 50–249	Large 250–999	Mega 1000+	Total
Alabama	51	47	7	1	107
Arizona	7	15	6	3	31
Arkansas	62	20	3	0	85
California	14	48	68	15	145
Colorado	33	14	11	1	59
Florida	13	37	37	17	104
Georgia	72	87	18	5	182
Idaho	26	11	3	0	40
Illinois	50	36	10	1	97
Indiana	31	51	11	1	94
Iowa	85	6	5	0	96
Kansas	76	16	4	0	96
Kentucky	41	45	7	0	93
Louisiana	28	47	18	5	98
Maine	7	7	1	0	15
Maryland	2	15	11	3	31
Massachusetts	0	11	8	1	20
Michigan	30	58	11	2	101
Minnesota	52	24	3	0	79
Mississippi	61	32	3	0	96
Missouri	96	22	6	1	125
Montana	37	5	0	0	42
Nebraska	59	8	1	0	68
Nevada	9	9	5	2	25
New Hampshire	1	7	2	0	10
New Jersey	2	8	12	4	26
New Mexico	20	17	4	1	42
New York	9	42	18	12	81
North Carolina	39	60	11	1	111
North Dakota	19	6	0	0	25
Ohio	62	46	11	2	121
Oklahoma	78	19	1	1	99
Oregon	13	23	5	0	41
Pennsylvania	9	41	23	4	77
South Carolina	22	25	8	0	55
South Dakota	22	7	1	0	30
Tennessee	53	49	8	2	112
Texas	142	83	41	13	279
Utah	11	14	4	0	29
Virginia	39	38	22	0	99
Washington	23	19	8	2	52
West Virginia	25	13	4	0	42
Wisconsin	32	36	9	2	79
Wyoming	15	7	0	0	22
Totals	1,579	1,231	449	102	3,360

Number of Facilities and Programs for Juveniles

as of June 30, 1998

	Institutions			Diagnostic/Reception				Community Based				Detention Centers				Psych				Medical/Homes				Camps				Other			
	M	F	C	M	F	C	L	M	F	C	L	M	F	C	L	M	F	C	L	M	F	C	L	M	F	C	L	M	F	C	L
AL	6		1					17	6																4	2						
AK																																
AZ																																
AR																																
CA	8		1	2		1																	1		4							
CO																																
CT																																
DE																																
FL																																
GA																																
HI			1																		2											
ID																																
IL	5	1																											1[1]			
IN	2	1		1				4																	1				7[2]			
IA																																
KS	3	1																														
KY	10	1		1											1						12	4									27[3]	
LA	3		1				1					4		14		7	3	10		12	15	20		1[4]						18[4]	
ME																																
MD	6	1					3	11	4	5	3	1		4	1	9	1	22	6	104	84	38						2[5]		6[5]	4[6]
MA																																
MI	16		1	2	1			4	1	1																						
MN	1	1																						1								
MS	1	1									8									1				2			5				
MO																																
MT	1	1						1		1																1		1[7]			
NE	1	1									7																				
NV																																
NH																																
NJ																																
NM																																
NY	11	2		1				11	5											8	4	111[8]						1		4[9]	
NC	4		1											9								6	1			7					
ND			1				1								1																
OH	9	1		1																1	1										
OK																																
OR	1		6					23	10	20										190	37			5		1					
PA	13	1																						2							
RI																																
SC																				1	1			1							
SD	1	1	1																												
TN	3		1	1				10	3																						
TX	9	1	2			1		7	1											1				1							
UT			6			6				66				11				1				5									
VT																																
VA	6		1				1							1						3		1		4		1					
WA	5		2					6	2	2										7										10[10]	
WV																																
WI																																
WY																																
Total	125	12	29	9	1	9	5	94	32	95	18	5	0	40	2	16	4	33	6	342	146	182	1	25	2	10	5	13	0	65	4
NYC						1								2	10																
MB	1		1																	2[11]	1[11]										
NF										10												25									
NS			1					1				1																			
VI			1				1															2									

Notes:

- C   Coed
- L   Located in other facilities
- 1. Boot Camp
- 2. Contract bed
- 3. Day treatment—Nonresidential
- 4. Day treatment and trackers
- 5. Spec. out of state
- 6. Impact
- 7. Sex offender treatment program
- 8. Foster care
- 9. Day treatment units (ERCs) and City Challenge
- 10. Community committment contracted with county detention
- 11. Open custody

Number of Juvenile Detention Facilities by Administration

As of March 31, 1997

	County Cmsn or Board	County Exec or Mgr	City Cmsn or Board	City Exec or Mgr	Juv or Fam Ct Judge(s)	State Juv Agency	State Judicial Agency	Sheriff or Police Chief	Private Con-tractor	Other
AL	4				1				2	1
AK						5			1	2
AZ	3				7					
AR	1	1		1				3		
CA	11	6			2					5
CO								1	1	
CT						1	1			
DE						2				
DC										
FL						5				
GA	1					11			1	
HI										
ID	4						1	2		
IL	5				4					3
IN					11	1		2	2	1
IA	5	1								
KS	11								2	
KY	2	2								2
LA	3	1	2			1			11	8
ME	2							6		1
MD						3				
MA						3			1	
MI	3	2			22	3		3		3
MN	3	2				1		3	2	2
MS	1			1	2			1		
MO	2				7		1			1
MT	1	2								1
NE	3								1	
NV	1				3					
NH										
NJ	6	4						1		
NM	4	3				1				
NY	2		1						8	2
NC	2					4				
ND						1		1		1
OH	10				17					1
OK	5								5	
OR	8					1				1
PA	11	1		1	1					1
RI						1				
SC	1	2				1		4		1
SD	3							1	2	
TN	2				4				2	
TX	11				11				1	4
UT						4			1	
VT						1				
VA	6	1	1	2	1			2		3
WA	2	2			5					1
WV	1					1			4	
WI	2				1			4		
WY	1							4		
Total	142	30	4	5	99	50	3	38	47	45

Note: Totals for above tables may not add up because of unavailable breakdowns for administration.

Adult Inmate Population in Institutions

as of June 30, 1998

	Total	WHITE		BLACK		HISPANIC		ALL OTHERS		PENDING IN COUNTY JAILS	
		M	F	M	F	M	F	M	F	M	F
AL	22,670	7,058	648	14,041	842	—	—	76	5	1,373*	
AK	3,522	1,531	125	459	41	114	8	1,172	72	—[1]	—[1]
AZ	25,000	10,651	975	3,442	297	7,802	413	1,320	100	247	0
AR	11,157	4,701	305	5,650	425	49	2	22	3	—[1]	—[1]
CA	159,563	42,946	4,339	46,116	3,810	51,519	2,719	7,497	617	—[1]	—[1]
CO											
CT	16,371	3,974	402	7,095	530	4,044	243	79	4	—[1]	—[1]
DE											
FL	67,224	22,850	1,442	34,873	1,864	5,700	184	275	36	—[1]	—[1]
GA	38,563	11,412	947	24,215	1,498	355	22	105	9	2,844	170
HI	4,880	908	136	176	20	93	7	3,186	354	—[1]	—[1]
ID	3,579	2,506	203	83	6	556	45	166	14	199	38
IL	42,788	9,740	656	26,287	1,794	4,128	162	1	20	0	0
IN	17,621	9,081	646	6,930	454	424	19	61	6	1,300	49
IA	8,186	5,631	375	1,504	110	320	18	120	108	—[1]	—[1]
KS	8,039	3,993	266	2,819	203	518	24	204	9	—[1]	—[1]
KY	11,106	6,427	370	3,916	288	76	4	24	1	3,196	234
LA	18,291	4,015	289	13,347	620	4	0	15	1	10,863	1,186
ME											
MD											
MA	10,264	4,450	331	2,846	132	2,224	140	139	2	393	0
MI											
MN	5,480	2,461	134	1,949	104	366	11	423	32	12	0
MS	16,483	3,652	403	11,581	756	57	3	29	2	—[1]	—[1]
MO	25,609	12,779	1,080	10,774	812	296	17	113	10	—[1]	—[1]
MT	1,846	1,231	0	32	1	63	2	488	29	137	17
NE	3,493	1,864	144	884	67	348	15	154	18	0	0
NV											
NH											
NJ	24,237	4,135	276	14,692	767	4,129	156	80	2	3,563	248
NM	5,052	112	103	538	57	2,636	163	420	23	—[1]	—[1]
NY	70,320	10,332	548	33,629	1,850	21,380	1,033	1,470	78	1,213	71
NC	32,231	9,689	826	19,430	1,085	—[1]	—[1]	1,140	61	—[1]	—[1]
ND	942	627	52	23	2	47	2	175	14	8	0
OH	49,126	20,509	1,239	24,586	1,619	896	44	226	7	—[1]	—[1]
OK	19,879[2]	9,775	1,052	6,040	773	733	42	1,323	141		
OR											
PA	36,143	11,508	607	19,582	745	3,359	127	201	14	4	14
RI	3,289	1,599	115	921	55	530	30	39	0	—[1]	—[1]
SC	20,924	5,773	473	13,711	842	90	9	24	2	338	25
SD	2,412	1,697	134	91	5	—[1]	—[1]	428	57	—[1]	—[1]
TN	15,605	7,065	396	7,803	229	67	3	37	5	4,957	594
TX	132,273	35,192	2,602	55,319	4,129	33,317	1,122	568	24	—[1]	—[1]
UT											
VT	1,400	1,293	40	47	2	0	0	22	0	—[1]	—[1]
VA	29,340[3]	9,186	612	18,316	967	111	4	137	7	3,437	508
WA	14,073	7,436	606	2,831	216	1,814	77	978	115	—[1]	—[1]
WV											
WI	18,653	7,344	483	8,325	616	1,139	47	645	54	—	—
WY	1,404	948	88	70	6	179	9	101	3	11	0
Total	999,038	318,081	24,468	444,973	28,639	149,483	6,926	23,683	2,059	34,095	3,154
FBP	109,872	30,459	2,516	39,238	2,975	28,897	2,240	3,303	244	—[1]	—[1]
NYC	18,335	1,078	141	9,325	1,135	5,808	481	329	38	—	—
PHL	6,229	871	144	4,107	428	569	58	46	6	0	0
MB	971	—	—	—	—	—	—	916	65	—[1]	—[1]
VI	260	2	0	195	7	55	1	0	0	0	0
YK	598*	—	—	—	—	—	—	—	—	—[1]	—[1]

Notes:

*   Ethnic and/or sex breakdown unavailable at time of publication
1. Data not available
2. County Jail inmates are included
3. Totals include 1,483 out-of-state contract inmates

Adult Inmate Population by Security

as of June 30, 1998

	Protective Maximum		Close		Medium		Minimum		Trusty		Unclassified		Custody		Other	
	M	F	M	F	M	F	M	F	M	F	M	F	M	F	M	F
AL	158[1]		192[1]		11,349[1]		5,229[1]		14[1]						5,728[1,2]	—
AK	49	1	809	20	1,059	64	896	92	—	—	457	66			6[3]	3[3]
AZ	3,189	75	3,072	503	8,425	501	6,683	425	—	—	445[4]	35[4]	288	5	1,092[5]	261[5]
AR	2,128	88	0	0	5,064	381	3,156	202	0	0	33	0	100	5	0	0
CA	24,806	*	39,922	*	38,808	*	23,673	*	—	—	20,846	*	23	*	—	11,485
CO																
CT	235	19	5,024	376	5,335	346	3,719	394	777	40	102	4	—	—	—	—
DE																
FL	369	4	27,279	463	20,005	936	14,789	2,064	—	—	822	58	434	1	—	—
GA	4,081	3	6,264	241	14,293	722	10,406	1,289	1,542	79	2,500	142	—	—	—	—
HI	12	2	153	12	1,178	110	1,283	101	0	0	25	5	6[6]	6[6]	0	0
ID	—	—	511	5	1,151	29	1,427	92	—	—	95	19	—	—	310[3]	122[3]
IL	4,953	130	0	0	13,354	887	21,437	1,514	0	0	0	0	0	0	412[7]	101[7]
IN	6,349		151	—	9,179	983	817	142	—	—	—	—	—	—	—	—
IA	545	5	—	—	5,465	379	1,008	150	—	—	—	—	—	—	557[8]	59[8]
KS	1,361	31	—	—	3,147	142	2,451	306	—	—	145	16	30	0	7,537[9]	502[9]
KY	222	8	1,261	60	5,845	320	1,556	139	1,204[3]	105[3]	0	0	0	0	355[10]	31[10]
LA	2,801	118	—	—	10,373	600	2,800	192	—	—	—	—	[11]	[11]	[11]	[11]
ME																
MD																
MA	819	0	727	0	6,386	491	1,438	73	—	—	—	—	—	—	132[12]	0
MI																
MN	284	2	1,631	74	2,669	116	335	49	—	—	280	40	—	—	—	—
MS	1,374	32	—	—	8,356	709	1,705	303	—	—	1,705	150	—	—	491[13]	3[13]
MO	3,476	156	5,343	97	3,022	251	7,534	825	2,464[14]	353[14]	—	—	—	—	—	—
MT	55	—	495	—	680	—	554	—	—	—	85	—	—	—	—	—
NE	820	46	—	—	1,167	57	884	86	379	54	0	0	108	0	0	0
NV																
NH																
NJ	4,222	150	1,838	13	8,696	359	8,280	679	—	—	—	—	—	—	—	—
NM	—	—	61	22	2,640	187	673	131	—	—	237	48	—	—	1,007	46
NY	20,779	810	—	—	39,507	1,913	6,525	786	—	—	—	—	—	—	—	—
NC	—	—	4,106	153	14,766	735	11,378	1,084	—	—	—	—	—	—	9	0
ND	121	22	125	3	312	19	263	26	0	0	51	0	0	0	0	0
OH	1,946	64	10,456	281	16,507	1,075	17,102	1,489	0	0	0	0	206	0	0	0
OK	1,598	122	0	0	8,533	637	5,741	697	1,345	186	0	0	75[15]	0	743[16]	277[16]
OR																
PA	801	17	5,866	209	11,763	621	12,322	450	768	65	3,130	131	—	—	—	—
RI	919	—	—	—	1,158	73	537	88	—	—	475[17]	39[17]	—	—	221[1,18]	
SC	1,099	11	961	33	1,297	47	15,865	1,182	—	—	369	54	6	0	—	—
SD	183	7	573[19]	37[19]	696[20]	32[20]	—	—	—	—	—	—	—	—	228[21]	17[21]
TN	890	5	441	18	3,791	123	7,754	306	2,087	175	9	6	[22]	[22]	—	—
TX	8,045	127	4,782	213	8,402	372	93,253	6,535	4,358	491	42	10	2,427	0	3,087[23]	129[23]
UT																
VT	0	0	24	0	398	1	320	1	281	11	349	13	—	—	—	—
VA	10,753	264	—	—	10,508	598	3,741	506	—	—	2,748	222	—	—	—	—
WA	176	2	1,461	75	2,944	185	7,499	682	0	0	525	56	120	0	334[24]	14[24]
WV																
WI	3,837	199	13	0	9,064	422	3,020	464	—	—	1,198	62	—	—	321[25]	53[25]
WY	26	11	442	30	355	24	387	41	0	0	42	0	14	0	32[26]	0
Total	110,471	2,531	123,986	2,938	317,647	15,447	308,440	23,586	15,219	1,559	36,715	1,176	3,831	11	22,501	13,203
	113,002		126,924		333,094		332,026		16,778		37,891		3,842		35,704	
FBP	13,847[27]	102[27]	23,685[27]	0	33,891[27]	2,317[27]	23,145	4,960	—	—	7,328	596				
NYC	48	0	1,858	83	8,927	1,187	1,197	0	—	—	1,850	195	570	43	582	281
PHL	0	0	1,175	88	1,335	160	2,322	300	0	0	478	58	0	0	283[3]	30[3]
VI	89	0	—	—	45	1	91	6	1	1	8	0	13	1		

Notes:
— Not available
* Numbers not broken by these groups
1. Combines male/female total
2. Community, quarantine, on-the-way, RCES, RCPV, others
3. Community
4. Detention
5. DUI, release centers
6. Protective custody included with each security
7. Pending
8. Work release and substance abuse
9. Administrative segregation—male, 22; female, 1
10. Restricted
11. These numbers are included in med. and max. levels
12. Treatment and support facilities
13. Supermax
14. Community release
15. Included in maximum figures
16. Contracted jails and halfway houses
17. Pretrial
18. Community confinement
19. Close is high medium
20. Medium is low medium
21. Includes disciplinary and administrative segregation, special needs, infirmary, etc.
22. PC inmates are distributed within other levels of security
23. Mental health, intellectually impaired, death row and medical
24. Administrative segregation
25. Intensive sanctions
26. Infirmary—males, 13; intensive supervision unit—males, 19
27. Maximum=high, close=meduim, medium=low

Adult Inmate Population by Age

as of June 30, 1998

	Under Age 16		Ages 16–18		Age 19–55		Ages 55–75		Over Age 75	
	M	F	M	F	M	F	M	F	M	F
AL	1		320	2	20,140	1,461	696	30	20	0
AK	—	—	72	2	3,058	236	141	8	5	0
AZ	11	1	337	21	21,885	1,730	956	35	24	0
AR	1	0	245	11	9,862	701	305	23	9	0
CA	138	2	2,508 [1]	64 [1]	141,237 [2]	11,194 [2]	4,165 [3]	220 [3]	—	—
CO										
CT	11	0	918	41	13,977	1,128	278	10	8	0
DE										
FL	20	3	1,317	52	60,056	3,380	2,214	88	91	3
GA	3	0	499	26	34,350	2,387	1,195	63	40	0
HI	0	0	20	1	4,152	504	136	6	5 [4]	0 [4]
ID	0	0	59	0	2,234	262	189	6	18	0
IL	0	0	963	37	38,359	2,561	799	34	35	0
IN	3	—	280	15	15,677	1,074	517	34	19	2
IA	*	*	*	*	*	*	*	*	*	*
KS	0	0	107	5	7,136	487	285	9	8 [5]	0 [5]
KY	0	0	0	2	9,820	636	599	25	24	0
LA	0	0	137	2	16,563	873	673	30	10	0
ME										
MD										
MA	1	0	135	11	9,107	585	408	9	8	0
MI										
MN	—	—	78	4	4,964	274	153	3	4	0
MS	8	1	337	11	14,346	1,146	409	30	11	1
MO	1	1	898	35	22,066	1,828	635	36	71	2
MT	—	—	—	—	—	—	—	—	—	—
NE	0	0	55	4	3,098	237	93	2	4	0
NV										
NH										
NJ	55 [6]	3 [6]	1,372 [7]	36 [7]	20,9188 [8]	1,142 [8]	691	20	—	—
NM	1	0	24	0	4,536	341	139	4	7	0
NY	0	0	1,104	38	63,536	3,342	1,834	79	50	0
NC	0	0	911	35	28,492	1,899	818	36	28	2
ND	0	0	3	0	850	70	19	0	0	0
OH	5	0	564	21	43,865	2,800	1,710	84	73	4
OK	0	0	199	8	16,947	1,961	695	37	30	2
OR										
PA	4	0	300	8	32,856	1,480	1,444	53	46	2
RI	—	—	39	4	2,957	195	90	1	3	0
SC	0	0	553	16	18,530	1,283	492	27	23	0
SD	—	—	—	—	—	—	—	—	—	—
TN	5	6	117	3	14,254	602	574	22	22	0
TX	0	0	902	30	115,390	7,515	6,056	268	2,048	64
UT										
VT	0	0	21	1	1,270	39	71	2	0	0
VA	3	0	244	8	26,616	1,559	850	22	38	0
WA	3	0	290	19	12,217	972	525	23	24	0
WV										
WI	4	0	496	35	16,477	1,161	450	14	26	0
WY	0	0	36	0	1,197	99	63	7	2	0
Total	278	17	16,500	608	872,994	59,147	31,367	1,399	2,834	82
	295		17,108		932,141		32,766		2,916	
FBP	0	0	76	10	95,040	7,498	6,671	461	106	6
NYC	0	0	1,146	55	15,068	1,725	323	15	3	0
PHL	12	1	248	7	5,247	627	75	2	5 [9]	0 [9]
VI	0	0	2	0	223	7	27	0	0	0

Notes:

— Not available
* Numbers not broken by these groups
1. Ages 18–19
2. Ages 20–54
3. Ages 55–70
4. Unknown—male, 51; female, 6
5. Age unavailable—male, 1; female, 1
6. Under 18 years
7. 18–20 years
8. 21–55 years
9. Age unknown—male, 6; female, 1

U.S. Prison Population—Historical View

Year	Prison Population	U.S. Population	Rate of Incarceration per 100,000 U.S. Citizens
1840	4,000	17,000,000	23.53
1850	7,000	23,000,000	30.44
1860	19,000	31,000,000	61.29
1870	33,000	40,000,000	82.50
1890	45,000	63,000,000	71.43
1900	57,000	76,000,000	75.00
1910	66,000	92,228,531	71.56
1920	76,000	106,021,568	71.68
1930	130,000	123,202,660	105.52
1940	166,000	132,165,129	125.60
1950	161,000	151,325,798	106.39
1960	210,000	179,323,175	117.11
1970	195,000	203,211,926	95.96
1980	320,613	226,504,825	141.55
1985	489,371	238,816,000	204.92
1986	509,015	241,625,000	210.66
1987	545,632	243,178,704	224.38
1988	578,322	245,602,000	235.47
1989	645,609	248,777,000	259.51
1990	716,172	250,630,000	285.74
1991	780,200	252,502,000	308.99
1992	849,900	254,521,000	333.92
1993	925,900	256,466,000	361.02
1994	945,240	260,100,000	362.74
1995	1,054,800	262,952,000	391.87
1996	1,164,360	265,804,000	421.00
1997	1,111,140	270,311,000	433.00
1998	1,277,870	271,548,000	452.00

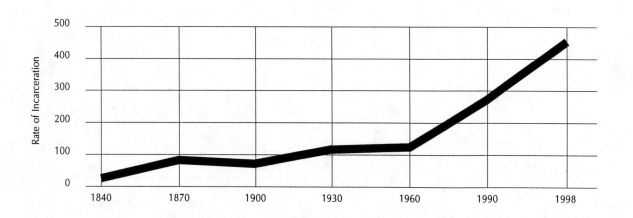

Death Sentence Survey

as of September 30, 1998

| | Death Sentence | | Death Row Maintained | | NUMBER OF PRISONERS SENTENCED TO DEATH | | | | | | | | | | | | | METHOD OF EXECUTION | | | | | No. Executions |
	Yes	No	Yes	No	Total	White M	White F	Black M	Black F	Hispanic M	Hispanic F	Asian/Pacific Islander M	Asian/Pacific Islander F	American Indian/Alaskan Native M	American Indian/Alaskan Native F	Other M	Other F	Lethal Injection	Hanging	Electrocution	Firing Squad	Gas Chamber	
AL	x		x		176	93	2	79	1	0	0	1	0	0	0	0	0			x			
AK		x			0																		x
AZ	x		x		118	82	1	12	0	17	0	0	0	6	0	0	0	x				x	
AR	x		x		44	18	1	19	0	0	0	0	0	5	1	5[3]		x		x			
CA	x		x		517	221	4	184	2	82	2	0	0	0	0	21	1	x				x	
CO																							
CT	x		x		6	3	0	3	0	0	0	0	0	0	0	0	0	x					
DE																							
FL	x		x		370	221	2	128	1							17	1			x			
GA	x		x		122	65	1	56	0											x			
HI		x																					x
ID	x		x		20	19	1											x					
IL	x		x		159	50	0	99	3	7	0	0	0	0	0	0	0	x					
IN	x		x		46	29	0	15	1	1	0	0	0	0	0	0	0	x					
IA		x																					x
KS	x			x	2	2												x					
KY	x		x		35	27	0	8	0	0	0	0	0	0	0	0	0	x		x			
LA	x		x		76	23	0	52	1									x					
ME																							
MD																							
MA		x																					x
MI		x																					x
MN		x																					x
MS	x		x		62	27	1	34	0	0	0	0	0	0	0	0	0	x					
MO	x			x	88	46	1	41	0	0	0	0	0	0	0	0	0	x					
MT	x			x	6	5								1				x					
NE	x		x		10	8	0	1	0	0	0	0	0	1	0	0	0			x			
NV																							
NH																							
NJ	x		x		14	8	0	6	0	0	0	0	0	0	0	0	0	x					
NM	x		x		4	3				1								x					
NY	x		x		2	0	0	1	0	1	0	0	0	0	0	0	0	x					
NC	x		x		188	74	3	103	0	0	0	0	0	5	0	3		x					
ND		x		x																			x
OH	x		x		188	89	0	94	0	5	0	0	0	0	0	0	0	x		x			
OK	x		x		150	82	2	45	1	7	0	3	0	10	0	0	0	x					
OR																							
PA	x			x	221	71	1	132	3	12	0	2	0					x					
RI		x																					x
SC	x		x		66	32	0	34	0	0	0	0	0	0	0	0	0	x		x			
SD	x			x	2	2	0	0	0	0	0	0	0	0	0	0	0	x					
TN	x		x		98	61	2	32		1		1		1				x[4]					
TX	x		x		457	167	5	187	2	92	0	0	0	0	0	0	0	x					
UT																							
VT		x																					x
VA	x		x		45[1]	21	0	24	0	0	0	0	0	0	0	0	0	x[2]		x[2]			
WA	x		x		14	11	0	3	0	0	0	0	0	0	0	0	0	x					
WV																							
WI																							
WY	x			x	2	2												x					
1997	33	7	26	7	2,718	1,369	21	1,115	15	109	1	4	0	23	0	59	1	29	0	9	0	2	
1996	37	13	27	11	3,105	1,541	27	1,326	16	180	2	18	0	18	0	33	0	30	2	12	2	4	42
1994	37	13	27	10	2,873	1,459	25	1,157	13	160	2	6	0	19	0	32	0	28	3	13	1	5	39
1993	36	14	28	8	2,761	1,406	22	1,106	13	149	2	4	0	19	0	40	0	25	3	12	1	5	30
1991	36	14	30	6	2,504	1,297	26	982	12	145	0	5	0	18	0	19	0	22	3	13	1	6	16
1988	36	14	32	4	2,147	1,114	15	856	4	103	0	3	0	15	0	23	0	20	3	14	1	6	11
1987	36	14	28	9	1,952	1,006	17	791	6	93	0	4	0	17	0	7	0	18	3	15	1	7	25
1985	38	12	29	9	1,597	821	15	641	5	92	0	2	0	7	0	14	0	16	4	16	2	6	18
FBP	x			x	20	4	0	14	0	1	0	1	0	0	0	0	0	x		x			

Notes:

1. Four black male inmates housed for the federal government.
2. Choice of method of execution made by inmate. If no choice made, defaults to lethal injection.
3. Held for the federal government.
4. Method of execution changed from electrocution to lethal injection on 7/1/98, felons sentenced to death prior to 7/1/98 can choose method of execution.

Movement of Prisoners in Adult Systems

as of September 30, 1998

| | ADMISSIONS | | | ESCAPES | RELEASES | | | | DEATHS | | | | |
| | Court Cmtd | Parole Violator | Other | Escaped/ Returned[1] | Cond | Sent Served | Court Order | Other | Ntrl[2] Causes M/F | AIDS[3] M/F | Murder[3] M/F | Sui- cide M/F | Accdt/[3] Other Totals |
State													
AL	7,676			306/204	2,644	2,738		3,078[4]	30[5]/			1/	2/
AK	4,495	299	27,129	/5	14,572	9,614	4,988	2,494	2/0	0/0	0/0	0/0	2/0
AZ	11,229	2,855	75	2/7	3,106	9,089	65	91[6]	49/2	4/0	1/0	7/0	7[7]/
AR	3,881	925	338	14/14	4,532	647	5	538[8]	30/0	0/0	1/0	3/0	1/
CA	66,994	72,061	17,760	319/209	128,737	5,118	—	16,177	—	—	—	—	—
CO													
CT	30,707[9]	—	—	2/2	26,450[9]				7/0	11/0	1/0	0/1	9/
DE													
FL	21,754	8	1,039[10]	144/167	4,531	17,581	359	562	122/6	71/6	3/0	5/0	3/1
GA	8,947	2,495	115	48/61	10,395	4,364	181	15,996[11]	76/0	10/0	1/0	9/2	5/
HI	2,495	416	7,295	43/48	3,076	1,871	—	4,609	2/0	1/0	1/0	3/0	0/
ID	2,406[12]			15/11	942	319			9/0	1/0	1/0	0/0	0/
IL	24,022	1,817		1,044/1,061	22,756	1,216	30	105	67/1	9/1	4/0	10/1	12/
IN	8,548	752	1,519	17/20	3,985	—	4,288	1,016	—	—	—	—	1/0
IA	3,427	484	923	1/1	1,745	906	225	2,121	6/0	0/0	0/0	1/0	0/0
KS	3,149	1,952	92[13]	37/27	4,521	279	139	25	23/0	0/0	0/0	1/0	0/0
KY	5,976	1,407	571	102/77	2,268	3,400	77	1,060[14]	21/2	0/0	1/0	1/0	0/0
LA	10,818	4,856	489[15]	102/96	12,560	562	49	139[16]	*/*	*/*	*/*	*/*	*/*
ME													
MD													
MA	2,920	599	990	17/22	1,169	2,478	73	584[17]	20/0	5/0	0/0	2/0	1/0
MI													
MN	3,140	1,167	—	13/11	3,011	693	32	—	5/0	1/0	1/0	1/0	0/0
MS	5,963	118	394	73/55	1,828	1,883	—	185	41/3	2/0	0/0	2/0	1/0
MO	7,399	1,906	3,337[18]	5/796	5,991	959	8	5,743[19]	37[5,20]/		0/0	4[5]/	4[5]/
MT													
NE	1,603	313	127	15/16	751	985	0	132	6/0	0/0	0/0	0/0	1/0
NV													
NH													
NJ	10,288	6,082	385	0/0	9,683	4,123	102	169[21]	34/2	15/1	1/0	2/0	14/0
NM	1,859	839	793	1,076[22]/13	1,685	1,200	0	302[23]	5/2	0/0	1/0	1/0	0/0
NY	20,203	6,300	2,990[24]	7/6	24,899	1,597	98	2,122[25]	136/9	39/0	1/0	13/1	12/2
NC	20,973	1,900	1,702	128/127	7,894	14,222	114		75/6	0/0	14/0	4/0	6/0
ND	699	62	9	4/5	447	136	6	16[26]	1/0	0/0	0/0	0/0	0/0
OH	17,681	1,379	1,213[27]	13/12	6,172	8,638	1,861	1,056	111/4	7/0	2/0	6/0	4/0
OK	6,972	70	—	107/127	3,250	3,915	83	66[28]	52/1	1/0	4/0	3/0	3/0
OR													
PA	6,476	3,302	256	71/68	5,935	2,546	12	377[29]	71/2	20/0	1/0	8/1	5/1
RI	3,102	219	1,251[30]	21/10	552	2,791	113	957[31]	4/0	3/0	0/0	0/0	4[32]/0
SC	9,017	1,276	1,299[33]	44/63	2,839	7,699	10	419	57/2	0/0	0/0	0/2	3/0
SD	1,065	148	118[34]	4/4	656	385	82	24[35]	1/0	0/0	0/0	1/0	0/0
TN	7,706	5,124	137	21/	8,485	3,612	—	197	40/3	5/0	2/0	5/0	1/0
TX	24,331	6,409	6,953[36]	11/10	10,638	2,498	19,112[37]	1,028	231/19	48/1	9/0	18/0	28/2
UT													
VT	1,067	6	—	5/4	2	594	—	—	3/0	0/0	0/0	1/0	0/0
VA	8,858	1,268	303[38]	3/3	2,424	7,339	93	108	19/1	9/0	0/0	1/0	27[41]/0
WA	6,371	36	780	141/126	43	5,190	—	766	32/1	2/0	0/0	2/0	0/0
WV													
WI	5,187	1,088	2,155	600/566	4,698	148	33	1,519	22/0	0/0	1/0	4/0	5/0
WY	472	233	4	13/6	400	221	19	41[40]	1/0	0/0	0/0	0/0	1/0
Total	389,876	130,171	82,541	4,588/4,060	350,272	127,556	32,257	63,822	1,448/66	264/9	51/0	119/8	213/2
FBP	42,946	2,979	12,184	112/107	1,393	37,503	252	4,258[41]	195/11	9/0	3/0	11/0	3/0
Cook	100,400	—	—	0/	—	—	—	—	—	—	—	—	—
NYC	23,450	7,157	96,323	3/3	1,925	39,612	27,757	59,562	26/4	—	1/0	4/1	—
PHL	27,643	—	—	48/	26,850	—	—	—	2/1	5/1	0/0	0/1	1/0
MB	4,200	—	3,859	43/	—	—	—	8,041	—	—	—	—	—
VI	259	4	1	0/0	55	75	0	0	1/0	0/0	0/0	0/0	0/0

Notes:

— Unknown

* Cause of death is not captured in the central inmate database

1. May include detainee, temp hold, arrested, bond, ISC, Ret. DCP, PV's for release parole returned, Evaluators and safekeepers, those returned by court order, new admissions, and probation violators
2. May include returned escapees and walkaways from previous years
3. May include furlough, federal release, non-criminal, house arrest, escapes, appeals bond, death, execution, shock probation release, new bail, supervised release, acquittal, emergency release, evaluators and safekeepers, warrant lifted, fine paid, court orders and transfers.
4. Act, 754; parole reinstated, death, other
5. Combines males and females
6. Deaths, 70; escapes/absconder, 12; transfer, 9
7. Pending investigation
8. Transfers, 27; Other includes bond, other juris, cond release (BC; Act 378), 511

9. Totals
10. Returned by court order, 572; Other, 567
11. Transfers, 528; Other, 15,468
12. Includes technical parole violators
13. Returned by court order, 73; interjurisdictional transfers, 19
14. Shock probation, 1,056; transfers, 4
15. Returned by court order, 435; Other, 54
16. Transfers, 75; conviction overturned, good time release without supervision, 64
17. Transfers, 584
18. Returned by court order, 2,262; Other, 1,075
19. Transfers, 19; Other, 5,724
20. Includes AIDS related
21. Deaths, 64; misc, 100
22. Institutions, 15; alternative programs, 1061
23. Transfers, 28; Other, 274
24. Returned by court order, 79; Other, 2,911
25. Transfers, 639; Other, 1,483
26. Transfers, 11; appeal bond, 5

27. Returned by court order—Judicial release violators and sentence reactivations, 816; Other, 397
28. Transfers, 2; deaths, 64
29. Transfers, 43; Other, 334
30. Returned by court order, 384; Other, 249; civil committments, 618
31. Transfers and temporary release weekend inmates, 339; Other—civil commitments, 618
32. Includes parole violators pending in which a decision has not been made
33. Returned by court order, 245; Other, 1,054
34. Returned by court order, 44; Other, 74
35. Transfers, 4; Other, 20
36. Returned by court order—mandatory supervision violators, 5,567; Other—shock probation violators, 1,386
39. Mandatory supervision violators
40. Out of state cases under contract all from Delaware
41. Autopsy pending
42. Transfers, 8; Other, 33
43. Transfers, 258; Other, 4000

Juveniles Under Supervision by Security

as of September 30, 1998

		SECURE								NONSECURE												
		Institutions Training Schools			Detention		Diagnostic		Other		Community Residential		Med/Drg Men Health		Specialty Facilities		Group/Foster Homes		Detention		Other	
	Total	Total	M	F	M	F	M	F	M	F	M	F	M	F	M	F	M	F	M	F	M	F
AL	1,253	569	460	109	—	—	—	—	—	—	515	62	—	—	107	0	—	—	—	—	—	—
AK	425[1]	158	—	—	83[2]						72[2]		11[2]		—	—	101[2]					
AZ†	1,683	500	472	28			41	3			105	16					88	14			772	116
AR†	430	125	27						129	2	32	17	8	4	86							
CA	8,563	7,919	7,610	309	170	7	23	1	0	0	24	0	6	0	322	0	0	0	0	0	88[3]	3[3]
CO†	1,549	721	667	54	394	75	53	6							75		45	24				
CT†	209		176	33																		
DE†	208	74	74		118	16							22	4	148	19	18	6	12	10		
FL†	5,595	253	253		1,601				126		1,756		20		155		132		1,129		423	
GA†	5,358	1,032	957	75	1,002	251			949	207	203	118	203	62	171	5	48	7	10	16	820	254
HI	85	73	63	10							2[4]		3				5	1				1[5]
ID†	125	110	105	5	13	2																
IL	2,110	2,110	1,971	139																		
IN	1,148	737	505	232	—	—	39		100[6]		131		—		26		—		—		115[6]	
IA†	187	180	180				7															
KS	2,137	541[2]			165[2]						852[2]						444[2]				135[2]	
KY	879	408	376	32	22[7]	3[7]	—	—	—	—	212	89	—	—	—	—	117	28	—	—	—	—
LA	3,094	1,645	1,473	172	187	30	92			3[8]	290	53	20	12	—	—	132	114	10	9	409[9]	88[9]
ME†	202	160	152	8	33	6												3				
MD	1,806	674	649	25	376	72					277	41	191	57	0	0	51	22	0	0	22[10]	23[10]
MA†	3,081	319	305	14	403	59	142		91	1	83	21	26	7	32		319	54				
MI	1,066	763	682	81	183	41					57	22										
MN	192	192	174	18											48[23]							
MS	1,043	600	504	96																	390[11]	53[11]
MO†	681	100	100								316	74					86				89	16
MT	120	103	86	17					20[12]	0	17	0										
NE	324	299	233	66			25[2]															
NV																						
NH	111	87	72	15	11	1											6	6				
NJ†	882	623	608	17							154	9	23	0	71	0						
NM	712	539	488	51			45	10			103	15	21	1								
NY	3,236	1,385	1,261	124							610	140					820	150			120[13]	11[13]
NC	1,456	936	832	104	123	33	0	0							282	31	34	7				
ND	514	68	56	12	6	0	5	5	5[14]	0	103	17	4	1	0	0	51	22	0	0	196[15]	31[15]
OH	1,995	1,995	1,845	150																		
OK†	193	178	166	12			15															
OR	802	760	689	71			27	15														
PA	825	584	541	43									241									
RI†	222	155	143	12							12	10					45					
SC	1,797	833	735	98	70	68	175	39	50[16]	9[16]					279	0	170	97			5[17]	2[17]
SD	508	186	150	36	2	2	43	8					24	8	120	0	54	61				
TN	5,415	713	680	33	391	52	151	55			167	43	59	19			293	210			2,309	963
TX	5,589	3,696	3,480	216	60	3	302	29	513	92	137	16	120	59	216	19	123	55	0	0	118	31
UT	2,588	223	212	11	259	52	73	18	18[18]	3[18]	495	98	8	1	43	1			189	36	57[19]	14[19]
VT																						
VA	1,300	1,114[20]	986[20]	128[20]			127[20]	17[20]							37[20]	5[20]						
WA	1,196	954	880	74							149	17					76	0				
WV†	142	142	135	7																		
WI†	932	894	820	74					38													
WY	410	180	90	90							101	49					47	23	7	3		
Total	52,699	31,044	27,783	2,562	2,108	364	1,127	197	711	104	4,312	662	708	158	1,480	56	2,525	796	206	48	3,964	1,220
			30,445		2,472		1,324		815		4,974		866		1,636		3,321		254		5,184	
DC†	516	181	161	20									96	20			126	11	71	11		
NYC	354	267	—	—			227	40											78	9		
AB†	456	397	360	37								3	11		60						70	10
BC†	375	193									12				170							
MB	299	94	86	8	72	17															97[21]	19[21]
VI	128	50	43	7	0	0	2[22]	4[22]									1	1				

Notes:

—	Not available
*	Totals may include ages over 18
†	Data as of 6/30/97
1.	Total includes 350 males and 75 females
2.	Combines males and females
3.	Other includes furlough, escape
4.	Adult facility, 1; secure treatment, 1
5.	Escape
6.	Contract bed facilities
7.	State operated centers only
8.	Absent offenders
9.	Day treatment
10.	Structured shelter care
11.	AOP
12.	Sex offender treatment program
13.	Day programs
14.	Time out
15.	Other includes: home/relatives/job/out-of-state
16.	Mental health
17.	Shelters
18.	Jail
19.	Hospital, shelters, AWOL
20.	Gender counts are estimates based on distribution of FY '98 admissions
21.	Open custody
22.	Crisis center
23.	Not included with other totals

Juveniles Under Supervision by Age

as of September 30, 1998

	Entering Offender (avg)	Under 16	16 to 18	18 and Over
	M&F	Total	Total	Total
AL	15	1,165	88*	15
AK	16	140	285*	63
AZ†	15.5	723	1,311	
AR†	15.4	261	169	
CA	17	282	8,281*	6,192
CO†	16.2	389	523	24
CT†		152	57	
DE†	15			
FL†	15.3			
GA†	15.49	3,215	2,090	53
HI	16.4	9	76*	26
ID†	16			
IL	15.6	535	1,619*	279
IN	16	437	778*	61
IA†		76	111	
KS	—	—	—	—
KY	14	—		
LA	15.2	1,109	1,985*	427
ME†	16.2			
MD	16.5	726	1,080*	86
MA†	15.3	657	2,007	173
MI	15.5	—	—	—
MN	16.9	19	173*	65
MS	15.0	217	383*	3
MO†	15.5	301	379	1
MT	—	—	—	—
NE	16	—		
NV				
NH	15.2	36	87*	—
NJ†	17	135	481	266
NM	16.6	298	414*	57
NY	15.4	1,317	1,919*	182
NC	15.5	1,105	255*	—
17	17	150	364*	73
OH	16.5	461	1,534*	442
OK†	15.7	65	116	12
OR	15.6	198	604*	188
PA	—	—	—	—
RI†	15	35	70	50
SC	15	—	—	
SD	15.5	223	285*	30
TN	15	1,766	3,648*	573
TX	15.9	1,297	4,292*	1,119
UT	16	570	1,018*	167
VT				
VA	15.8[1]	299[1]	1,001[1]	247[1]
WA	15.6	332	864*	313
WV†	16	14	118	10
WI†	15.2	190	548	194
WY	15	279	121*	1
TOTAL	15.7 (avg.)	12,970	31,154	10,609
DC†	15	139	217	160
NYC	15	228	26*	1
AB†	15–16	209	226	21
BC†	16.1	99	21	80
MB	—	95	204*	40
VI	—	18	29*	6

Notes:
— Not available
* Totals may include ages over 18
† Data as of 6/30/97
1. Age counts are estimates based on distribution of FY '98 admissions

Profile of State Prisoners under Age 18 (1985–97)

PERSONS UNDER 18 HELD IN STATE PRISON AT YEAR-END

	Number Held	Percent of All Inmates
1985	2,300	0.5%
1990	3,600	0.5
1993	4,700	0.6
1995	5,300	0.5
1997	5,400	0.5

- On December 31, 1997, less than 1% of inmates in State prison were under age 18, a proportion that has remained stable since the mid-1980's.

PERSONS UNDER 18 ADMITTED TO STATE PRISON

	Number of Admissions	Violent Percent
1985	3,400	52%
1990	5,100	45
1993	6,300	52
1995	7,600	57
1997	7,400	61

- The number of offenders under age 18 admitted to State prison has more than doubled from 3,400 in 1985 to 7,400 in 1997, consistently representing about 2% of new admissions in each of the 13 years.

- In 1997, 61% of persons admitted to State prison under age 18 had been convicted of a violent offense compared to 52% in 1985.

- The violent arrest rate for persons under age 18 did not change dramatically between 1980 and 1988, but increased over 60% from 1988 and 1994, then fell 23% from 1994 to 1997.

CHARACTERISTICS OF STATE PRISONERS UNDER 18 IN 1997

	Admitted to Prison	Held in Prison
Gender		
Male	97%	92%
Female	3	8
Race/Hispanic origin		
White non-Hispanic	25%	19%
Black non-Hispanic	58	60
Hispanic	15	13
Other	2	8
Most serious offense		
Violent	61%	69%
Property	22	15
Drugs	11	11
Public-order	5	5

Source: Bureau of Justice Statistics

NEW COURT COMMITMENTS TO STATE PRISON, 1985–97

Persons under age 18

Number of State prisoners

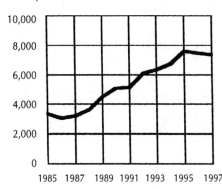

ESTIMATED AGE OF RELEASE FOR PERSONS UNDER AGE 18 ADMITTED TO STATE PRISON

Percent released based on minimum time to be served

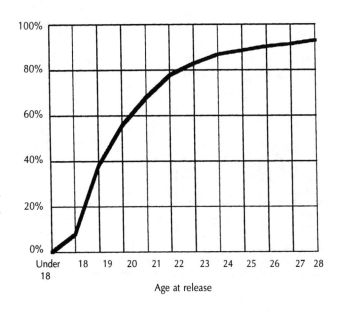

Age at release

Note: Minimum time served was provided in 51% of all cases involving persons admitted to State prison under 18 in 1997 (National Corrections Reporting Program). The expected age of release was estimated by adding age at admission to minimum time to be served. These calculations are estimates of the earliest possible release age and are not the actual age of release from prison.

Jail and Detention Facility Populations

as of June 30, 1999

(Excludes States with Combined Jail/Prison Systems)

| | | SMALL | | | | MEDIUM | | | | LARGE | | | | MEGA | | | |
| | | Adult | | Juvenile | | Adult | | Juvenile | | Adult | | Juvenile | | Adult | | Juvenile | |
	Total	M	F	M	F	M	F	M	F	M	F	M	F	M	F	M	F
AL	4,402	212	11	0	0	1,266	120	1	0	1,549	134	9	0	973	127	0	0
AZ	366	0	0	0	0	312	46	3	1	0	0	0	0	0	0	4	0
AR	2,107	1,089	105	17	0	454	40	22	9	311	55	5	0	0	0	0	0
CA	10,904	0	0	0	0	0	0	0	0	4,548	371	0	0	5,166	816	0	3
CO	4,230	179	15	0	0	1,011	91	1	0	1,025	80	6	0	1,650	166	6	0
FL	45,517	74	5	0	0	1,436	440	35	15	11,133	2,230	211	10	26,195	2,887	838	8
GA	18,872	201	18	0	0	6,065	863	83	14	3,237	402	1	0	7,039	892	56	1
ID	1,051	114	12	1	0	313	28	0	0	521	62	0	0	0	0	0	0
IL	4,598	293	31	0	0	1,741	198	5	0	2,088	242	0	0	0	0	0	0
IN	4,277	231	16	3	0	2,019	146	8	0	1,664	177	13	0	0	0	0	0
IA	1,595	456	39	5	0	417	48	0	0	548	68	12	2	0	0	0	0
KS	2,507	403	39	1	0	501	38	2	0	1,339	176	8	0	0	0	0	0
KY	3,566	172	16	0	0	1,060	148	10	2	1,870	238	43	7	0	0	0	0
LA	4,779	26	6	0	0	1,324	85	2	1	2,102	176	0	0	954	103	0	0
ME	559	109	4	0	0	240	18	10	1	163	14	0	0	0	0	0	0
MD	5,309	0	0	0	0	666	63	0	9	1,883	198	9	0	2,178	245	58	0
MA	5,534	0	0	0	0	595	28	0	0	3,002	121	0	0	1,595	193	0	0
MI	7,071	415	34	0	0	2,166	191	7	0	2,726	331	22	0	1,030	149	0	0
MN	3,072	539	37	2	1	994	107	5	0	1,270	117	0	0	0	0	0	0
MS	2,640	1,130	90	3	1	1,031	120	18	1	222	24	0	0	0	0	0	0
MO	3,743	519	62	0	1	964	162	3	2	1,824	186	20	0	0	0	0	0
MT	417	124	18	1	0	239	35	0	0	0	0	0	0	0	0	0	0
NE	1,759	426	45	8	1	562	70	6	0	585	56	0	0	0	0	0	0
NV	4,804	642	158	0	0	347	51	0	0	370	106	0	0	2,678	422	29	1
NH	18,084	0	0	0	0	462	16	8,321	0	799	72	8,414	0	0	0	0	0
NJ	12,625	0	22	0	0	1,049	170	0	0	7,027	701	10	1	3,246	399	0	0
NM	3,510	163	26	3	0	831	86	78	15	866	129	0	0	1,154	159	0	0
NY	28,701	482	82	150	26	2,147	143	161	7	6,929	381	178	14	15,948	1,847	193	13
NC	6,493	289	26	9	0	2,567	262	18	0	2,552	206	32	0	477	55	0	0
ND	348	98	10	6	0	196	31	6	1	0	0	0	0	0	0	0	0
OH	23,933	421	30	0	0	4,970	774	7	1	12,151	2,189	26	3	2,882	452	27	0
OK	2,962	415	53	4	0	478	61	8	0	766	136	21	0	816	146	54	4
OR	4,578	96	8	1	0	2,006	220	14	2	1,920	304	6	1	0	0	0	0
PA	23,710	277	24	0	2	2,869	467	11	1	14,251	1,663	135	2	3,762	244	2	0
SC	6,683	363	8	0	0	1,798	152	3	0	3,860	422	71	6	0	0	0	0
SD	536	159	29	3	0	61	10	0	0	242	32	0	0	0	0	0	0
TN	8,659	378	73	0	0	3,474	328	6	0	1,671	265	8	0	2,316	50	90	0
TX	25,483	745	78	0	0	2,624	325	0	0	5,337	471	0	0	13,901	1,975	24	3
UT	1,344	49	4	0	0	560	94	0	0	600	36	1	0	0	0	0	0
VA	12,778	578	61	7	2	3,711	469	15	0	6,900	1,015	19	1	0	0	0	0
WA	8,032	158	11	0	0	1,115	127	1	0	2,429	333	12	0	3,353	462	31	0
WV	733	81	13	0	0	261	26	0	0	299	53	0	0	0	0	0	0
WI	10,210	897	144	1	0	3,545	495	8	4	2,223	577	26	13	2,182	48	47	0
WY	606	254	21	17	0	252	35	25	2	0	0	0	0	0	0	0	0
Totals	354,441	13,413	1,490	242	34	62,659	7,855	8,905	88	119,199	14,590	9,318	60	103,032	12,027	1,492	37

"0" entries mean one of two things: If the "adult" entry is *also* "0", the state has no facilities of that size. If there is an adult entry with a "0" juvenile or female entry, there are no juvenile or female inmates in facilities of that category.

Juvenile Detention Population by Sex and Race

As of March 31, 1997

	TOTAL POPULATION			WHITE Not of Hispanic Origin		BLACK Not of Hispanic Origin		HISPANIC White and Black		ALL OTHERS	
	Total	Male	Female	Male	Female	Male	Female	Male	Female	Male	Female
AL	366	308	58	81	21	228	35	2			
AK	119	99	20	39	8	12	1	3		45	11
AZ	648	535	113	199	61	99	18	213	26	24	8
AR	121	89	32	50	22	36	10			3	
CA	4,778	4,182	596	622	162	153	156	1,867	198	291	33
CO	10	10		2		2		6			
CT	930	294	12	2	3	8	4	11	3	1	3
DE	114	102	12	29	5	68	6	3	1	2	
DC											
FL	754	362	78	134	26	206	47	22	5		
GA	1,456	1,295	161	370	70	913	87	6	2	6	2
HI											
ID	101	81	20	61	14	2	0	15	5	3	1
IL	955	852	103	158	32	602	61	85	9	9	1
IN	458	386	72	260	49	105	15	9	2	3	
IA	88	74	14	45	9	18	3	10		1	2
KS	264	197	67	95	40	51	11	21	8	9	
KY	149	145	4	47	4	98					
LA	594	462	132	77	39	364	91	8	1	4	1
ME	59	53	6	49	6	4					
MD	201	147	54	62	21	67	32	12		6	1
MA	112	112		36		29		35		12	
MI	721	596	125	241	58	314	61	34	3	8	3
MN	416	371	45	198	24	101	9	17	2	44	6
MS	72	59	13	9	3	50	10				
MO	330	282	48	114	28	169	20	2		7	
MT	53	39	14	27	12	1		6	1	5	1
NE	126	95	31	53	20	33	10	5	1	4	
NV	274	237	37	102	22	61	4	68	6	6	5
NH											
NJ	778	703	75	82	28	495	34	125	10	1	3
NM	138	111	27	34	7	8	4	64	15	5	1
NY	122	80	42	47	21	29	15	12	4	2	1
NC	88	76	12	18	6	58	6				
ND	17	11	6	10	5						
OH	1,174	943	231	498	136	392	80	31	6	4	1
OK	216	183	33	80	12	80	16	9		8	5
OR	615	580	35	430	31	51		63	1	36	3
PA	671	561	110	185	42	309	54	46	9	10	3
RI	297	273	24	94	11	75	6	61	6	43	1
SC	110	100	10	22	4	75	6			3	
SD	241	209	32	92	17	62	3	20	1	31	15
TN	246	210	36	78	19	129	17			3	
TX	777	638	139	145	44	196	39	277	52	9	3
UT	182	146	36	108	32	3		30	3	7	1
VT	16	16									
VA	544	444	100	166	49	258	38	12	8	8	5
WA	551	459	92	259	62	89	16	62	10	49	4
WV	78	58	20	35	18	20	1	2		1	1
WI	176	135	41	87	28	24	8	11	1	13	4
WY	37	34	3	28	4			4		1	
Total	21,209	17,302	2,969	5,627	1,333	6,057	1,034	3,280	399	726	129

Note: Totals for above tables may not add up because of unavailable breakdowns for population.

HEALTH CARE

1998 Inmate Populations and Health Care Budgets

	Report Period	Average Daily Population	No. of New Inmates Processed	Total DOC Budget (Millions)	Percentage Allocated for Inmate Health Care	Actual Expenditure for Inmate Health Care	Actual Amount Spent Per Inmate	Change from Previous Year	Comments (Due to: Population Changes, Budget Cuts, Medical Costs, Etc.)
AL	FY '98	22,386	7,676	$197.3	11	$22,221,816	$94	Increase	Population changes
AK	No Response								
AZ	FY '98	24,935	12,987	$486.7	12.3	$54,081,082	$2,319	Increase	
AR	FY '98	9,426	6,022	$146.4	16.9	$24,757,262	$2,626	Increase	Population changes
CA	No Response								
CO	FY '98	13,242	4,288	$343.5	9.6	$32,107,280	$2,499	Increase	Population changes
CT	FY '99	16,673	9,477	$415.8	12.4	$51,652,385	$3,099	Increase	Population changes, increased costs relative to HIV treatment
DE	FY '99	5,720	22,934	$141.2	13.03	$10,988,224	$1,921	Increase	Population per diem costs, contract increases
DC	No Response								
FL	FY '98	66,280 (6/30)	22,654	$1,736.2	12 approximately	$220,000,000 approximately	$3,493	Decrease	Budget cuts
GA	No Response								
HI	FY '98	4,086	10,206	$106.0	9.23	$9,784,269	Unavailable	Increase	Population changes, opening of expansion projects
ID	FY '99	Unavailable	2,700	$7.4	10 approximately	$7,492,670	$2,141	Increase	Population changes, HIV treatment regimens, contract increases
IL	FY '98	38,862	25,839	$928.9	10	$68,107,900	$1,753	Increase	Population changes
IN	CY '98	18,617	5,982	$409.8	6.7	$26,157,120	$1,445	Increase	Population changes, privatization of medical services (expected to subsequently decrease)
IA	FY '98	6,985	4,734	$197.9	5.13	$10,164,689	$1,460	Increase	Population changes, pharmacy cost increases
KS	FY '99	7,931	5,220 (CY '98)	$217.4 est.	9.4	$20,654,285	$2,548	Increase	Population changes, contract increases
KY	FY '98	14,390	6,090	$158.0	10	$15,645,000	Unavailable	Increase	Merit pay increase for staff
LA	FY '99	19,085	7,170	$349.7	11	Unavailable	Unavailable	Increase	
ME	No Response								
MD	FY '98	26,500	Unavailable	$613.0	8.4	$49,000,000	$2,160	Increase	Population changes, cost increases
MA	No Response								
MI	CY '98	44,791	9,424	$1,382.4	13.7	$188,836,556	$4,150	Decrease	Partial year's implementation of managed care
MN	CY '98	5,766 (6-mo avg.)	4,037	$289.0	7.4	$21,451,555	$3,875	Increase	
MS	FY '98	16,250	7,649	$201.0	9	$19,041,355	$1,785	Decrease	

1998 INMATE POPULATIONS AND HEALTH CARE BUDGETS, continued

	Report Period	Average Daily Population	No. of New Inmates Processed	Total DOC Budget (Millions)	Percentage Allocated for Inmate Health Care	Actual Expenditure for Inmate Health Care	Actual Amount Spent Per Inmate	Change from Previous Year	Comments (Due to: Population Changes, Budget Cuts, Medical Costs, Etc.)
MO	FY '98	23,877	1,281	$439.8	10	$44,505,876	$1,697	Increase	Population changes, Mental Health included for the first time
MT	FY '99	2,540	Unavailable	$95.2	Unavailable	$6,557,183	Unavailable	Increase	Population changes
NE	FY '99	3,454	1,791	$84.9	9.8	$7,897,225	$2,224	Increase	Population changes
NV	FY '99	9,201	4,394	$162.3	18	$28,500,000	$3,291	Increase	Population changes
NH	FY '98	2,160 (CY '98)	1,056	$49.9	9	$4,512,106	$2,684	Decrease	
NJ	FY '99	26,622	16,800	$691.5	12	$85,817,000	$3,224	Increase	Population changes, contract increases, AIDS treatment
NM	FY '98	4,917	3,600	$1500	11.3	$16,983,100	$3,581	Increase	Population changes, inflation
N	FY '98	69,885	28,871	$1,629.2	10.4	$167,675,402	$2,362	Increase	Population changes, drug costs
NC	FY '98	32,236	25,156	$921.5	7.4	Unavailable	Unavailable	Increase	
ND	CY '98	903	774	$18.5 (FY '98)	16.1	$1,147,335 (FY '98)	$1,398 (FY '98)	Increase	Population changes, aging with increased illnesses, higher medical
OH	FY '99	47,972	21,142	$1,233.3	7.5	$91,945,752	$1,911	Decrease	Budget cuts, internal cost reductions
OK	No Response								
OR	FY '98	8,765	5,110	$364.11	5.68	$16702613	$1,905	Static	
PA	FY '98	35,757	10,578 (CY '98)	$1,027.9 (CY '98)	12.6	$121,181,097	$3 413	Increase	Population changes
RI	FY '99	3,384	14,644	$129.4	Unavailable	Unavailable	Unavailable	Unavailable	
SC	FY '98	20,656	11,321	$330.8	14.5	$46,822,601	$2,267	increase	Population changes, contract
SD	FY '99	2,424	1,047	$49.4	9	$4,426,031	$1,825	increase	Population changes, inflation
TN	FY '98	15,243	4,773	$425.6	8	$33,754,300	$2,243	Increase	Population changes, additional beds at central hospital
TX	FY '98	129,620	37,693	$2,078.3	12 approximately	$288,077,919	$2,223	Increase	Population changes
UT	No Response								
VT	No Response								
VA	FY '99	26,255	8,858	$618.0	10.78	$49,210,038	$1,815	Increase	Opening new facilities
WA	FY '98	13,315	4,272	$424.2	11.2 (excludes sex offender treatment and chemical dependency)	$46,315,365	$3,359	Increase	Population changes, higher medical cost
WV	No Response								
WI	FY '98	13,544	7,354	$667.0	4	$28,471,808	$2,100	Increase	Population changes
WY	CY '98	1,413	497	$44.3	10.1	$4,495,978	$53	Increase	Population changes
FBP	No Response								
MB	FY'98	1,071	8,530	1$35.3	13	$1,260 000	Unavailable	Static	

	Report Period	Average Daily Population	No. of New Inmates Processed	Total DOC Budget (Millions)	Percentage Allocated for Inmate Health Care	Actual Expenditure for Inmate Health Care	Actual Amount Spent Per Inmate	Change from Previous Year	Comments (Due to: Population Changes, Budget Cuts, Medical Costs, Etc.)
NF	CY'98	327.5	1,510	Unavailable	Unavailable	Unavailable	Unavailable	Static	
ON	FY '98	7,689	32,815	$348.1	Unavailable	$21,966,692	$2,759 approximately	Unavailable	Funding for nurses was removed over a two-year period
YK	FY'99	73.42	187 est.	$6.2	Unavailable	Unavailable	Unavailable	Static	

Notes:
1. OREGON: Budget determined by Legislature on biennial basis. Total appropriated for period 1997-99: $728,248,363. 2 WISCONSIN: Figures do not include contracted facilities within or outside of the state.

1998 Health Care Staffing

Internal / Contracted

	M.D.	Nurse Practitioner	P.A.	Psychiatrist	Psychologist	M.H. Therapist	RN	LPN	EMT	Dentist	Dental Tech.	Pharmacist	Records Clerk	Other	Changes from Previous Year	Factors for Change
AL	0/20.2	0/0	0/4	0/9	18/0	/4.2	0/42.8	0/153.8	0/0	0/6.6	0/8.6	0/0	0/26.8	0/23.5	Static	
AK	No Response															
AZ	29/0	19/0	0/0	15/0	28/0	1/0	206/registry	RN fill-ins	0/0	27/0	39/0	24/0	27/0	0/4	5.0% increase	Population shifts
AR	0/11.7	0/9		5/0	5/0	47/0	2/30.2	4/130.2	0/0	0/9.3	0/8.3	0/0	0/33.5	15/33.5	Static	
CA	No Response															
CO	10.4/.5	7/0	14/	3/2.7	13.7/0	0/0	101.2	29/0	0/0	10/3	7.3/.3	5/1	10.5/6	0/0	5.2% increase	Population shifts
CT	11/18	16/1	1/0	2/11	9/0	33/0	190/0	80/0	0/0	19/1	0/0	8/0	10/0	216/0	4.2% increase	Population shifts; MH Staff expansion
DE	7/1	2/0	2/0	3/0	2/0	0/0	28/16	21/4	0/0	6/0	4/0	1/2	12/0		4.3% increase	Budgetary; acuity increase
DC	No Response															
FL	115/0	42/0	0/0	49/0	354/0	45/0	521/0	470/0	0/0	78/0	133/0	44/0	81/0	0/0	5.0% decrease	Budgetary
GA	No Response															
HI	2.5/3	3/0	0/0	1/.5	1/0	8/0	42/vary	11/vary	0/0	3.5/6	0/0	0/0	6/0	5/1	7% decrease	Legislative adjustment
ID	All contracted staff				12/0	All contracted staff									8.0% increase	Additional infirmary beds
IL	2/42.2	0/0	0/7.5	0/13.7	16/23	0/0	117/149.1	0/78	108/0	75/25.9	12/29.8	0/2.8	16/15	2/63.2	15.2% increase	Population shifts
IN	Breakdown unavailable															
IA	14/0	0/0	1/0	0/0	13/0	0/0	73/0	0/0	0/0	5/0	7/0	3/0	0/0	0/0	12% increase, est.	New facility opening
KS	0/8.4	0/1	0/0 26.7	0/3.7	0/58.8	0/19.6	0/	0/50.6	0/0	0/9.5	0/9.5	0/2	0/11.4	0/1	Static	
KY	9	8	1	1 5	13	12	37	1 28	0	6	1 2	10	1	20	Static	
LA	11/32	1/0	5/0	1/9	3/6	45/0	71/0	98/0	2	13/5	8/0	12/6	24/0	0/16	5.0% increase (internal); 10.0% decrease (contracted)	Population shifts; budgetary
ME	No Response															

	M.D.	Nurse Practitioner	P.A.	Psychiatrist	Psychologist	M.H. Therapist	RN	LPN	EMT	Dentist	Dental Tech.	Pharmacist	Records Clerk	Other	Changes from Previous Year	Factors for Change
MD	1/20	1/2	0/15	1/6	36/2	0/0	12/	0/40	5/0	1/12	0/12	0/0	0/80	0/0	Static	
MA	No Response															
MI	29/ 19.5	0/1	7/ 10.5	0/0	95/4	0/0	378.2 /47.8	51/0	0/0	39.6/ 6.4	62/9	19/3	41/0	9318/ 94.2	6.9% increase	Population shifts
MN	0/7	2/3	0/0	0/11	27/0	8/0	80/0	8/0	0/0	9/0	7/0	0/0	7/0	0/0	Unavailable	Contract revision
MS	12/7	4/0	NA	1/4	1/1	10/0	69/2	35/0	0/0	8/0	6/0	7/0	6/9	0/0	Static	
MO	0/27.4	0/2	0/0	3/0	28/0	0/0	6/ 103 5	0/ 188.9	0/0	0/ 20.3	0/ 21.6	0/0	0/53.5	33/0	10.0% increase	Population shifts
MT	1/2	0/0	0/2	0/0	1/0	0/3.5	10/ 2.6	11/ vary	7/0	1/ vary	1/0	0/2	4/0	2/0	Static	
NE	2 5/2	0/0	6/0	1/3	0/0	0/0	0	7.510	0/0	3/0	3/0	3/2	3/0	23/2	Static	
NV	9/0	0/0	2/0	7/0	34/0	0/0	99/0	0/0	0/0	6/0	8/0	7/1	9/0	133/0	Static	
NH	1/1	3/0	0/0	0/6.3	0/0	0/0	30/0	0/0	0/ 18.5	1/2.3	3.8/0	2/.6	1.6/0	3/0	Static	
NJ	0/19.5	0/11.9	0/0		0/ 39.3	0/90	0/ 164.4	0/ 126.2		0/ 22.5	0/ 29.6	0/1	0/32.1	0/55	2% increase	Population shifts, increased support staff
NM	1/8.4	0/6	0/5	.8/4	0/0 69.4	0/0	1/	0/47.2	0/0	0/5.7	0/0	0/1	0/9	0/vary	10% increase	Population shifts
NY	106/0	15/0	32/0	0/0	0/0	0/0	0	83/0	0/0	105/0	100/0	117/0	78/0	195/0	Unavailable	Population shifts
NC	0/0	0/0	0/0	7/41	110/8	50/0	0/0	0/0	0/0	0/0	0/0	0/0	82/0	33/7	3% increase plus 5% increase, MH	Population shifts
ND	0/4	0/0	0/0	0/4	1/0	0/0	9.5/0	1.8/0	0/0	0/1	0/1	1/.5	0/.5	0/1	Static	
OH	1/47	0/0	0/1	6/59	69/3	169/13	345/0	98/0	5/3	2/35	5/21	10/23	6/0	104 civil service	1.0% increase	Population shifts est.
OK	No Response															
OR	8/14	5/2	0/1	0/0	0/0	0/0	95.3/ 0	0/0	0/0	8.4/0	14.9/	6.5/0	0/0	47/0	20% increase est.	Population shifts
PA	2/vary	0/0	0/ vary	3/vary	23/0	0/0	422/ vary	166/ vary	0/0	37/0	46/0	0/vary	55/vary	132/ vary	Static	
RI	Break down unavailable															
SC	17/10	4/0	0/2	1/2	1/0	83/7	83/ 121	67/89	0/0	11/8	17/8	9/0	16/10	43/53	Static	
SD	0/4	0/2	0/2	0/3	0/1	0/9	0/35	0/13	0/0	0/7	0/7	0/1	0/4	0/0	Static	
TN	Breakdown unavailable															
TX	Breakdown unavailable for approximately 4,400 staff														Static	
UT	No Response															
VT	No Response															
VA	8.5/5/27	284.5/0	10/0	4/0	73/0	69/0	2/0	4/0	0/0	20/0	28.6/0	2/0	0/0	75/0	Static	

1998 HEALTH CARE STAFFING, *continued*

	M.D.	Nurse Practitioner	P.A.	Psychiatrist	Psychologist	M.H. Therapist	RN	LPN	EMT	Dentist	Dental Tech.	Pharmacist	Records Clerk	Other	Changes from Previous Year	Factors for Change
WA	3/5	33/8	0/0	3/3.5	27/.75	10/0	150/1	44/0	0/0	13/2	21/0	26/2	17/0	94/.5	4% increase	Population shifts
WV	No Response															
WI	20/4	7/0	3/1	11/5	0/0	0/0	122/7	14/0	0/0	24/1	26/1	5/0	6/2	65/1	22% increase	Population shifts; new facility
VV	0/5	0/0	0/0		1 0/1		0/13 0/6		0/0	0/3	0/3	0/0	0/2.5	0/2	Static	
FBP	No Response															
MB	0/7	0/0	0/0	0/2	2/0	0/0	16/25	0/0	0/0	0/1	0/0	0/0	0/0	18/35	10% increase	Population shifts
NF	0/1	0/0	1 0/1	0/0	0/0	0/0	1 0/1	0/0	0/0	0/0	0/0	0/0	0/1	0/0	Static	
ON	0/47	2/0	0/0	0/35	35/4	1/0	162/179	2/0	0/0	2/0	3/1	0/1	0/0	1/0	10% increase	Budgetary, added use of casual agencies and temps
YK	0/1	0/0	0/0	0/ vary	0/ vary	0/ vary	3/0	0/0	0/0	0/0	0/0	0/0	0/0	1/0	Static	

Notes:
1. KENTUCKY: Number of contracted staff in all categories is unavailable.
2. LOUISIANA: Security officers are trained to provide EMT services.

1998 Inmate Health Care Services and Medical Co-Pays

	When Tested for Communicable Disease (Except HIV/AIDS)	Treatments Included in Budget	TREATMENTS (Percentage)		Contracted Out Types Of services	Medical Co-Pay in Operation
			On-Site	Off-Site		
AL	Intake; physician request	Dental, MH, OBGYN, TB	NA	NA	Medical staffing and management, pharmacy, lab, radiology, dental, eye exams, MH hospitalization, transportation	$3
AK	No Response					
AZ	Intake; inmate or physician request	Dental, sex offender, MH, OBGYN, TB	85	15	Lab, radiology, eye exams, hospitalization, transportation, PT	$3 per visit; waived for certain conditions by statute
AR	Intake; inmate or physician request; routine surveillance (i.e., TB); infection outbreak	Alcohol and drug, dental, sex offender, MH, OBGYN, TB, acute/chronic care, secondary care, et al	75	25	Medical staffing and management, pharmacy, lab, radiology, dental, eye exams, hospitalization, transportation, PT	No
CA	No Response					
CO	Intake; inmate or physician request	Alcohol and drug, dental, sex offender, MH, OBGYN, TB, full range of other health care services	78	22	Medical staffing and management, lab, radiology, eye exams, some MH, hospitalization, PT, drug and alcohol services	$.50, outpatient or internal "no show" or dental; $3, eye exam, OTC medications or off-site "no show"
CT	Intake; inmate or physician request	Dental, sex offender, MH, OBGYN, TB, cardiology, dermatology, endocrinology, ENT, hematology, dialysis, neurology, ophthalmology, optometry, orthopedic, podiatry, pulmonary, surgical	99.9	.1	Medical staffing and management, pharmacy, lab, radiology, dental, eye exams, MH, hospitalization	$3, sentenced offender only
DE	Intake; inmate or physician request; STD's or TB	Alcohol and drug (detox only), dental, sex offender, MH, OBGYN, TB	90	10	Hospitalization, MRI, CT scan, radiation treatment	$4, first occurrence only; $2, OTC medications
DC	No Response					
FL	Intake; physician's request	Dental, MH, OBGYN, TB	75	25	Medical staffing, lab, some radiology, eye exams, hospitalization, PT	$4
GA	No Response					
HI	Inmate or physician request	Dental, MH, OBGYN, TB	80	20	Supplemental medical staffing, pharmacy, lab, radiology, hospitalization, PT, conditional eye exams	$3
ID	Intake; inmate or physician request	Dental, MH, OBGYN, TB	97	3	Pharmacy, lab, hospitalization, transportation, PT	$3, self-initiated; $2, prescriptions
IL	Inmate or physician request	Alcohol and drug, dental, MH, OBGYN, TB	98	2	Medical staffing and management, pharmacy, radiology, dental, hospitalization	$2, off-site non-emergency
IN	Intake; inmate or physician request	Alcohol and drug, dental, sex offender, MH, OBGYN, TB	NA	NA	Medical staffing and management, pharmacy, lab, radiology, dental, eye exams, MH, hospitalization, PT	$5

1998 INMATE HEALTH CARE SERVICES AND MEDICAL CO-PAYS, continued

	When Tested for Communicable Disease (Except HIV/AIDS)	Treatments Included in Budget	TREATMENTS (Percentage) On-Site	Off-Site	Contracted Out Types Of services	Medical Co-Pay in Operation
IA	Intake; physician request	Alcohol and drug, dental, sex offender, MH, OBGYN, TB	95	5	Medical staffing and management, pharmacy, lab, radiology, dental, eye exams, MH, hospitalization	$3, self-initiated; free, staff initiated or annual physical
KS	Intake; physician request; court order	Alcohol and drug, dental, sex offender, MH, OBGYN, TB	NA	NA	Radiology, hospitalization	$2, non-emergency
KY	Intake; inmate or physician request	Dental, MH, OBGYN, TB	60	40	Lab, eye exams, hospitalization, PT	$2
LA	Intake; inmate or physician request	Alcohol and drug, dental, sex offender, MH, OBGYN, TB	91.5 est.	8.5 est.	Hospitalization through state charity facilities	$3, self-initiated (medical, dental, MH); $2, most new prescriptions
ME	No Response					
MD	Intake; inmate or physician request	Alcohol and drug, dental, MH, OBGYN, TB, infectious diseases, chronic care, oncology, asthma, neurology	85	15	Medical staffing and management, pharmacy, lab, radiology, dental, eye exams, MH, hospitalization, PT	$2, self-initiated
MA	No Response					
MI	Intake; inmate or physician request; when warranted	Alcohol and drug, dental, sex offender, MH, OBGYN, TB	NA	NA	Lab, radiology, eye exams, MH, PT; partial pharmacy, dental, hospitalization, transportation	$3, self-initiated; free, physician request; full cost, self-inflicted injuries
MN	Intake; inmate or physician request	Dental, MH, OBGYN, TB, other general medical care	80	20	Medical staffing and management, pharmacy, lab, radiology, eye exams, hospitalization, PT, dietician, other therapies	$3 (first occurrence only in chronic cases)
MS	Intake, inmate or physician request	Dental, MH, OBGYN, TB	90	10	All services provided by local university medical center	$3
MO	Intake; annually for TB	Alcohol and drug, dental, sex offender, MH, OBGYN, TB	99.3	.7	Medical staffing and management, pharmacy, lab, radiology, dental, eye exams, hospitalization, PT	None
MT	Intake; inmate or physician request	Dental, MH, OBGYN, TB	80	20	Medical staffing, pharmacy, lab, hospitalization	None
NE	Intake	Alcohol and drug, dental, sex offender, MH, OBGYN, TB	NA	NA	Medical staffing, pharmacy, lab, radiology, dental, eye exams, MH, hospitalization, transportation, PT	None (but under consideration)
NV	Intake; physician request	Alcohol and drug, dental, sex offender, MH, OBGYN, TB	85	15	Lab, hospitalization, PT	$4; $2, prescriptions
NH	Physician request	Dental, MH, OBGYN, TB	85	15	Lab, radiology, eye exams, hospitalization, PT, specialty care	$3, visit; $5, on-site "no shows"; full cost, off-site "no shows", free, indigent

	When Tested for Communicable Disease (Except HIV/AIDS)	Treatments Included in Budget	TREATMENTS (Percentage) On-Site	Off-Site	Contracted Out Types Of services	Medical Co-Pay in Operation
NJ	Intake; inmate or physician request; annually for TB	Alcohol and drug, dental, sex offender, MH, OBGYN, TB	90	10	Medical staffing and management, pharmacy, lab, radiology, dental, eye exams, MH, hospitalization, transportation, PT, some substance abuse	$5, self-initiated; $1, prescriptions
NM	Intake; physician request	Alcohol and drug, dental, MH, OBGYN, TB, HIV treatment	90	10	Medical staffing and management, pharmacy, lab, radiology, dental, eye exams, hospitalization, PT	None
NY	Intake; inmate request; annually	Dental, OBGYN, TB	All but acute care		Medical staffing, pharmacy, dental, eye exams, hospitalization (for acute care)	$3 (exempt for chronic care)
NC	Intake; inmate or physician request; when warranted; annually for TB	Alcohol and drug, dental, MH, OBGYN, TB	NA	NA	Lab, hospitalization, transportation	$3, first occurrence; $5, falsely declared emergency; free, staff-initiated
ND	Intake; inmate or physician request	Alcohol and drug, dental, sex offender, MH, OBGYN, TB	90	10	Some medical staffing, lab, some radiology, hospitalization	15% for dental prosthetics
OH	Intake; physician request	Dental, OBGYN, TB	Unavailable	Unavailable		
OK	No Response					
OR	Intake; inmate or physician request; when warranted	Dental, OBGYN, TB, chronic illness (cancer, diabetes, etc.)	80	20	Lab, routine radiology, routine eye exams, hospitalization	Full charge for prosthetics and commissary items
PA	Intake; physician request	Alcohol and drug, dental, sex offender, MH, OBGYN, TB	90	10	Medical staffing and management, pharmacy, lab, radiology, eye exams, MH, hospitalization, transportation, PT	$2
RI	Breakdown unavailable					
SC	Intake; some inmate request; physician request; court ordered; when warranted	Alcohol and drug, dental, sex offender, MH, OBGYN, TB, developmental disabilities	95 est	5 est.	Eye exams, MH for females, hospitalization, transportation (ambulance only), PT, specialty care; minor lab, radiology and dental	Legislatively approved but not implemented
SD	Intake; inmate or physician request	Alcohol and drug, dental, sex offender, MH OBGYN TB	Unavailable	Unavailable	$2	
TN	Intake; physician request	Alcohol and drug, dental, sex offender, MH, OBGYN, TB, limited hepatitis-B	90	10	Medical staffing, lab, radiology, eye exams, hospitalization, PT	$3; $5, prosthetics
TX	Intake; inmate or physician request	Dental, MH, OBGYN, TB	60	40	Medical staffing and management, pharmacy, lab, radiology, dental, eye exams, MH, hospitalization, transportation, PT, specialty services	$3, self-initiated
UT	No Response					
VT	No Response					

1998 INMATE HEALTH CARE SERVICES AND MEDICAL CO-PAYS, *continued*

	When Tested for Communicable Disease (Except HIV/AIDS)	Treatments Included in Budget	TREATMENTS (Percentage)		Contracted Out Types Of services	Medical Co-Pay in Operation
			On-Site	Off-Site		
VA	Intake, STD's & TB; inmate or physician request; hepatitis B & C	Alcohol and drug, dental, sex offender, MH, OBGYN, TB	90 est.	10 est.	Medical staffing and management, pharmacy, lab, radiology, dental, eye exams, MH, hospitalization	$5; $2, medications; many exceptions
WA	Intake; inmate or physician request	Alcohol and drug, dental, sex offender, MH, OBGYN, TB	80	20	Lab, hospitalization, specially care	$3
WV	No Response					
WI	Intake; physician request	Dental, limited MH, OBGYN, TB	90 est.	10 est.	Lab, radiology, eye exams, limited MH, hospitalization, special-needs transportation, PT, occupational therapy, communication therapy, oral surgery	$2.50
WY	Intake; physician request	Dental, MH, OBGYN, TB	75	25	Medical staffing and management, lab, pharmacy, radiology, hospitalization, PT	None
FBP	No Response					
MB	Intake; inmate or physician request	Dental, OBGYN, TB	95	5	Lab, radiology, dental, eye exams	None
NF	Inmate or physician request	Dental, MH, TB	NA	NA	Pharmacy, lab, radiology, dental, eye exams, hospitalization, PT	None
ON	Physician request; hepatitis	Alcohol and drug, dental, sex offender, MH, TB	NA	NA	Pharmacy, lab, radiology, dental, eye exams, MH, hospitalization, PT	None (Ontario Health Insurance Plan in effect)
YK	Intake; inmate or physician request	Alcohol and drug, dental, MH, OBGYN, TB	40	60	Medical staffing, pharmacy, lab, radiology, dental, eye exams, MH, hospitalization, PT	None

Notes:
1. SOUTH CAROLINA: About 60 percent of services are provided on-site by departmental staff; about 40 percent of services are contracted out.

Specialized Inmate Health Care Services—1998

	DRUGS		ALCOHOL		Percent 55 or Older	ELDERLY		CHRONICALLY / TERMINALLY ILL		
	Number Treated	Treatment Provider	Number Treated	Treatment Provider		Special Provisions for Elderly Inmates	Laws in Place for Early Release	Percentage of Inmate Population	Special Provisions	Laws in Place for Early Release
AL	3,700 combined; provided by treatment division				3.3	Segregation as necessary	No	< 1	Hospice cells at some facilities	No
AK	No response									
AZ	Unavailable	N/A	Unavailable	N/A	4.1	None specific for elderly inmates	No	Unavailable	Special housing; medical furlough	Yes
AR	1,916	MH/Substance Abuse Treatment	1,010	MH/Substance Abuse Treatment		Chronic care clinics; focused housing units	No	7.6	Maintenance of required therapy; prescriptions; palliative care	Yes, if criteria met
CA	3,513 combined; provided by outside contractors				Approx. 2.7	Special housing; medically necessary	No	Unavailable	Medically necessary; chronic care program being implemented; hospice	Yes, compassionate release provisions
CO	1,067	Clinical Services, MH and Alcohol and Drug Office	Approx. half of all inmates	Clinical Services, MH and Alcohol and Drug Office	3.6	Full range of cervices; chronic care clinic	No	Unknown	Hospice at Colorado Territorial Correctional Facility	No, unless compassionate discharge granted
CT	12,024 combined; provided by Addiction Services Unit				1.9	LOFT housing program	No	< 0.1	Dedicated infirmary; super-skilled care	No, unless qualification for medical parole
DE	2,420 combined; Bureau of Management Services; Correctional Medical Services				2.5	Chronic care clinic; Nursing Home Center	No	Unavailable	Chronic care clinic; inpatient hospice care; extended family visiting for terminally ill	No
DC	N/A	N/A	N/A	N/A	< 1	Special, separated housing	Yes, Medical and Geriatric Parole Act	Unavailable	Transfer to outside hospital for tertiary care, as needed	Yes, Medical and Geriatric Parole Act
FL	15,215 combined; provided by DOC staff				3.5	No	No	1.7	Relocation as medically necessary	Yes
GA	Unavailable	DOC counseling services	Unavailable	DOC counseling services	25 >40 yrs.	Geriatric services	No	Unavailable	Chronic care; terminal care	Yes, if criteria met
HI	No response									
ID	Unavailable				Unavailable	Dedicated beds and units	No	6	Infirmary; specialized care	Yes, but very rigid

SPECIALIZED INMATE HEALTH CARE SERVICES—1998, continued

	DRUGS / ALCOHOL		ELDERLY			CHRONICALLY / TERMINALLY ILL		
	Number Treated	Treatment Provider	Percent 55 or Older	Special Provisions for Elderly Inmates	Laws in Place for Early Release	Percentage of Inmate Population	Special Provisions	Laws in Place for Early Release
IL	5,858 combined; provided by contractors or CADC-certified staff		2	Dedicated unit; special needs provisions	No	0.2	Infirmary care; clinics; renal dialysis; medically necessary	No
IN	6,586 combined; provided by Substance Abuse Department		3.4	None	No	20.5	Some hospice services; advanced directives; special visitation rules	Yes
IA	Number and provider unavailable			Medically necessary	No	Unavailable	Infirmary care	No
KS	Number unavailable; provided by outside contractor		4	Medically necessary devices and placements	No	23	Chronic care clinics; hospice	No
KY	Numbers and providers unavailable		Not known	State-licensed nursing care facility	Yes, if terminal or in latter stage of chronic disease	Unknown	State-licensed nursing care facility with 24 hour nursing	Yes
LA	1,085 combined; Department of Health and Hospitals, Division of Alcohol and Drug Abuse		7.4	Health screening; special housing under construction	No	Approx. 20-25	Infirmary care; hospitalization as required; hospice	Yes, medical furlough
ME	Data unavailable at this time							
MD	2,500 combined; Department of Public Safety			Chronic care hospice	Yes, medical parole		Chronic care protocols, hospice	Yes, medical parole
MA	No response							
MI	15,972 combined; Substance Abuse Program Services		3.9	Long-term hospital beds; special housing and nursing home units	No		Long-term hospital beds; special housing and nursing home units	Yes, if mentally or physically incapacitated
MN	1,047 combined; Faculty Division and Sex Offender/ICD Support Unit		3	Special housing unit	No	Unavailable	Special housing unit; hospice; chronic care clinics	Yes
MS	1,680 combined; Alcohol and Drug Department		3	Special housing unit; geriatric medications and support	No	1	Extended care unit; hospital with long-term care capabilities	Yes
MO	8,882 combined; Division of Offender Rehabilitative Services		3.7	Chronic care clinics; handicap access	Yes	Approx. 17	Chronic care clinics	Yes
MT	218 combined; Montana State Prison Chemical Dependency Program		Approx. 6	Chronic care health system; over-50 wellness program	No	10	ADA housing unit; chronic care system	Yes, medical parole in extreme cases
NE	1,216 combined; Nebraska Correctional Treatment Center		3	Provide for needs	No	Unavailable	None	No

	DRUGS Number Treated	DRUGS Treatment Provider	ALCOHOL Number Treated	ALCOHOL Treatment Provider	ELDERLY Percent 55 or Older	ELDERLY Special Provisions for Elderly Inmates	ELDERLY Laws in Place for Early Release	CHRONICALLY / TERMINALLY ILL Percentage of Inmate Population	CHRONICALLY / TERMINALLY ILL Special Provisions	CHRONICALLY / TERMINALLY ILL Laws in Place for Early Release
NV	140	Private contractors	309	Private contractors; NDOP staff	5.3	None specific to elderly inmates	No	1	Extended care unit	No
NH	Number unavailable; residential programs at two prisons				9	None	No	10 cases	Community placement; inpatient terminal care	No
NJ	2,174 combined; DOC Office of Drug Program Operations, via private contractor				2.1	Infirmary; extended care unit; inpatient hospital; as needed	No	15	Clinics; specialists, infirmaries; extended care unit; acute care hospital, as needed	Yes, medical parole and executive clemency, but rarely used
NM	Unavailable	Health Services	Unavailable	Health Services	Not known	Medically necessary	Yes, geriatric parole	< 1	Individual services/ treatment plan; in-patient long-term care	Yes, geriatric parole
NY	29,978 combined; Bureau of Substance Abuse Treatment Services				2.6	Based on prevailing policies	No	Unavailable	Regional medical units	Yes, medical parole
NC	Data unavailable				Not known	Data unavailable			None	No
ND	212 combined; provider unavailable				3	Individual care plans	No	0	7-bed infirmary	No
OH	11,763 combined; Bureau of Recovery Services				3.7	Long-term care units at two institutions	No	Unavailable	Long-term care; hospice	Yes
OK	1,865	Programs	Unknown	Programs	3.4	None	No	Unknown	Infirmary services; chronic care clinics	Yes
OR	2,378 combined (est.); Counseling and Treatment Services				5.4	None specific to elderly inmates	Yes	1.1	Hospice; self-care and maintenance education	Yes
PA	12,537 combined; DOC staff and contracted vendors				Not known	Long-term and personal care	No	0.3	Hospice; infirmary care; long-term care	Yes, for treatment unavailable in prison
RI	275	Outside contractors	Unavailable	Outside contractors	3.5	Chronic medical clinics	No	< 1	Hospice	yes
SC	7,500 combined (est.); SCDC staff and contracted staff				1.3	Handicap housing units; chronic infirmary care	No	Unknown	Handicap housing units; chronic infirmary care	Yes, medical furloughs
SD	106 combined; Department of Human Services				4	Medically necessary; hospitalization; reduced sentence	Yes	< 1	Medically necessary; hospitalization; reduced sentence	Yes
TN	No response									
TX	78,588 combined; Programs and Services/Substance Abuse Treatment Program				3.7	60-bed geriatric facility	Yes, Special Needs Parole Process	Unavailable	Hospice; chronic clinics; specialty consultation and services; continuity of care; hospitalization	Yes, special needs parole process
UT	No response									

SPECIALIZED INMATE HEALTH CARE SERVICES—1998, *continued*

	DRUGS		ALCOHOL		ELDERLY			CHRONICALLY / TERMINALLY ILL		
	Number Treated	Treatment Provider	Number Treated	Treatment Provider	Percent 55 or Older	Special Provisions for Elderly Inmates	Laws in Place for Early Release	Percentage of Inmate Population	Special Provisions	Laws in Place for Early Release
VT	400 combined; DOC				2	Medical furlough	No	1	Medical furlough	Yes
VA	1,800 combined (funded); DOC and AA/NA volunteers				5.8 >50 yrs.	Geriatric dorm; assisted living unit	No	Unavailable	Medical units at facilities	No
WA	7,325 combined; Pierce County Alliance, Damon Counseling, BHR Recovery, Lakeside Milum				12	None	No	30	Dialysis at one facility; assisted living facility	Yes
WV	No response									
WI	2,541 combined; DOC Social Service Department and community treatment providers				0.4	None specific to elderly inmates	No, but may apply for compassionate parole	24	24-hour infirmary; periodic monitoring	No, but may apply for compassionate parole
WY	62	Contract with Wexford Health	50	Contract with Wexford Health Services	7	None	No	< 1	Housed in infirmary	No, but may apply for medical parole
FBP	33,997 combined; Psychology				10.9	Community standard	No	30.4	Community standard	Yes
MB	100 est.	Corrections Department	500 est.	Corrections Appropriation	4	None	No	Unknown	None	No, but may apply for compassionate release
NF	N/A	N/A	N/A	N/A	8	Handicap cell; one wheelchair	No		Medications; hygiene and comfort care; referrals to outside hospitals for treatment	No
ON	Unavailable	In-house and community-based programs	Unavailable	In-house and community-based programs	5.5 est. >50 yrs.	Medically necessary	Yes, Temporary Absence Program and Parole	Unavailable	Institution health care units; community hospital treatment	Yes, parole and temporary absence
YK	50% of population approx.	Nursing staff; Alcohol/Drug Services; case managers	Approx. 75% of population	Nursing staff; case managers; Alcohol/Drug Services	0	None, but could be arranged	None specific for elderly inmates	1	Medically necessary; hospitalization; medication	Yes, if authorized by designated medical practitioner

Female Inmate Health Services—1998

	Number	COSTS		Higher/Lower Than For Males	SPECIFIC PROGRAMS PROVIDED			New Pregnant Inmates Entering System	Number of Births	Newborns Allowed To Remain With Mothers	Other Services Provided
		Health Care	Per Inmate		Ob/Gyn	Prenatal/Post Partum	Mammography				
AL	2,329	Unavailable	Unavailable	Unavailable	Yes	Yes	Yes	12	12	No	WIC
AK	No response										
AZ	1,653	Unavailable	Unavailable	Unavailable	Yes	Yes	Yes	12	73	No	Unavailable
AR	600	Unavailable	Unavailable	Static	Yes	Yes	Yes	6	17	No	
CA	11,425	$39,344,973	$3,444	Higher	Yes	Yes	Yes	Unavailable	254	Yes[1]	Prisoner Mother Program; dietary services; antenatal surveillance; family planning
CO	1,019	$3,194,261	$2,993	Higher	Yes	Yes	Yes	13	13	No	On-site post-partum care
CT	1,126 ADP	$8,670,422	$7,895	Lower	Yes	Yes	Yes	186	33	No	Parenting education
DE	353	Unavailable	Unavailable	Unavailable	Yes	Yes	Yes	173 est.	21	No	Education
DC	NIA	N/A NIA	NIA	NIA	No	NIA	NIA	NIA	No	NIA	
FL	3,512	$18,900,000	$7,840	Higher	Yes	No	Yes	330	62	No	As needed
GA	2,335	Unavailable	Unavailable	Unavailable	Yes	Yes	Yes	53	53	No	Project REACH
HI	No response										
ID	285	$950,000	$3,755	Higher	Yes	Yes	Yes	60	14	No	Prenatal counseling; ultrasound, C-section PRN
IL	2,522	Unavailable	Unavailable	Unavailable	Yes	Yes	Yes	111	81	Yes, 24 furs.	Women and Children's Residential Program
IN	1,081	Unavailable	Unavailable	Unavailable	Yes	Yes	Yes	32	21	No	Counseling; child placement; parenting classes
IA	430	Unavailable	Unavailable	Unavailable	Yes	Prenatal only	Yes	15	15	No	Prenatal and post-partum counseling
KS	502	Unavailable	Unavailable	Unavailable	Yes	Yes	Yes	Unavailable	14	Yes, 23 furs.	
KY	584	$374,950	$642	Lower	Yes	Yes	Yes			Yes, only while hospitalized	Parenting program; bonding visits
LA	2,187	$2,176,204	$2,323	Higher	Yes	Yes	Yes	34	32	No	High-risk OB/GYN annual breast self-exam class
ME	Data unavailable at this time										
MD	1,000	Unavailable	Unavailable	Higher, possibly	Yes	Yes	Yes	80	40	No	Post-delivery care
MA	No response										
MI	2,052	Unavailable	Unavailable	Unavailable	Yes	Yes	Yes	46	33	No	
MN	308	$855,657	$3,304	Lower	Yes	Yes	Yes	26	14	No	Prenatal education, social services; bonding program

FEMALE INMATE HEALTH SERVICES—1998, continued

	Number	COSTS Health Care	COSTS Per Inmate	Higher/ Lower Than For Males	SPECIFIC PROGRAMS PROVIDED Ob/Gyn	Prenatal/ Post Partum	Mammo-graphy	New Pregnant Inmates Entering System	Number of Births	Newborns Allowed To Remain With Mothers	Other Services Provided
MS	1,341	Unavailable	Unavailable	Unavailable	Yes	Yes	Yes	26	20	No	Counseling, literature medical supplements
MO	1,864	$3,248 929	$1,799	Static	Yes	Yes	Yes	82	44	No	
MT	253	$786,5i8	Unavailable	Higher	Yes	Yes	Yes	10	6	No	Well-baby checks; immunizations; child care, parenting, birthing classes
NE	250	Unavailable	Unavailable	Higher	Yes	Yes	Yes			Yes, 18 most	
NV	736	$480,486	$3,291	Static	Yes	Yes	Yes	21	20	No	As needed
NH	109	Unavailable	$2,684	Unavailable	Yes	Yes	Yes	5	3	No	Post-partum visiting
NJ	1,220	$3,932,718	$3,224	Unavailable	Yes	Yes	Yes	35	24	Yes, only while hospitalized	Counseling regarding termination options
NM	376 ADP	$1,283,800	$3,424	Higher	Yes	Yes	Yes	6	6	No	Medically necessary
NY	3,565 ADP	$8,926,255	$2,599	Higher	Yes	Yes	Yes	Unavailable	Unavailable	Yes, 1 1/2yrs.	Pre- and post-natal care; parenting, as needed
NC	Data Unavailable	Yes	Yes	Yes	Data Unavailable						
ND	71	Unavailable	Unavailable	Unavailable	Yes	Yes	Yes	9	3	No	
OH	2,821	$8,174,142	$2,891	Higher	Yes	Yes	Yes	113	79	No	
OK	2,095	Unavailaible	Unavailable	Higher	Yes	Yes	Yes	43	35	No	Post-natal visitations
OR	473	$1,784,156	$3,772	Higher	Yes	Yes	Yes	19	14	No	Prenatal classes; post-partum group
PA	1,464	$8,039,026	$5,490	Higher	Yes	Yes	Yes	31	22	No	Parenting program; post natal; Project Impact; speakers
RI	200	Unavailable	Unavailable	Higher	Yes	Yes	Yes	100 est.	5-10/yr.	No	Parent-child visitations
SC	1,313	Unavailable	Unavailable	Higher	Yes	Yes	Yes	51	28	Yes, about 6 hrs.	Prenatal; post-partum; lab per protocol; genetic testing; high risk OB/GYN
SD	203	Health Care budgeting is not broken down by sex			Yes	Yes	Yes	9	4	No	Medically necessary as deter mined by contracted provider
TN	No response										
TX	10,333	Unavailable	Unavailable	Higher	Yes	Yes	Yes	Unavailable	205	Yes, few hrs placement	Pre- and post-natal care; child
UT	No response										
VT	60	$350,000	$7,000	Higher	Yes	Yes	Yes	5	2	No	None
VA	1,904			Yes	Yes	Yes		Unavailable	No	No	
WA	886	$5,700,000	$6,433	Higher	Yes	Yes	Yes	Unavailable	15	No	
WV	No response										
WI	963	$1,762 950	$1,830	Lower	Yes	Yes	Yes	36	16	No	

	Number	COSTS		Higher/ Lower Than For Males	SPECIFIC PROGRAMS PROVIDED			New Pregnant Inmates Entering System	Number of Births	Newborns Allowed To Remain With Mothers	Other Services Provided
		Health Care	Per Inmate		Ob/ Gyn	Prenatal/ Post Partum	Mammo- graphy				
WY	136	Unavailable	Unavailable	Unavailable	Yes	Yes	Yes	10	7	Yes, 24 hrs.	Counseling
FBP	8,872	Unavailable	Unavailable	Unavailable	Yes	Yes	Yes	95	56	No	MINT program for low-risk offenders
MB	983	$250,000	$250	Higher	Yes	Yes	No		3	Yes, 10 mos	Parenting program; post-natal
NF	64			Yes	Yes	Yes	2	0	No	No	Medical temporary absence
ON	144 ADP	Unavailable	Unavailable	Unavailable	Yes	Yes	Yes	Unavailable	0	Yes, varies	
YK	59	Unavailable	Unavailable	Unavailable				1	0	No	Counseling

Notes:
1. CALIFORNIA: Only while hospitalized. If enrolled in mother/infant program, child may remain with mother until age 6

HIV/AIDS Testing, Infection Rates and Services—1998

	When Tested	Number Known to be Infected	PERCENT		Percentage of Total Population	Treatment Offered	Infected Inmates Segregated	Condoms Distributed	Other Preventive Measures
			Male	Female					
AL	Data unavailable at this time								
AK	No response								
AZ	Inmate or physician request	105	91	9	0.4	Community standard	No	No	In-service training in prevention and treatment
AR	Intake; inmate or physician request; sexual assault/rape	104	98.1	1.9	0.98	Multiple-drug; specialty clinics; support groups; post-release networking	No, unless behavior warrants	No	Continuing education through multimedia resources and special drug events
CA	Inmate or physician request	1,651	76.9	23.1	1	Follows CDC guidelines and prevention standards	No	No	HIV/AIDS Peer Education program
CO	Intake; inmate or physician request	105	90	10	0.7	Contemporary care under supervision of contracted specialist	No	No	Patient teaching
CT	Intake or physician request; court order	640	83	17	3.8	Follows CDC and NIH guidelines	No	No	Health education; peer support groups
DE	Inmate request	294	89	11	5	Follows CDC guidelines; community standard	No	No	Education
DC	Inmate request	225	100	0	6-7	Follows CDC and U.S. Public Health services guidelines	No	Yes	None
FL	Inmate or physician request	2,274	90	10	4	Latest medication regime; volunteers may participate in testing of FDA-approved medication	No	No	None
GA	Intake	900	89	11	3	Community standard	No	No	Prevention of transmission
HI	No response								
ID	Intake; inmate or physician request; suspicion	12	100	0	.0032	Follows CDC guidelines	No, unless predatory or victimized	No	Universal precautions; education and training; counseling
IL	Inmate or physician request	700	90	10	1.6	Medically necessary, including anti-retroviral therapy, clinics, infirmary care, hospital care, discharge planning, community linkages	No	No	Extensive peer education group, educational programs and counseling
IN	Inmate or physician request	120	93	7	0.9	Community standard	No	No	
IA	Intake; inmate or physician request; reappraisals	38	80	20	< 1	Medically necessary, including HAART	No, unless behavior warrants	No	Education
KS	Inmate or physician request	39	N/A	N/A	04	Preventive; anti-retroviral medications; opportunistic disease treatment; medically necessary	No	No	Education

	When Tested	Number Known to be Infected	PERCENT		Percentage of Total Population	Treatment Offered	Infected Inmates Segregated	Condoms Distributed	Other Preventive Measures
			Male	Female					
KY	Inmate or physician request	78	92	8		Current FDA-approved medications	No	No	Education
LA	Inmate or physician request; following altercation; following positive TB testing	456	94.7	5.3		Follows CDC and NIH guidelines; medically necessary	No	No	
ME	Data unavailable at this time								
MD	Intake; inmate or physician request	950	85	15	3.6	Community standard	No	No	
MA	No response								
MI	Intake; inmate or physician request; exposure	422	94.3	5.3	0.09	Community standard; early combination therapy and prophylaxis for opportunistic infections	No	No	Peer education programs, prevention education; health education and HIV/AIDS/STD booklets; resource booklet and condoms to discharging and paroling inmates
MN	Inmate or physician request	28	96	4	0.04	Community standard	No	No	HIV, STD and Hepatitis prevention education
MS	Intake; inmate or physician request	182	84	16	1	Medications; HIV clinic	Yes, in special unit	Yes	Literature, counseling
MO	Intake	247	90	10	< 1	All necessary care, includes NRTI, NNRTI, PI	No	No	Education
MT	Inmate or physician request	11	91	9	.004	Full range of services; triple-load anti-retroviral	No	No	Wellness program
NE	Intake; inmate or physician request; court order	22	100	0	0.6	Community standard	No	No	
NV	Intake; physician request; exposure	106 (males)	100	0	1.2 (males)	Community standard; anti-retroviral medications; discharge follow-up coordination	Yes	No	Prevention education
NH	Intake; physician request	17	88	12		Current medications; treatment of acute diseases including hospitalization	No	No	Preventive INH if test positive for TB; annual flu shots for at risk; recurrent exams
NJ	Inmate request; physician request if inmate consents	1,000	90	10	3.8	Community standard	No	No	Education; counseling; prohibitions of drug use and sexual activities
NM	Inmate request; high-risk, intake (voluntary)	34	94	6	0.6 approx.	Full services; medically necessary	No	No	Counseling
NY	Inmate or physician request	9,000 approx.	91	8	13	FDA-approved therapies	No	No	Counseling; testing; general and peer education
NC	Inmate request; indication of disease	526	91	9	1.6	Community standard; UNC-Chapel Hill physician specialist offering clinics	No	No	Education class on high-risk behavior

HIV/AIDS TESTING, INFECTION RATES AND SERVICES—1998, *continued*

	When Tested	Number Known to be Infected	PERCENT		Percentage of Total Population	Treatment Offered	Infected Inmates Segregated	Condoms Distributed	Other Preventive Measures
			Male	Female					
ND	Intake	2	100	0	< 0.5	Community standard	No	No	Facts on HIV course; peer counseling
OH	Intake; inmate or physician request; court order	412	93	6	1.7	Protease inhibitors; MAC drugs; pneumonia medications	No	No	Administrative control placement if behavior warrants, AIDS education
OK	Intake; inmate or physician request; post-exposure	Unavailable	Unavailable	Unavailable	Unavailable	Counseling; medications; lab monitoring	No	No	Annual TB screening; intake screening for TB, syphilis, chylamydia, gonorrhea
OR	Inmate or physician request	35	Unavailable	Unavailable	0.4	Protease inhibitors; lab work; counseling	No	No	Education
PA	Inmate request	977	95.4	4.6	2.7	Community standard	No	No	AIDS education
RI	Intake; inmate or physician request; sentencing	Approx. 100	94	6	3 est.	Infectious disease specialists; discharge planning; support groups	No	No	Public health education
SC	Intake; physician request; some inmate request; suspicion; court order; post-exposure; PPD conversion >5mm	639	92	8	3	Community standard; discharge/release planning	Yes, at separate facilities	No	HIV education; policies against conjugal visits and homosexual activity; monitoring of syringes; zero drug tolerance
SD	Inmate request; physician request if inmate consents; high-risk	3	Unavailable	Unavailable	< 1	Community standard	No, unless behavior warrants	No	
TN	No response								
TX	Inmate or physician request; high-risk	2519	88.9	11.1	1.7	Community standard	Yes, as medical condition or behavior warrants	No	Education and preventive counseling programs
UT	No response								
VT	Inmate or physician request	15	80	20	1	Triple drug therapy; social services; medically necessary	No	Yes	Education; peer counseling
VA	Inmate or physician request	453			Approx. 1.5			No	
WA	Inmate request; court order	80	90	10	0.6	Drug therapy; counseling; medically necessary	No	No	
WV	No response								

	When Tested	Number Known to be Infected	PERCENT		Percentage of Total Population	Treatment Offered	Infected Inmates Segregated	Condoms Distributed	Other Preventive Measures
			Male	Female					
WI	Inmate request; physician request if inmate consents	117	92	8	.87	Outpatient and inpatient care and medications are provided by specialists	No	No	HIV and blood borne pathogen education; universal precautions
WY	Intake; physician request	2	100	0	< 1	Appropriate medications, vitamins and protein supplements	No	No	Education; counseling; chronic clinic
FBP	Intake; inmate or physician request; random or serial commitment sample exposure	1,013	93	7	0.9	FDA-approved medications; follows US Public Health Service guidelines	No	No	Mandatory education; pre and post-testing counseling; universal precautions
MB	Inmate or physician request	Not known			Approx. 6	Pre- and post-testing counseling	No	No	Health and lifestyle education
NF	Inmate or physician request	2 or 3	100	0		Medications; follow-up care by specialist; AIDS committee; dietary	No, unless behavior warrants	Yes, if requested	Prevention education
ON	Physician request	97 (1994)	99	1	1	Acute care; special needs activities and programs	Yes, as required	Yes	Dental dams and lubricant; education; exit kits; universal precautions
YK	Inmate request	Not known	Not known	Not known	Not known	Counseling; vitamins; continuation of medications	Yes, if medically necessary	Yes	Education; immunizations

MANAGEMENT ISSUES

Components of Sentencing Guidelines

as of February 1999

State	Date in Place	Reasons for Adopting	Set by	Options for Judicial Consideration	Judicial Departure from Guidelines	3-Strikes Law in Place	Alternatives to Incarceration
AK	1980[1]	Equal sentencing	Contained in the law	Circumstances of crime and offenders criminal history	Yes, to specified degree	Yes, not only for violence	No
AR	1-1-94	Equal sentencing; harsher penalties for habitual violence; proportionally and appropriate use of resources	Grid structure in law based on actual numbers by Commission	Offenders criminal history	Yes	Yes, for violence	Yes; short-term confinement in regional punishment facilities for non-violent offenders
CA	No Response						
DE	1987	Equal sentencing; harsher penalties for habitual violence.	Decided by Commission	Circumstances of crime	Yes	Yes, not only for violence	Yes, intensive supervision, electronic monitoring, residential treatment, standard probation, community service
	1991	Truth-in-Sentencing	Contained in the law	Offender's criminal history			
DC	No Response						
FL	1983	Equal sentencing; Truth-in-Sentencing; harsher penalties for habitual/violence	Contained in the law	Offender's criminal history; current conviction; victim injury; legal status of offender	Yes	Yes, for violence	Yes, probation, community control, county jail
IN		Equal sentencing; harsher penalties for habitual/violence; switch to determinate sentencing	Contained in the law	Circumstances of crime; offender's criminal history and social background; offenders cooperation, and more	No (not supposed to)	Yes, not only for violence	Yes, diversion through community correction programs (e.g., electronic monitoring, day reporting)
KS	7-1-93	Equal Sentencing, Truth-in-Sentencing harsher penalties for habitual/violence; qualify for federal funds (subsequent motivation)	Contained in the law	Offenders criminal history and severity level of crime of conviction	Yes	No	Yes; community supervision and correctional boot camp
MD	1987	Equal sentencing; Truth-in-Sentencing; expand judicial knowledge base; promote increased visibility and understanding	Decided by a Commission	Unavailable	Yes	Yes, for violence	Unavailable
MI	1999	Truth-in-Sentencing	Contained in the law	Circumstances of crime; offender's criminal history and social background	Yes	No	Yes; consistent with the current law on probation
MN	1980	Equal sentencing; Truth-in-Sentencing; harsher penalties for habitual/violence	Maintained by a Commission	Circumstances of crime; offender's criminal history	Yes	Yes, for violence	No
MO	1997	Equal sentencing	Decided by a Commission	Offender's criminal history; offense severity; correctional resources	Yes	No	Yes; probation
MT	No Response						

COMPONENTS OF SENTENCING GUIDELINES, *continued*

	Date in Place	Reasons for Adopting	Set by	Options for Judicial Consideration	Judicial Departure from Guidelines	3-Strikes Law in Place	Alternatives to Incarceration
NM	1977	Equal sentencing; harsher penalties for habitual/violence (added in 1983)	Contained in the law	Circumstances of crime	Yes, by 113 of the presumptive sentence for aggravating or mitigating circumstances	Yes, for a limited number of very serious violent felonies	Yes, probation, intensive supervision, community corrections, fines, community service
NC	1994	Truth-in-Sentencing; prioritize prison resources for the most violent offenders	Contained in the law	Circumstances of crime; offender's criminal history	No	Yes	Yes
OH	7-1-96	Harsher penalties for habitual/violence, end parole release and good time 2	Contained in the law	Circumstances of crime; offender's criminal history, presumptive criteria 3	Yes	No	Yes; community residential; continued significant expansion of state funding for community corrections
OK	NA	Truth-in-Sentencing	Contained in the law	Circumstances of crime; offender's criminal history and social background	No	No	Yes; graduated sanctions and a list of most known intermediate sanctions
OR	1989	Equal sentencing; Truth-in-Sentencing	Decided by a Commission	Offender's criminal history	Yes	No	No
PA	1982	Equal sentencing, harsher penalties for habitual violence	Decided by a Commission	Circumstances of crime; offender's criminal history	Yes	Yes, for violence	Yes; intermediate punishments and drug and alcohol treatment in lieu of jail; boot camp
RI	1981	Equal sentencing geared to Superior Court; harsher penalties for habitual violence	Set by state law and Superior Court benchmarks	Circumstances of crime; offender's criminal history and social background	Yes	No	Yes; fines when jail sentence not prescribed
TN	1989	Equal sentencing	Contained in the law	Circumstances of crime; offender's criminal history	No	Yes, for violence	Yes; fines, restitution, probation, periodic and/or split confinement community corrections
UT	1985	Equal sentencing	Decided by a Commission	Circumstances of crime; offender's criminal history	Yes	Yes and must have been imprisoned for 2 priors	Yes; electronic monitoring day reporting, probation
VA	1-1-95	Equal sentencing; Truth-in-Sentencing; harsher penalties for habitual violence	Decided by a Commission	Circumstances of crime; offender's criminal history	Yes	Yes, and also for three drug-	Yes; detention and diversion centers; boot camp related
WA	7-1-84	Equal sentencing, to rectify perceived problems with parole	Contained in the law	Offender's criminal history; seriousness of offense	Yes	Yes, not only for violence	Yes; work release; community service, work crews
FBP	1987	Fair sentencing, Truth-in-Sentencing; uniform and proportionality in sentencing	Contained in the law and decided by a Commission	Circumstances of crime; offender's criminal history	Yes	Yes, not only for violence	Yes; probation community confinement, home confinement

Notes:
1. INDIANA: General Assembly sets guidelines by statute enacted over the course of several years
2. OHIO: This preceded federal push for Truth-in-Sentencing and the VOI/TIS bill. The Ohio guidelines met the TIS concerns and were eligible for federal funds.
3. OHIO: Presumptive criteria options for (1) in/out decisions; (2) expectation for minimum option for most first-timers; and (3) requirements for maximum.

Impact/Effects of Sentencing Guidelines

as of February 1999

	Organized Opposition	Parole Abolished	Initial Effect[1] (by Numerical Code)	OFFICIAL ASSESSMENT			Restructured	Additional Changes Under consideration
				Policy	Advantages	Disadvantages		
AK	No	No	5/6/7/8/9	Hard to say		Increased length of sentence means overcrowding	Yes, adding harsher sentences	
AR	No	No	8/12 (small and being studied)				No	None at present time
DE	No	Yes; 6 month probation imposed	4/618	Improvement	Non violent population reduced	Judges retain release authorization, limiting DOC discretion	Yes, Truth-in-sentencing 1991	
FL	Yes, by state attorneys and sheriffs, since resolved	Yes; Conditional release for specified violent offenders	Due to numerous changes, It is unknown what is attributable to guideline implementation	No opinion yet	Admission predictability that allows for adequate funding/planning		Yes, many times	None
IN	No	No, but limited extremely	Unsure	No opinion yet	More accurate population projections increased diversion for non-violent criminals	Less control over releases; must rely on court-ordered modifications to veer from statutory guidelines	Yes; changed parole eligibility requirements for some[2]	Cut all misdemeanants from the state system to county
KS	Yes, by district judges and some prosecutors	Yes; 2- or 3-year supervision based on severity level of offense	1/6/7/8/9/10	Improvement	Fewer non-violent offenders incarcerated; enhanced ability to project populations	Offenders serving under different sentencing laws; mixed sentence administration	Yes; most serious sentences have been increased	Comprehensive 13 point plan has been introduced to 1999 legislative session
MD	No	No	11	No opinion yet	Unknown	Unknown	Yes, Formulated 6-stage mission statement	
MI	No	No	4/7/8/9/12 (all speculation since impact not yet realized)	No opinion yet	None	Overcrowding anticipated due to longer sentences, though fewer will be sentenced to prison	No	NA
MN	No	Yes; supervised release	3/6/8/12 (disparity in sentencing decreased)	Improvement over past policy	Less criticism of DOC release decisions; able to more accurately predict future population, viewed as more equitable	Unknown	Yes, modified annually by the Commission	None
MO	No; guidelines are voluntary	No	12 (too early to tell since it is voluntary)	Improvement over past policy	More consistent sentencing by state's judges; ability to plan for growth in population	None (but some uncertainty in the level of usage by judges)	No	
NM	Unknown	No	5 (habitual offenders)	Enacted too long ago to compare	Easier to project population growth		Yes; added habitual offender and firearm enhancements	Expanding 3-strike list of offenses and overhauling sentence categories[3]

IMPACT/EFFECTS OF SENTENCING GUIDELINES, *continued*

	Organized Opposition	Parole Abolished	Initial Effect[1] (by Numerical Code)	OFFICIAL ASSESSMENT			Restructured	Additional Changes Under consideration
				Policy	Advantages	Disadvantages		
NC	No	Yes	4/6/7/8/10	Improvement over past policy	Predictability of release; lower admissions	Fewer incentives for good behavior; increasingly violent population	No	
OH	Yes; by individual prosecutors and appeals court judges (all minor)	Yes (for most crimes); required 3 or 5 years post-release control for serious violent offenders and all imprisoned felony sex offenders	4/8/9/12 (better community alternatives; repeat misdemeanor petty theft stays same; caps on sentences, parole release; limits on consecutives; good time ends)	Improvement in community sentencing; not affecting sentencing trends	Easier sentence calculation; fewer sent to prison; better choices for prison; better community corrections options	Increase in imprisoned violent offenders; fewer incentives to "program"; fewer incentives generally to promote good institutional behavior	No	A major revision of misdemeanor sentencing is presently before the Legislature
OK	No	No	11	No opinion yet	Not yet implemented	Not yet implemented	NA	Repeal being considered
OR	Yes, individual circuit court judges	Yes; mandatory post-release supervision imposed	3/6/7/8/9	Improvement over past policy	Far more certainty regarding length of prison sentences; improves planning for future growth		No	
PA	Yes; District Attorneys Association	No	5/12 (more consistent statewide sentencing)	Improvement over past policy	Greater reliability in projecting population; useful tool for targeting offenders for alternatives; stability regarding policies	Recommendations to increase severity of sentences for targeted offenders may result in increased prison population	Yes, eight times; increased recommendations for violent offenders consistent with Special Session on	None
RI	No	No; benchmark ranges specify terms to which defendants should be sentenced	11	Improvement over past policy	Consistency in sentencing increased, thereby improving population projectors	No connection between bed space and guidelines	Yes, increased bench marks; presumptive sentencing law; GA statutes requiring certain mandatory minimum	
TN	No	No	1/3/4/6/8	Improvement over past policy	Consistency in sentencing	None	Sentences incarceration for certain violent offenses, provide Truth-in-sentencing qualify for federal funds	None
UT	No	No	11/12 (no intensive analysis conducted on effects of guidelines on sentencing practice)	Improvement over past policy	Benchmark for measuring sentencing activity, allowing for enhanced planned capacity	None	Yes, incorporated intermediate sanctions and to adjust matrix to reflect current sentencing practice	None

	Organized Opposition	Parole Abolished	Initial Effect[1] (by Numerical Code)	OFFICIAL ASSESSMENT				Additional Changes Under consideration
				Policy	Advantages	Disadvantages	Restructured	
VA	No	Yes; but mandatory post-release supervision not imposed	3/6/8	No opinion yet			Yes, judicial feedback, legislative code changes; age of victims; more community programs	
WA	Yes, trial lawyers and certain victims' groups	Yes, mandatory post-release supervision imposed	3/5/6/7/8/12 (First, decrease; then, increase in population; more equitable sen-	NA	Accurate population projections and simulations of policy impacts	Lack of flexibility	No, but special sentencing options and Truth-in-sentencing aspects added	Considering establishing comprehensive guidelines for length of
FBP	Unknown	Yes, supervised release added	2/3/5/6/7/8/9 (resulting from combination of guidelines, mandatory minimum sentences and statutory directives	affecting sentencing/population trends	Consistency in sentencing	Managing rapidly increased population; managing reactions to longer sentences or sentences perceived as inordinately long	Yes, but minor	Supervision after release

Notes:
1. INITIAL Effect CODES: 1 = Early release for some prisoners; 2 = Fewer offenders in general placed on probation; 3 = Fewer offenders in general receiving incarceration; 4 = More offenders placed on probation; 5 = More offenders in general receiving incarceration; 6 = More violent offenders receiving incarceration; 7 = Longer sentences in general; 8 = Longer sentences for violent offenders; 9 = Increased prison population; 10 = Decreased prison population; 11 = No known effect; 12 = Other
2. INDIANA :Also expanded aggravating/mitigating circumstances; allows lowes' felonies to be sentenced as misdemeanors; expands eligibility for community corrections.
3. NEW MEXICO: Four category changes — (a) presumptive prison; (b) no presumption; (c) presumptive non-prison; (d) presumptive fines and penalties

Systems Not Using Sentencing Guidelines

as of February 1999

	Primary Reason	Being Proposed	If so, by	Implementing a 3-Strikes Provision	Comments
AL	Judicial Study Commission to make final recommendation	Yes	Attorney General	Already implemented	Habitual Offender statute in effect
AZ	Lack of legislative support	No		No	Truth-in-Sentencing model in place
CO	Judicial discretion valued as sentencing foundation	No		No	Habitual sentencing provisions already implemented
CT	All guidelines imposed by statute	Yes	Legislature	No	Truth-in-Sentencing in place; inmates do "day for day."[1]
GA	Courts are independent, with judicial discretion	No		Already implemented	
HI	Neither proposed nor considered	No		No; studies undertaken that could lead to legislative action	
ID	Court discretion as set out in state law	No		No	
IL	Already moved to structured policy of determinate sentencing in 1978	No		No	Habitual Criminal Act in place Feb. 1, 1978
IA	Indeterminate sentencing deemed satisfactory	Legislative sentencing commission established to consider guidelines along with other structure channel.		No; rejected in the past in favor of other sentencing enhancements	
KY	State has jury sentencing	No		No	
LA	Revoked by Legislature three years ago	No		No	Habitual Offender sentencing provision in place
ME	Higher state courts informally provide guidelines by hearing appeals	No		Yes, proposed bill before the Legislature this session	
MA	Legislation pending	Yes	Legislature and Sentencing Commission	Already implemented	
MS	No legislative authority	No		No	
NE	Historically not an issue	No		No	
NV	No legislative action	No		No	Habitual Criminal statute in place[2]
NH	Lack of political will and support	No		No	
NJ	Unknown	Unknown		Already implemented in 1995	
NY	Considered but abandoned in mid-80's[3]	No		No	
ND	Active opposition by the courts	No		No	
SC	No previous legislative action	Yes, 2/22/99	Legislature and Sentencing Commission[4]	No a 2-strike version for violent offenders in place 111/96 as specifically defined in the SC Criminal Code	Truth-in-Sentencing in place
SD	Lack of legislative interest	No		No	Habitual Offender laws in place
TX	Past lack of legislative interest	Yes, changes proposed to the Penal Code	Legislature	Already implemented	

	Primary Reason	Being Proposed	If so, by	Implementing a 3-Strikes Provision	Comments
VT	Regardless of judicial approval, Sentencing Commission recommended denial in 1987	No		No	
WV	Lack of need for consideration	No		No	Habitual Offender statute in place and general sentencing provisions already utilized by the courts
WI	Unknown	Yes	Criminal Penalties Study Committee making recommendations	Yes, for those who committed three violent felonies	Truth-in-Sentencing new law taking effect 12/31/99 to include Committee recommendations
WY	Not considered by the Legislature	No		No	

Notes:

As reported by Manitoba, Newfoundland, Nova Scotia, Ontario, Saskatchewan, and Correctional Service Canada, Sentencing Guidelines have not been enacted by the Canadian Parliament which has complete jurisdiction over criminal law legislation. The Provinces are responsible for the administration of justice.

1. CONNECTICUT: Parole Board sees nonviolent offenders serving sentences more than two years after 50% of time served Violent offenders must serve 85% of their sentence before review.

2. NEVADA: Codes revised in 1995, with mandatory minimum sentences imposed that cannot be reduced by sentence credits Each crime carries a wide range of "min-max" sentences; parole and probation considers options using a risk-assessment tool they developed.

3. NEW YORK: Initially considered because of disparate sentencing practices between upstate and downstate, but abandoned after public hearings when no agreements were reached.

4. SOUTH CAROLINA: Both the DOC and Department of Probation, Parole and Pardons, work with the Commission to do impact analysis for the Legislature on guideline versions.

Departments & Institutions Under Court Order/Consent Decree

as of September 30, 1998

	ADULT					JUVENILE				
	Entire Dept. Under Order	Master or Monitor Assigned	One or More Inst. Under Order to Imprv Cond	Master or Monitor Assigned	Number of Institu-tions	Entire Dept. Under Order	Master or Monitor Assigned	One or More Inst. Under Order to Imprv Cond	Master or Monitor Assigned	Number of Institu-tions
AL	Yes [1]	No	No	No	—	Yes [2]	No	—	—	—
AK	Yes [3]	Yes	Yes	Yes	13	No	—	No	—	—
AZ*	Yes	*	No	No	—					
AR	No	—	No	—	—					
CA	Yes	Yes	Yes	Yes	33					
CO										
CT	Yes [19]	Yes	Yes	Yes	4					
DE										
FL	No	—	Yes [4]	No	2					
GA	No	—	Yes	Yes	8					
HI			Yes	Yes	1	No	—	No	—	—
ID	Yes [5]	No	No	—	—					
IL	No	No	Yes	Yes	1					
IN	Yes [6]	No	No	No	—					
IA	No	—	No	—	—					
KS	No	—	No	—	—					
KY	Yes [7]	No	No	—	—	Yes [8]	Yes	Yes	Yes	11
LA	No	—	Yes	Yes	1	No	—	Yes	Yes	3
ME										
MD										
MA										
MI	No	—	Yes	—	6	No	—	No	No	—
MN	No	—	No	—	—					
MS	Yes [9]	No	No	—	—	No	—	No	—	—
MO	No	—	Yes	No	5					
MT	No	—	Yes	Yes	1					
NE	No	—	No	—	—	No	—	No	—	—
NV										
NH						Yes/No [10]	No	Yes	No	1
NJ	Yes	Yes	No	—	—					
NM	No	Yes	No	—	—	No	No	No	No	—
NY	No	—	Yes	Yes	[20]	No	—	Yes	Yes	1
NC	No	—	No	—	—	No	—	No	—	—
ND	No	—	No	—	—					
OH	Yes [11]	Yes	No	—	—	No	—	No	—	—
OK	Yes [7]	No	Yes	No	2					
OR	No	—	No	—	—					
PA	No	—	No	—	—					
RI	No	—	—	—	—					
SC	No	—	—	—	—	No [12]	Yes	Yes	—	14
SD	No	—	No	—	—					
TN	No	—	No	—	—	Yes	No	Yes	No	4
TX	Yes [13]	No	Yes	No	—	No	No	No	No	—
UT	No	No	No	No	—					
VT	No	—	No	—	—					
VA	No	No	No	—	—	No	—	No	—	—
WA	Yes [14]	No	Yes	No/Yes	2	No	—	Yes	Yes	1
WV										
WI	Yes	No	Yes	No	1	No	—	No	—	—
WY	No	—	No	—	—	No	—	No	—	—
FBP	No	—	Yes	No	1					
Cook	Yes [15]	Yes	No	—	—					
DC										
PHL	Yes [7,15,16]	Yes	Yes	Yes	[17]					
NYC						No	—	No	—	—
VI	Yes [15,18]	Yes	Yes	Yes	2					

Notes:
* Disciplinary rules and regulations—monitor/master assigned, No; mail policy—monitor/master assigned, Yes; quality of prison life—monitor/master assigned, No; mental health—monitor/master assigned, Yes
1. Failure to remove state inmates
2. Delivery improvement of services
3. Institutional overpopulation
4. Limited to death row exercise
5. Religious practices
6. Caps on prison pupulation
7. Conditions of confinement
8. CRIPA violations
9. Settle issues concerning HIV and Muslims
10. Court order—overpopulation/consent decree—educational services
11. Improvement of mental health care for inmates
12. Unconstitutional conditions of confinement
13. Overcrowding and related issues, Mail system—inmate correspondence, In-cell integration
14. High school diplomas for anyone under 21, Washington state penitentiary—no master/monitor, Washington corrections center for women—yes master/monitor
15. Overcrowding
16. Assaults on inmates
17. Entire system
18. Safety and health violations
19. AIDS and HIV medical/mental health care
20. Some court orders/consent decrees apply system-wide; others can apply to a particular facility

Death Penalty: Legislation, Change, Methods of Execution

as of July 1999

	IN EFFECT			DEATH PENALTY OPTIONS			
	Currently	Pre-1973	Changes	Moratorium Proposals	Life Without Parole	Straight Life	Methods of Execution and Those Charged with Conducting the Executions
AL	Yes	Yes	None being considered	None	Yes	No	Electric chair; by staff
AK	No	Yes	Abolished 1957; being reconsidered	NA	NA	NA	NA
AZ	Yes	Yes	Eliminated 1972; reinstated 1973; ruled unconstitutional 1978; reinstated 1979	None	Yes	No	Gas; lethal injections added in 1992; by staff
AR	Yes	Yes	Reinstated in 1973; no changes being considered	None	Yes	Yes	Electric chair; lethal injection added in 1993; by staff and outside person
CA	Yes	Yes	None being considered	None	Yes	Yes	Lethal injection; gas if inmate requests;
CO	Yes	Yes	None being considered	None	Yes	Yes	Lethal injection; gas added in 1988; by staff
CT	Yes	Yes	Reinstated in 1973; no changes being considered	None	Yes	Yes	Lethal injection since 1995; by staff and/or outside person
DE	Yes	No	None being considered	None	Yes		Lethal injection after 1986; by hanging unless injection requested and if sentenced previously; by staff
DC	No Response						
FL	Yes	Yes	Reinstated in 1976; no changes being considered	None	Yes	Yes	Electric chair; by staff and private citizen (executioner)
GA	No Response						
HI	No	Yes	None being considered	NA	NA	NA	NA
ID	Yes	Yes	Reinstated in 1977; no changes being considered	None	Yes	Yes	Lethal injection or firing squad; hanging eliminated in 1973
IL	Yes	Yes	Reinstated in 1977; no changes being considered	Yes, one year proposed	Yes	No	Lethal injection; changed from electric chair in 1983; by staff
IN	Yes	Yes	Reinstated in 1977; no changes being considered	None	Yes	Yes	Lethal injection; changed from electric chair in 1995
IA	No	Yes	Eliminated in 1964; no changes being considered	NA	Yes	No	NA
KS	Yes	Yes	Reinstated in 1994; no changes being considered	None	No[1]	No	Lethal injection; changed from hanging in 1993
KY	Yes	Yes	Reinstated in 1976; no changes being considered	Yes, to life without parole	Yes		Electric chair and lethal injection (injection added in 1998)
LA	Yes	Yes	Reinstated in 1976; no changes being considered	Yes, to indefinite term	Yes	No	Lethal injection; changed from electric chair; by confidential sources
ME	No	Yes	Death penalty provisions not utilized since late 1800s; changes are being considered in the current legislature	NA	NA	NA	NA
MD	Yes	Yes	Reinstated in 1987; no changes being considered	None	Yes	Yes	Lethal injection; changed from gas; by staff
MA	No Response						
MI	No	No	NA	NA	Yes	Yes	NA
MN	No	Yes	Eliminated in 1911 and unused since 1906; no changes being considered	NA	Yes	Yes	NA
MS	Yes	Yes	Reinstated in 1977; no changes being considered	None	Yes		Lethal injection; by staff and/or outside person
MO	Yes	Yes	Reinstated in 1977; no changes being considered	None	Yes	Yes	Lethal injection; by staff
MT	Yes	Yes	No changes being considered	Yes, two years proposed	Yes	Yes	Lethal injection; changed from hanging; by staff and/or outside person
NE	Yes	Yes	Reinstated in 1976; no changes being considered	Yes, three years proposed	Yes	Yes	Electric chair; by confidential sources
NV	Yes	Yes	Reinstated in 1979; no changes being considered	None	Yes	Yes	Lethal injection; changed from gas; by staff
NH	Yes	Yes	No changes being considered	None	Yes	Yes	Lethal injection added in 1986 or by hanging; by staff

DEATH PENALTY: LEGISLATION, CHANGE, METHODS OF EXECUTION, *continued*

	IN EFFECT			DEATH PENALTY OPTIONS			Methods of Execution and Those Charged with Conducting the Executions
	Currently	Pre-1973	Changes	Moratorium Proposals	Life Without Parole	Straight Life	
NJ	Yes	Yes	Reinstated in 1982; changes are being considered in current legislature	None	Yes	Yes	Lethal injection; changed from electric chair in use from 1907 to 1972; by discretion of the Commissioner
NM	Yes	Yes	Reinstated in 1979; no changes being considered	None	No		Lethal injection; by outside persons
NY	Yes	Yes	Reinstated in 1995; changes are being considered in current legislature	None	Yes	Yes	Lethal injection, changed from electric chair; by staff
NC	Yes	Yes	Reinstated in 1977; changes are being considered in current legislature	None	Yes	Yes	Lethal injection, changed from gas; by staff
ND	No	No	NA	NA	Yes	Yes	NA
OH	Yes	Yes	Reinstated in 1981; no changes being considered	None	No	No	Electric chair or lethal injection, at inmate's option; by staff
OK	Yes	Yes	Reinstated in 1977; no changes being considered	None	Yes	Yes	Lethal injection; by outside person
OR	Yes	Yes	Reinstated in 1984; no changes being considered	None	Yes		Lethal injection, used for first time in 1996; by staff and/or outside person
PA	Yes	Yes	No changes being considered	Yes; unspecified	Yes	Yes	Lethal injection, changed from electric chair in 1990; by outside person
RI	No	Yes	Eliminated in 1852	None	No	No	NA
SC	Yes	Yes	Reinstated in 1977; no changes being considered	None	Yes	Yes	Lethal injection added in 1995, or electric chair; at inmate's option; by staff
SD	Yes	Yes	Reinstated in 1979; no changes being considered	No	Yes	Yes[2]	Lethal injection, changed from electric chair in 1984, by undetermined source
TN	Yes	Yes	No changes being considered	No	Yes	Yes	Lethal injection for offenses prior to 1-1 99; electric chair or lethal injection for offenses after 1-1-99, at inmate's option; by staff
TX	Yes	Yes	No changes being considered	No	No	No	Lethal injection changed from electric chair by staff
UT	Yes	Yes	No changes being considered	No	Yes	Yes	Lethal injection or firing squad; eliminated hanging; by staff and outside
VT	No	Yes	Eliminated in 1966; no changes being considered	NA	Yes	No	NA
VA	Yes	Yes	Reinstated in 1978; no changes being considered		Yes	Yes	Lethal injection; electric chair if original sentence so states or by injection at inmate's option; by staff
WA	Yes	Yes	No changes being considered	No	Yes	No	Lethal injection; or hanging at inmate's option; by outside person
WV	No	Yes	Eliminated in 1969; no changes being considered	NA	NA		NA
WI	No	Yes		NA	Yes	Yes	NA
WY	Yes	Yes	No changes being considered	No	Yes	Yes	Lethal injection unless held to be unconstitutional; gas then used; by outside person
FBP	Yes	Yes	Reinstated in 1988; changes currently are being considered	No	Yes		Lethal injection, unless for those cases covered under 18 U.S.C. 3596 that mandates method to be used as determined by the state in which the sentence was imposed

Notes:

CANADIAN PROVINCES: The death penalty was abolished throughout all the provinces of Canada in 1976. The Solicitor General of Canada is responsible for court imposed sentences of two years or more, including any action involving a death penalty. Correctional Service Canada states that legislation is pending for repealing the death penalty for a few remaining military offenses. This legislation will come into law Sept. 1, 1999. Six provinces (Manitoba, Newfoundland, Nova Scotia, Ontario, Saskatchewan and Yukon Territory) plus Correctional Service Canada responded to this survey.

1. KANSAS: Enacted a "Hard 50" that requires 50 years to be served before parole-eligible.

2. SOUTH DAKOTA: Straight Life sentence is an option if the governor commutes the sentence to a fixed number of years followed by parole.

Death Penalty: Numbers, Exclusions and Past Executions

as of July 1999

	UNDER DEATH SENTENCE AS OF 6-1-99			AGES		Racial / Ethnic Makeup	Exclusions	SINCE 1973		YEARS ON DEATH ROW	
	Total	Men	Women	Oldest/ Youngest	Longest Stay (Years)			Number Executed	Racial/Ethnic Makeup	Long	Short
AL	181	179	2	61/0	21	95 Caucasian; 86 African-American; one Asian	Under 14; mentally ill; mentally retarded	18	6 Caucasian; 12 African-American	22	NA
AK	NA	NA	NA	NA	NA	NA	NA	NA	NA	NA	NA
AZ	115	114	1	83/22	20	80 Caucasian; 13 African-American; 18 Hispanic; four Native American	Under 15; mentally incompetent to be executed; mentally retarded; pregnant	18	13 Caucasian; 3 Hispanic; 2 Native American	27	7
AR	40	39	1	59/20	19	17 Caucasian; 22 African-American; one Hispanic	Mentally retarded	19	14 Caucasian; 4 African-American; 1 Hispanic	18	2
CA	539	529	10	69/22	21	229 Caucasian; 193 African-American; 97 Hispanic; 23 Asian, Native American and Pacific Islander	Under 18; insane at time of execution; mentally retarded at time of execution; during pregnancy	7	5 Caucasian, 1 African-American; 1 Asian	16.8	9.6
CO	4	4	0	41/20	12.5	1 Caucasian; two African-American, one 1 Hispanic	Under 18 at time of offense	1	1 Caucasian	10	NA
CT	5	5	0	52/29	9.7	2 Caucasian; 3 African-Americans	Under 18; mentally impaired at time of offense	0	NA	NA	NA
DE	18	18	0	49/21	17	9 Caucasian; 9 African-American	Under 18 at time of offense	9	5 Caucasian; 3 African-American; 1 Native American	17	3
DC	No Response										
FL	376	372	4	72/21	26	228 Caucasian; 134 African-American; 14 Hispanic	Under 16 at time of offense; deemed insane at time of execution; mentally retarded and no understanding of death penalty	44	27 Caucasian; 16 African-American; 1 Hispanic	16	2
GA	No Response										
HI	NA	NA	NA	NA	NA	NA	NA	NA	NA	NA	NA
ID	20	19	1	NA	NA	20 Caucasian	None	1	1 Caucasian	NA	NA
IL	162	159	3	61/21	19	51 Caucasian; 103 African-Americans 8 Hispanic	Under 18	12	7 Caucasian; 5 African-American	17	6
IN	46	45	1	65/26	20	29 Caucasian; 16 African-Americans; 1 Hispanic	Under 18 at time of offense; pregnant	6	3 Caucasian; 3 African-American	15	1.1
IA	NA	NA	NA	NA	NA	NA	NA	NA	NA	NA	NA

DEATH PENALTY: NUMBERS, EXCLUSIONS AND PAST EXECUTIONS, *continued*

	UNDER DEATH SENTENCE AS OF 6-1-99			AGES		Racial / Ethnic Makeup	Exclusions	SINCE 1973		YEARS ON DEATH ROW	
	Total	Men	Women	Oldest / Youngest	Longest Stay (Years)			Number Executed	Racial / Ethnic Makeup	Long	Short
KS	2	2	0	43/23	1.3	2 Caucasian	Under 18; mentally ill with mitigating factors; mentally retarded as determined by court	0	NA	NA	NA
KY	39	39	0				Under 16; mentally ill or mentally retarded[1]				
LA	81	80	1	57/19	16	23 Caucasian; 57 African-American; 1 Hispanic	Under 14	25	13 Caucasian; 11 African-American; 1 Hispanic	14.3	1
ME	NA	NA	NA	NA	NA	NA		NA	NA	NA	NA
MD	17	17	0	54/25	18	5 Caucasian; 12 African-American	Juveniles; mentally ill, mentally retarded	3	1 Caucasian; 2 African-American	11	4
MA	No Response										
MI	NA	NA	NA	NA	NA	NA	NA	NA	NA	NA	NA
MN	NA	NA	NA	NA	NA	NA	NA	NA	NA	NA	NA
MS	60	59	1	61/19	28	26 Caucasian; 34 African-American	Juveniles; mentally ill; mentally retarded, pregnant	4	1 Caucasian; 3 African-American	9	8
MO	81	80	1	78/23	17	45 Caucasian; 36 African-American	15 at time crime committed; mentally ill, if incapable of knowing and appreciating nature, quality or wrongfulness of his conduct; mentally retarded; in first degree murder where facts do not show statutory aggravating circumstances	40	22 Caucasian; 18 African-American	15	6
MT	6	6	0	45/27	16	5 Caucasian; 1 Caucasian/Native American	Under 18 (effective 10/99);	2	Caucasian	20	10
NE	10	10	0	66/25	20.9	8 Caucasian; 1 African-American; 1 Native American	Under 18 at time of crime; mentally ill (incompetent); mentally retarded, with IQ below 70	3	1 Caucasian 2 African-American	19.4	11.7
NV	84	83	1	70/22	19.8	45 Caucasian; 34 African-American; 5 Hispanic	Under 16; if found insane or retarded after judgement of death	8	Unknown		
NH	0	0	0	NA	NA	NA	Under 18; mentally ill (as a mitigating factor)	0	NA	NA	NA
NJ	15	15	0	69/21		9 Caucasian; 6 African-American	Under 18	0	NA	NA	NA
NM	4	4	0			3 Caucasian; 1 Hispanic	Some exclusions apply, but not necessarily by death statute	0	NA	NA	NA
NY	2	2	0	29/27	1	1 African-American; 1 Hispanic	Under 21; lack capacity, the nature and effect of death penalty; mentally retarded, pregnant	0	NA	NA	NA

| | UNDER DEATH SENTENCE AS OF 6-1-99 | | | AGES | | Racial / Ethnic Makeup | Exclusions | SINCE 1973 | | YEARS ON DEATH ROW | |
	Total	Men	Women	Oldest/ Youngest	Longest Stay (Years)			Number Executed	Racial/Ethnic Makeup	Long	Short
NC	192	188	4	73.5	19.6	78 Caucasian; 105 African-American; 7 Native American 2 Elias Syriani/Angel Guevara	None	12	Caucasian	16	2
ND	NA	NA	NA	NA	NA	NA	NA	NA	NA	NA	NA
OH	196	196	0	73/20	17	94 Caucasian; 97 African-American; 5 Hispanic	Under 18; mentally ill[2]; mental disease or defect is mitigating circumstance, pregnant	1	Caucasian	8.9	8.9
OK	149	146	3	72/22	19	84 Caucasian; 48 African-American; 6 Hispanic; 9 Native American; 1 Iraqi	Under 16; by statute, mentally ill or mentally retarded competency must be determined	17	13 Caucasian; 1 African-American; 1 Asian; 1 His panic; 1 Native American	16.2	2.3
OR	25	25	0	65/20	8	22 Caucasian; 2 Hispanic; 1 Native American	Under 15	2	Caucasian	4.5	3.8
PA	227	223	4	63/20	18	72 Caucasian; 140 African-American; 2 Asian; 13 Hispanic	Mentally ill[3]	3	Caucasian	13	9
RI	NA	NA	NA	NA	NA	NA	NA	NA	NA	NA	NA
SC	67	67	0	47/21	17	33 Caucasian; 34 African-American	Juveniles; mentally ill; mentally retarded	22	14 Caucasian, 8 African-American	21	B
SD	3	3	0	NA	NA	Caucasian	None	0	NA	NA	NA
TN	101	99	2	70/23		64 Caucasian; 33 African-American; 1 Asian; 2 Hispanic; 1 Native American	Under 18; mentally ill can be a mitigating factor; mentally retarded[4]	0	NA	NA	NA
TX	458	450	8	62/18	24	167 Caucasian; 190 African-American; 97 Hispanic; 4 other	Under 16	177	90 Caucasian; 56 African-American; 29 Hispanic; 2 other	24.6	.69
UT	12	12	0	57/23	16	7 Caucasian; 2 African-American; 2 Hispanic; 1 Native American	Under 14; mentally ill or retarded could be a defense	5	3 Caucasian 2 African-American	18	4
VT	NA	NA	NA	NA	NA	NA	NA	NA	NA	NA	NA
VA	34	34	0	57/20	12.6	17 Caucasian; 17 African-American	NA	67	31 Caucasian, 34 African-American; 2 Hispanic	15.3	1.1
WA	14	14	0	56/28	10.5	11 Caucasian; 3 African-American	Under 18	3	2 Caucasian, 1 Hispanic	12.6	2.5
WV	NA	NA	NA	NA	NA	NA	NA	NA	NA	NA	NA

DEATH PENALTY: NUMBERS, EXCLUSIONS AND PAST EXECUTIONS, *continued*

	UNDER DEATH SENTENCE AS OF 6-1-99			AGES	Longest Stay (Years)	Racial / Ethnic Makeup	Exclusions	SINCE 1973		YEARS ON DEATH ROW	
	Total	Men	Women	Oldest/ Youngest				Number Executed	Racial/Ethnic Makeup	Long	Short
WI	NA	NA	NA	NA	NA	NA	NA	NA	NA	NA	NA
WY	2	2	0	30/29	1	Caucasian	Under 16, mentally ill or retarded[5]	1	Caucasian	13	13
FBP	20	20	0	49/22	11	5 Caucasian; 14 African-American; 1 Asian	Under 18; mentally ill or retarded[6]	0	NA	NA	NA

Notes:

1. KENTUCKY: For both mentally ill and mentally retarded, inmate must be considered as "serious"
2. OHIO: "Insane," which does not merely mean "mentally ill" but that the inmate does not have "sufficient intelligence to understand the nature of the proceedings..., what he was tried for, the purpose of his punishment, the impending fate that awaits him," knowledge of any facts which might assist in his defense and the ability to convey information to an attorney or judge. In re: Keaton, 19 0 App 2d 254 (1969).
3. PENNSYLVANIA: McNaghten Rule from Common Law covers those unable to appreciate the nature or consequences of their actions.
4. TENNESSEE: Persons with (1) significantly subaverage general intelligence as evidenced by a functional IQ of 70 or below; (2) deficits in adaptive behavior; (3) manifested during the developmental period, or by age 18.
5. WYOMING: Persons not having the "requisite mental capacity" or ability to understand the nature of the death penalty and the reasons it was imposed.
6. FEDERAL BUREAU OF PRISONS: 18 U.S.C. 3596(c), mental capacity — a sentence of death shall not be carried out upon a person who, as a result of mental disability, lacks the mental capacity to understand the death penalty and why it was imposed on the person.

Death Penalty: Location, Accommodations, Longest Confinement, Movement and Visitations

as of July 1999

	Specific Death Row Unit(s)	Female Housing Breakdown	Physical Cell Accommodations	Allowed Outside Cell Per Day	Population Mingling	VISITATIONS		
						Number Per Week	Length in Hours Per Visit	Type
AL	Yes, 3 facilities	1 separate facility	Individual cells	Under 1 hour	No	1	6	Contact
AK	NA	NA	NA	NA	NA	NA	NA	NA
AZ	Yes, separated from general population	1 separate facility	Individual cells	1 hour, 3 per week	No	Up to 5	2, unless special	Noncontact
AR	Yes, specific unit	1 woman housed at alternate unit	Individual cells	3+ hours	No	1	3	Contact, depending on inmate
CA	Yes, in one facility	Women's prison	Individual cells	Maximum of 6 hours, 7 days per week, depending on inmate	No	4	Varies by space available and number of visitors at a given time	Grade "A" inmates, contact; grade "B" inmates, noncontact
CO	No specific unit	NA	Individual cells	1 hour	No	1	4	Noncontact
CT	Yes, in cells separated by divider wall	NA	Individual cells	1 hour outside rec; 1 hour in evening; phone calls, work duties, visits	No	3	1	Contact for legal; noncontact for social
DE	No specific unit	NA	Individual cells	1 hour	No	1	1	Noncontact
DC	No Response							
FL	Yes	Separate facility	Individual cells	Twice weekly for 2 hours each	No	Socially, on weekends	6	Contact or noncontact, depending on inmate
GA	No Response							
HI	NA	NA	NA	NA	No	NA	NA	NA
ID	Yes, a tier at maximum security unit	Women's prison	Individual cells	1 hour	No	NA	NA	Noncontact
IL	Yes, 3 facilities	1 separate facility	Individual cells	Varies from 1-3 hours by facility	No	2	2, if space available, or 1 if segregation status	Contact or noncontact, depending on inmate
IN	Yes, 4 separate cell blocks	1 separate facility	Individual cells	3 or more hours	No	No limit	2-4, if space available	Contact
IA	NA	NA	NA	NA	NA	NA	NA	NA
KS	No	NA	Individual cells	1 hour	No	1.5	3.5 mornings and 2.5 afternoons	Noncontact

DEATH PENALTY: LOCATION, ACCOMMODATIONS, LONGEST CONFINEMENT, MOVEMENT AND VISITATIONS, *continued*

	Specific Death Row Unit(s)	Female Housing Breakdown	Physical Cell Accommodations	Allowed Outside Cell Per Day	Population Mingling	VISITATIONS		
						Number Per Week	Length in Hours Per Visit	Type
KY	Yes, in general population cell house, segregated by safety glass and confined	NA	Individual cells	1 hour normally, but can vary	No	1	6	Contact
LA	Yes, 1 cell block	1 separate facility	Individual cells	1 hour	No	2 per visit or month; 10 visitors on list per inmate	2-4	Contact or noncontact, depending on inmate
ME		NA	NA	NA	NA	NA	NA	NA
MD	Yes	NA	Individual cells	3 or more hours	No	8 per month	30 minutes	Noncontact
MA	No Response							
MI	NA	NA	NA	NA	NA	NA	NA	NA
MN	NA	NA	NA	NA	NA	NA	NA	NA
MS	Yes, in a maximum security unit	1 separate facility	Individual cells	1 hour	No	1	1	Noncontact
MO	No separate unit	No separate unit	2 per cell	3 or more hours	Yes	20	7	Contact
MT	No separate unit	NA	Individual cells	1 hour	No	5		Noncontact
NE	Yes, same as for general population but reserved for death row	NA	Individual cells	2 hours	No	2	2.8	Contact, but could vary, depending on inmate
NV	Yes	1 separate facility	Individual cells	3 or more hours	No	2	6	Contact
NH	Yes, section of maximum security facility	Same area as males	Single cells	3 or more hours	No	2	1	Noncontact
NJ	Yes, self-contained unit (single lock)	Same area as males	Individual cells	2 hours; inside and outside recreation every other day	No	2	1	Noncontact
NM	Yes, north unit of state penitentiary	NA	Individual cells	Varies based on classification	No	Unlimited	2	Depends on the inmate
NY	Yes, section of maximum security facility	Separate unit at female maximum facility	Individual cells	1 hour	No	1	Several hours	Contact
NC	Yes, separate sections and floors of pods	Women's prison	Individual cells	3 or more hours[1]	No	NA	NA	Noncontact
ND	NA	NA	NA	NA	NA	NA	NA	NA
OH	Yes, maximum security cell block at a different prison than where sentence is carried out	NA	Individual cells	1 hour	No	3; 5 maximum per month	3	Noncontact

	Specific Death Row Unit(s)	Female Housing Breakdown	Physical Cell Accommodations	Allowed Outside Cell Per Day	Population Mingling	VISITATIONS		
						Number Per Week	Length in Hours Per Visit	Type
OK	Yes, separate high security area, including administrative segregation	Separate facility	Single or double; usually double	1 hour, five days per week for exercise; 3 times (15 min.) per week for showering	No	8 per month and state holidays	2	Noncontact
OR	Yes, tier in disciplinary segregation unit at state penitentiary; overflow in administrative segregation	NA	Individual cells	2 hours	No	2 on weekends	2 2-hour family visits	Noncontact
PA	Yes, special housing units at 5 institutions	Separate facility	Individual cells	1 hour, five days per week	No	1	1 hour, unless extended to 2 hours with approval	Noncontact
RI	NA	NA	NA	NA	NA	NA	NA	NA
SC	Yes, separated from general population	NA	Individual cells	1 hour	No	First come first served	2	Noncontact
SD	Yes, separated from general population	NA	Individual cells	45 minutes recreation per weekday	No	2	Varies	Noncontact
TN	Yes, one unit containing four pods	Women's prison	Individual cells; double cells for women based on adapting to the system	Varies, depending on program level	Yes; females, based on behavior	2, males; females[2]	Per Visit 1-3 hours, males	Depends on the inmate
UT	Yes, a series of attached cells	NA	Individual cells	Varies based on classification	No	1	1.5	Noncontact
VT	NA	NA	NA	NA	NA	NA	NA	NA
VA	Yes	NA	Individual cells	Unavailable	No	Unavailable	NA	NA
WA	Yes, Intensive Management Unit first year and special unit determined by behavior	NA	Individual cells	1 hour	No	2	2 approximately	Noncontact
WV	NA	NA	NA	NA	NA	NA	NA	NA
WI	NA	NA	NA	NA	NA	NA	NA	NA
WY	Yes, isolated in separate block	NA	Individual cells	1 hour 15 minutes	No	1	2	Noncontact
FBP	Yes, one special confinement unit	NA	Individual cells	2 or more	No	2 plus legal	2 for social	Noncontact for social; may be contact for legal

Notes:
1. NORTH CAROLINA: Cells opened at 6:00 a.m. and can be in day room until lockdown at 11:00 p.m. Death row inmates go to dining hall together.
2. TENNESSEE: Of the two current female inmates on death row, one can have two visits per month of two visitors for two hours and the second female follows guidelines of general population. One female is allowed outside one hour per day and the other is out approximately 15 hours per day.

Death Penalty: Programs and Problems

as of July 1999

	Recreation	Work Programs	Education	COUNSELING		Legal Assistance	General Problems
				Religious	Mental Health		
AL	Outside yard, inside day room, TV, radio	No		General population chaplain	Yes	Library; outside attorneys	Lack of staff
AK	NA	NA	NA	NA	NA	NA	NA
AZ	Inside concrete pen	No	Correspondence; institutional TV	General population chaplain; contractors/community volunteers	Yes	Outside attorneys; contract paralegal	Staffing
AR	Outside yard, 12 hours per week in 2-hour increments	2-hour shifts, if approved	Available upon request and approval	General population chaplain		Law library; outside attorneys	Discipline; staffing; security
CA	Outside yard, inside day room, TV, radios, chess, cards, board games, basketball, no free weights	No	Correspondence; outside college courses offered by satellite	General population chaplain	Yes	Law library; outside attorneys; "pocket" law libraries in two facilities	Overcrowding; discipline; staffing
CO	Exercise yard; TV	May apply as barbers or janitors in their pods	Regular classes; individual tutoring; GED preparation; ESL; post high school classes	General population chaplain; outside ministers; volunteers	Yes	Law library (without physical access); outside attorneys; inmate legal counsel	None
CT	Exercise yard; inside day room; TV; radios	Cleaning details; barbers	Correspondence; or via assigned teacher	General population chaplain	Yes	Outside attorneys; inmate legal counsel; loose collection of legal books	None to present
DE	Outside yard; inside day room; radios	No	None	General population chaplain; outside ministers with warden's consent	Yes	Law library; outside attorneys	Discipline; security
D C	No Response						
FL	Outside yard; TV	No	None	Death row chaplain; general population chaplain; outside ministers	Yes	Law library; outside attorneys	None
GA	No Response						
HI	NA	NA	NA	NA	NA	NA	NA
ID	Outside yard; inside day room; TV and radio (if purchased from commissary)	No	TV programming	Outside ministers	Yes	Outside attorneys; paralegals	Security

	Recreation	Work Programs	Education	COUNSELING		Legal Assistance	General Problems
				Religious	Mental Health		
IL	Outside yard; inside day room; TV; radios	No	Correspondence	Death row chaplain; general population chaplain; outside ministers; volunteers	Yes	Law library; outside attorneys; inmate legal counsel; inmate law clerk	Discipline; staffing
IN	Outside yard; inside day room; TV; radios	For limited number (approximately percent)	Correspondence	Death row chaplain; outside ministers	Yes, upon request or recommendation	Law library; outside attorneys; inmate legal counsel	Security, on occasion
IA	NA	NA	NA	NA	NA	NA	NA
KS	Outside yard; TV; radios; hobby craft; books; phone	No	Individual tutoring; GED preparation	General population chaplain; outside ministers if on visiting list	Yes, if requested or need observed by staff	Law library; outside attorneys; inmate legal counsel; Legal Services for Prisoners, Inc	None
KY	Outside yard; IV; radios	Yes, but jobs cannot interact with general population	Correspondence	General population chaplain; outside ministers	Yes	Law library, outside attorneys; inmate legal counsel	None
LA	Outside yard; radios; tier time; TV outside cells	No	Correspondence; literacy course with staff supervision	Death row chaplain; outside ministers	Yes	Law library, outside attorneys, inmate legal counsel	None
ME	NA	NA	NA	NA	NA	NA	NA
MD	Outside yard; inside day room, including TV and VCR, board games and cards; TV; radios	Barbers and sanitation	Correspondence	General population chaplain; outside ministers	Yes	General library, outside attorneys, inmate legal counsel; Maryland law on CD Rom; day room computer; librarian visits daily; LASI, PSM	None
MA	No Response	NA	NA	NA	NA	NA	NA
MI	NA	NA	NA	NA	NA	NA	NA
MN	NA	NA	NA	NA	NA	NA	NA
MS	TV; radios	No	Correspondence	General population chaplain	Yes	Outside attorneys	None
MO	Outside yard, inside day room; TV; radios	Yes	Regular classes; correspondence; individual tutoring	Death row chaplain; general population chaplain; outside ministers	Yes	Law library; outside attorneys; inmate legal counsel	None
MT	Outside yard; inside day room; TV; radios (all depending on behavior)	In the school	Self-study	General population chaplain	Yes	Law library, outside attorneys	None
NE	Outside yard; inside day room; TV; radios; books, magazines, newspapers	Porter duties on a rotating basis	Correspondence; individual tutoring	General population chaplain assigned to entire institution	Yes	Law library; outside attorneys, inmate legal counsel; University Law School	None

DEATH PENALTY: PROGRAMS AND PROBLEMS, *continued*

	Recreation	Work Programs	Education	COUNSELING		Legal Assistance	General Problems
				Religious	Mental Health		
NV	Outside yard; inside day room; TV; radios	No	Correspondence	General population chaplain; outside ministers	Yes	Law library, outside attorneys	Overcrowding
NH	Outside yard; inside day room; TV; radios	Sewing project	Regular classes	General population chaplain; outside ministers	Yes	Law library, outside attorneys, inmate legal counsel	None
NJ	Outside yard; inside day room; TV; radios; word processor	No	Individual tutoring	Death row chaplain	Yes	Outside attorneys, inmate legal counsel	None
NM	Outside yard; TV; radios	Unit porters	Regular classes via ETV; correspondence; individual tutoring	General population chaplain; outside ministers	Yes	Law library, outside attorneys, inmate legal counsel	None
NY	Outside yard; TV on the unit	No	In-cell study	General population chaplain	Yes	Law Library; outside attorneys	None
NC	Outside yard; inside day room, with TV; radios	No	Correspondence, at inmate's expense	Death row chaplain	Yes	Outside attorneys; inmate legal counsel	At present, 29 sleeping on bunks in day rooms
ND	NA	NA	NA	NA	NA	NA	NA
OH	Outside yard; inside day room; TV; radios	May apply for unit jobs on a 6-month rotating basis	Correspondence; individual tutoring	General population chaplain; outside ministers	Yes	Law library, outside attorneys	Overcrowding
OK	Outside yard/ inside day room (females); men[1]; TV; radios	No	Correspondence; material provided for self study; GED preparation	General population chaplain; outside ministers; volunteers	Yes	Law library; outside attorneys	None
OR	Outside yard; TV; radios; open area on tier with tables	Custodial on tier	Materials for self study, if requested	General population chaplain; outside ministers	Yes	Law library; outside attorneys; inmate legal counsel	None
PA	Outside yard; inside day room; TV; radios	Yes, but restricted to special housing unit	Basic literacy; post-secondary opportunities at inmate's expense; ABE; GED preparation; self-study program	General population chaplain	Yes	Law library, with inter-library loan services; inmate legal counsel or other capital case inmates held in same housing unit, precluding security issues	None
RI	NA	NA	NA	NA	NA	NA	NA
SC	Outside yard; TV (if incarcerated pre 1995)	No	Unavailable	Death row chaplain; general population chaplain; outside ministers	Yes	Law library; outside attorneys	None
SD	Outside yard; TV; radios	No	None	General population chaplain; outside ministers, if on visiting list	Yes	Outside attorneys; inmate legal counsel	None

	Recreation	Work Programs	Education	COUNSELING		Legal Assistance	General Problems
				Religious	Mental Health		
TN	Outside yard; inside day room; TV; radios	Level A inmates have first choice, primarily custodial; 20 are assigned to prison industries doing data entry	Maximum security level would require individual tutoring	Death row chaplain; outside ministers	Yes	Law library; outside attorneys; inmate legal counsel	Due to small number of females, the system is unable to provide separate living area or services
TX	Outside yard; inside day room	Garment factory; SSI orderlies or clerks; barbers (but all jobs currently suspended)	None	Inmate may choose an advisor who does not count towards general visits	Yes	Law library; outside attorneys; inmate legal counsel	None
UT	Outside yard; inside day room; TV (for some), radios	Pending	Correspondence	General population chaplain	Yes	Outside attorneys	None
VT	NA	NA	NA	NA	NA	NA	NA
VA	Unavailable	Unavailable	Unavailable	Unavailable	Unavailable	Law library; outside attorneys	None
WA	Outside yard; inside day room; TV and radios (earned privileges)	Special housing units and possibility of stamping return address on envelopes	Correspondence	Death row chaplain; outside ministers, depending on religious preference	Yes	Law library; outside attorneys; inmate legal counsel	None
WV	NA	NA	NA	NA	NA	NA	NA
WI	NA	NA	NA	NA	NA	NA	NA
WY	Outside yard; TV; radios	No	Regular classes; correspondence	General population chaplain	Yes	Law library; outside attorneys	None
FBP	Outside yard; TV; radios; inside recreation	Phases I and II programs offering opportunities such as laundry orderlies and sewing machine operators	Closed circuit TV for educational programming	General population chaplain; Closed circuit TV available for BOP-recognized faith groups	Yes, through MH exams every 30 days or sooner	Law library; outside attorneys; inmate legal counsel	None (too soon to tell since Bureau program open only a few weeks)

Note:
1. OKLAHOMA: Exercise yard for men is inside a building, but with a mesh screen on top for openness.

Computerization in Departments of Correction

as of March 1999

	Share Information With Other CJ Agencies	Internet Accessibility	Maintenance	Website	Y2k Compliant	Security Concerns
AL	Working out details at present; Extranet basis	Staff, limited; no to inmates	Primarily in-house; some units contracted out	Yes, with webmaster on site, part time	Modification underway; completion by August	Limited general access to inmates is blocked, with no access to networks
AK	Courts; criminal history/warrants by Public Safety; not Extranet	Limited to administration and supervisors; no to inmates	In-house by data processing staff; outside network support	Yes, with webmaster on-site, part time	Yes	At final testing stage for departmental firewall service
AR	With ACIC/NCIC; not Extranet basis	Certain staff in certain areas; no to inmates	In-house	Yes, with part-time webmaster through internet	Yes	Experienced inmate tampering and unauthorized software and access
CT	State Police, collect system; NCIC, FBI; judicial, Megan's Law; Extranet basis	Staff, subject to approval by DOC security division; no to inmates	In-house, with MIS Division responsible for WAN installation and support and system development	Yes, with part-time webmaster on-site	Yes, for all major system components	Installation of firewalls to prevent access to DOC WAN
DE	DELJIS (Delaware Justice Info System) with police, courts, corrections, attorney general public defender, parole board and local law enforcement; on Extranet basis	Staff, based on need; no to inmates	In-house, with network support staff deployed through a help desk	Yes, with part-time webmaster on-site	Yes	Password sharing where not enough hardware exists; education is lacking; staff tries to get their jobs done any way they can, sometimes violating security
FL	Courts, Sheriffs, Juvenile Justice, Florida Department of Law Enforcement; on Extranet basis	Staff limited by sites and lockout based on topic/content; no to inmates	Primarily in-house, in combination with state staff and outside contractor	Yes, with full-time webmaster on-site	Yes	
GA	Crime Info Center for criminal history; on Extranet basis	Staff limited to work-related; no to inmates	In-house, with several technical support staff	Yes, with full-time webmaster on-site	Working on it	
HI	Access to OBTS, courts and NCIC; not on Extranet	Yes, on a very limited basis; no to inmates	Combination of staff, maintenance and contracts and part-time contracted personnel	No	Progressing and anticipate compliance by Oct. 1, 1999	None at this time
ID	Annual reports, studies, www sites, not on Extranet	Staff; no to inmates	In-house	Yes, with part-time webmaster on-site	Yes	None
LA	Policy analysis; offender tracking; background check; Extranet in development stage	Staff, if work related; no to inmates	In-house	Yes, through state system	Yes	
KS	Currently faxed; on Extranet basis soon	Staff, if work related; no to inmates	Off-site, primarily warranty hardware work	Yes, with part-time webmaster on-site	Working on it and anticipate compliance	Inmate telephone security continues to be an ongoing problem
KY	All court orders pertaining to felons; not on Extranet	Staff; no to inmates	Primarily in-house, with local support staff	No	Yes	

	Share Information With Other CJ Agencies	Internet Accessibility	Maintenance	Website	Y2k Compliant	Security Concerns
LA	Clerk of the Court; Sheriffs; State Police; FBI; detainer/warrants from other law enforcement agencies; on Extranet basis	Staff, if approved by Unit Head; no to inmates	In-house	No	Anticipate compliance by June 30, 1999	Dedicated data circuits leased from Bell South in conjunction with CISCO security firewall.
ME	Yes, but on a paper system; not on Extranet basis	Staff, based on proper use policies; no to inmates	In-house	Not directly; have a page and access to the state's website	Working on it and anticipate compliance	Network security is monitored periodically and adjustments made to permissions, etc., as needed
MD	Yes via shared mainframe with all Public Safety agencies; Yes on Extranet	Staff is limited, same as would apply to phones; no to inmates	In-house	Yes	Anticipate compliance by Sept 30, 1999	No major problems
MO	Yes, with courts, on a manual basis; fingerprint ID with law enforcement is manual but being automated, not on Extranet basis	Staff is very limited; no to inmates	In-house for application software that is not purchased; hardware maintenance is contracted out	Yes, through payment to another state agency for maintaining	Anticipate compliance	Severely restrict access from private network to the public network, and vice versa
MT	Not at present, but expected within two years; not on Extranet basis	Yes, limited to business use; no to inmates	Primarily in-house, with manufacturer's assistance as required	Yes, with a part-time webmaster	Working towards compliance	All Montana DOC policies are accessible via their website
NE	Crime Commission; CJIS; DB/2 status to share with State Patrol; on Extranet basis	Staff; no to inmates	In-house	Yes, with part-time webmaster contracted out	Yes	None
NJ	County state end federal criminal management interfaces; on Extranet basis	Staff, only on approved business-related sites (NJDOC tracks and logs all www activity); no to inmates	In-house for Tier1; outside vendors for Tiers 2 and 3	Yes, with part-time webmaster on-site	Yes	None
NM	Not currently, but being considered; not on Extranet	Staff, with supervisor approval; no to inmates	In-house for routine maintenance; outside support by specialized contractor	Yes, using State Information Systems Division as webmaster	Yes	New LAN/WAN system has state of-the-art built-in security (firewalls); staff training on security matters will be conducted
NC	Yes, on individual offenders; on Extranet basis	Staff, for state business only; password protected and changed monthly; no to inmates	In-house	Yes, with full-time webmaster (PIO specialist) on-site	Yes, after recent testing	Virus plagued past ten years; now, includes virus software and showing only minor problems
ND	Yes, from the courts; not on Extranet	Certain staff; no to inmates	In-house	No	Anticipate compliance	
OH	Yes, on sex offenders and gang members; not on Extranet	Staff, if work related and on justified need; no to inmates	In-house	Yes, with full-time webmaster on-site	Yes	Legislation pending to allow restricted internet use by inmates for educational applications
OK	NCIC and legal documents from courts; on Extranet basis	Staff; no to inmates	Primarily in-house for internally produced system; outside vendor for purchased system	Yes, with webmaster on-site	Anticipate compliance by Oct. 30, 1999	
OR	LEDS (Law Enforcement Data System) for background checks; CIS input by counties for inmate information; not on Extranet	Staff restricted to business use only; no to inmates	Primarily in-house: support by ISSD (Information Systems and Services Division); and some out-sourcing	Yes, via State Department of Administrative Services	Yes	Separate networks are employed in any area where inmates have access to PCs and no inmate networks have access to the outside

COMPUTERIZATION IN DEPARTMENTS OF CORRECTION, *continued*

	Share Information With Other CJ Agencies	Internet Accessibility	Maintenance	Website	Y2k Compliant	Security Concerns
PA	JNET statewide integrated system; on Extranet basis	Staff limited to units outside secure perimeter and signing responsibility forms; no to inmates	Primarily in-house; partially contracted out	No	Yes	Utilizing digital certificates in the statewide, integrated CJ system
SD	No	Staff, with some restrictions; no to inmates	Maintained by Bureau of Information and Telecommunications based off-site	Yes, with webmaster on-site	Yes	
TN	Criminal histories from the police; judgement orders from the courts; not on Extranet	Staff restricted to business use only; no to inmates	In-house for LAN and PC maintenance	Yes, with part-time webmaster on-site	Yes	Multi-level security employed for TOMIS access; staff has allowed non-secure individuals access to secure data and is being addressed by administrative policy, procedures and training
TX	State-ready program, using intake process; not on Extranet basis	Staff; no to inmates	In-house through Data Services	Yes, with full-time webmaster on-site	Yes	
VT	Court and Public Safety websites; not on Extranet	Staff; no to inmates	In-house	Yes, with part-time webmaster on-site	Yes	None
WA	Arrests flagged into State Patrol site; not on Extranet	Staff, for business use only; no to inmates	Primarily vendor-based contracts, augmented in-house	Yes, with part-time webmaster on-site	Yes	
WV	NIJ; not on Extranet	Staff; limited; no to inmates	In-house, unless serious hardware problems occur	Yes, with webmaster and page operated via state website	Yes, after elimination of older system	In library, inmates may use stand-alone units, without disks
WY	Yes, court documents and enforcement reports; not on Extranet basis	Some staff, limited to job functions on an "as needed" basis; no to inmates	In-house for software; hardware maintenance by another state agency	No	Yes	Utilize e-mail virus and internet access control
BC	Yes	Staff, limited; no to inmates	Primarily in-house	Yes, with part-time webmaster on-site	Yes	
MB	Court dispositions for offenders, with various no-contact prohibitions; police criminal interface (read only); on Extranet basis	Some staff, preventive security personnel, and authorized employees (based on need); no to inmates	Contracted by government to private vendor	Yes, with part-time webmaster on-site	Yes	Isolated incidents of minor staff tampering, resulting in unauthorized file access
NF	CPIC, OMS; not on Extranet basis	Neither staff nor inmates	Maintained by IT division of provincial government	No	Yes	New operating system and program currently being installed
NS	Court dockets and criminal records; not on Extranet basis	Staff; no to inmates	In-house and handled through the MIS component	No	Yes	
YK	Federal Crown's office, court services, RCMP, probation services and secure-custody facilities; not on Extranet	Staff; no to inmates	In-house for system administration and technical support; network services by Government Services Branch	Yes, with systems administrator employed by Department of Justice	Yes	

Computer Usage In DOC Central Office

as of March 1999

	Access to Direct Use, Extranet Capability	Computer Usage	LAN (Local Area Network) Usage	WAN (Wide Area Network) Usage	Unique Applications or General Comments
AL	Administration; Managers; Supervisors; Line Staff	Word processing; e-mail; internet; management info; payroll (state and local); tracking transfers; release dates; budgets; legal briefs; policies/procedures; interfacing (parole in future); computer-based training (outside department); (developing) teleconferencing	Yes	Yes	
AK	Administration; Managers; Supervisors; Line Staff	Word processing; e-mail; internet; management info; payroll; tracking transfers; release dates; budgets; policies/procedures; interfacing	Yes	Yes	
AR	Administration; Managers; Supervisors; Line Staff	Word processing; e-mail; internet; management info; payroll; staff scheduling; budgets; legal briefs; policies/procedures; teleconferencing; time keeping; ID badges	Yes	No	
CT	Administration; Managers; Supervisors; Line Staff	Word processing; e-mail; internet; management info; payroll; tracking transfers; release dates; staff scheduling; budgets; policies/procedures; interfacing; computer-based training; teleconferencing; central help desk; electronic DOC newsletter; inmate photo image system; electronic filing of personnel applications	Yes	Yes	
DE	Administration, Managers; Supervisors Line Staff	Word processing; e-mail; internet; management info; payroll; budgets; interfacing	No	Yes	Under major design changes: inmate management system; human resources; payroll; accounting; procurement
FL	Administration; Managers, Supervisors; Line Staff	Word processing; e-mail; internet; management info; tracking transfers; release dates; staff scheduling; budgets; policies/procedures; interfacing; computer-based training	No	Yes	
GA	Administration, Managers; Supervisors; Line (limited)	Word processing; e-mail; internet; management info; payroll; tracking transfers; release dates; budgets; legal briefs; policies/procedures; interfacing; computer based training; sentence computation; purchasing	Yes	Yes	
HI	Administration; Managers; Supervisors; Line Staff	Word processing; e-mail; internet (limited); management information; payroll; tracking transfers; release dates; staff scheduling (available, but not regularly used); budgets; policies/procedures (available, but not regularly used); interfacing (limited)	Yes	Yes (limited to e-mail and selected programs)	
ID	Administration; Managers; Supervisors; Line Staff	Word processing; e-mail; internet; management info; payroll; tracking transfers; release dates; budgets; legal briefs; policies/procedures; computer-based training	Yes	No	
IA	Administration; Managers Supervisors; Line Staff	Word processing; e-mail; internet; management info; payroll; tracking transfers; release dates; staff scheduling; budgets; legal briefs; policies/procedures; interfacing; computer-based training; (last three uses are via outside service)	No	Yes	
KS	Administration; Managers; Supervisors; Line Staff	Word processing; e-mail; internet; management info; payroll; tracking transfers; release dates; staff scheduling; budgets; legal briefs; policies/procedures	Yes	Yes	
KY	Administration; Managers; Supervisors; Line Staff	Word processing; e-mail; internet; release dates; budgets; legal briefs; computer-based training; teleconferencing	No	Yes	

COMPUTER USAGE IN DOC CENTRAL OFFICE, *continued*

	Access to Direct Use, Extranet Capability	Computer Usage	LAN (Local Area Network) Usage	WAN Wide Area Network) Usage	Unique Applications or General Comments
LA	Administration Managers; Supervisors, Line Staff	Word processing; e-mail; internet; management info; payroll; tracking transfers; release dates; staff scheduling; budges; legal briefs; policies/procedures; interfacing, computer-based training	Yes	Yes	Staff has developed an interactive, multimedia training system using LOTUS NOTES software. The system has customized lesson plans and they are complete with built-in testing and random questions, geared towards complying with ACA standards for training.
ME	Administration; Managers; Supervisors; Line Staff	Word processing; e-mail; internet; management info; payroll; release dates; budgets; policies/procedures	Yes	Yes, (connected LANs)	
MD	Administration; Managers; Supervisors; Line Staff	Word processing; e-mail; internet; management info; payroll; budgets; policies/procedures; interfacing	Yes	Yes	
MO	Administration; Managers Supervisors; Line Staff	Word processing; e-mail; internet; management info; payroll; tracking transfers; budgets; legal briefs; policies/procedures; interfacing	Yes	Yes	
MT	Administration; Managers; Supervisors; Line Staff	Word processing; e-mail; internet; management info; payroll; tracking transfers; release dates; staff scheduling; budgets; legal briefs; policies/procedures; interfacing; computer-based training	Yes	Yes	
NE	Administration; Managers Supervisors; Line (limited)	Word processing; e-mail; internet; management info; payroll; tracking transfers; release dates; staff scheduling; budgets; legal briefs; policies/procedures; interfacing; computer-based training; CAD-CAM; project management; presentations; training; victim notification	Yes	Yes	
NJ	Administration; Managers; Supervisors; Line Staff	Word processing; e-mail; internet; management info; payroll; staff scheduling; budgets; legal briefs; policies/procedures; interfacing; computer-based training	Yes	Yes	
NM	Administration; Managers; Supervisors; Line Staff	Word processing; e-mail; internet; management info; payroll; tracking transfers; budgets; legal briefs; policies/procedures; interfacing	Yes	Yes	Not currently
NC	Administration; Managers; Supervisors; Line Staff	Word processing; e-mail; internet; management info; payroll; tracking transfers; release dates; staff scheduling; budgets; legal briefs; policies/procedures; interfacing; computer-based training; teleconferencing	Yes (including parole/probation)	Yes (including parole/probation)	On website, can specialize requests down to individuals; can download to spread sheet; extract of OPUS files; system open to the press and public (parole/probation specifically); recently expanded sex offender information via the internet.
ND	Administration; Managers; Supervisors	Word processing; e-mail; internet; management info; payroll; budgets; policies/procedures	Yes	Yes	
OH	Administration; Managers; Supervisors	Word processing; e-mail; internet; management info; payroll; tracking transfers; release dates; staff scheduling; budgets; legal briefs; policies/procedures; interfacing; computer-based training; teleconferencing	Yes	Yes	
OK	Administration; Managers; Supervisors; Line Staff	Wordprocessing; e-mail; internet; management info; payroll; staff scheduling; budgets; legal briefs; policies/procedures; interfacing; computer- based training	No	Yes	
OR	Administration; Managers; Supervisors; Line Staff	Word processing; e-mail; internet; management info; payroll; release dates; staff scheduling; budgets; legal briefs; policies/procedures; interfacing; computer-based training; tele-conferencing	Yes	Yes	

	Access to Direct Use, Extranet Capability	Computer Usage	LAN (Local Area Network) Usage	WAN Wide Area Network) Usage	Unique Applications or General Comments
PA	Administration; Managers; Supervisors; Line Staff	Word processing; e-mail; internet; management info; payroll; tracking transfers; release dates; staff scheduling; budgets; legal briefs; policies/procedures; interfacing; computer-based training	Yes	Yes	Random drug testing program
SD	Administration; Managers; Supervisors;	Word processing; e-mail; internet; management info; payroll; tracking transfers; release dates; staff scheduling; budgets; policies/procedures	Yes	Yes	
TN	Administration; Managers; Supervisors, Line Staff	Word processing; e-mail; internet; management info; payroll; tracking transfers; release dates; staff scheduling; budgets; legal briefs; policies/procedures; computer-based training; sentence computation	No	No (will be on-line within 18 months)	TOMIS (Tennessee Offender Management Information System) is one of few systems nationally that tracks felony-convicted persons from courtroom's request for pre sentence investigation reports to expiration of sentence on probation or parole. TOMIS consists of twelve functional sub-systems: conviction/sentencing; incarceration; treatment; field supervision in probation/parole.
TX	Administration; Managers; Supervisors; Line Staff	Word processing; e-mail; internet; management info; payroll; tracking transfers; release dates; staff scheduling; budgets; legal briefs; policies/procedures; interfacing; computer-based training; teleconferencing	Yes	Yes	Fuginet: computerized database, an investigative tool for law enforcement in identifying parolees and facilitating apprehension of parole violators
VT	Administration; Managers; Supervisors; Line Staff	Word processing; e-mail; internet; management info; payroll; tracking transfers; release dates; budgets; legal briefs; policies/procedures; interfacing	No	Yes	
WA	Administration; Managers; Supervisors; Some Line Staff	Word processing; e-mail; internet; management info; payroll; tracking transfers; release dates; budgets; policies/procedures; interfacing; computer-based training;	No	Yes	In the Legislature, system allows listening to committees and floor action
WV	Administration; Managers; Supervisors	Word processing; e-mail; internet; management info; payroll; tracking transfers; release dates; staff scheduling; budgets; legal briefs; policies/procedures; interfacing; computer-based training; teleconferencing	Yes	Yes (state wide)	
WY	Administration; Managers; Supervisors; Line Staff	Word processing; e-mail; internet; management info; payroll; tracking transfers; release dates; staff scheduling; budgets; legal briefs; policies/procedures; computer-based training	No	Yes	
BC	Administration; Managers; Supervisors; Line Staff	Word processing; e-mail; internet; management info; release dates; budgets; policies/procedures; computer-based training	Yes	Yes	Victim notification
MB	Administration, Managers; Supervisors; Line Staff	Word processing; e-mail; internet; management info; payroll; tracking transfers; release dates; staff scheduling; budgets; legal briefs; policies/procedures; interfacing; computer-based training	Yes	No	Tracking gang members
NF	Administration, Managers; Supervisors; Line Staff	Word processing; management info; tracking transfers; release dates; staff scheduling; legal briefs; policies/procedures	No	No	
NS	Administration; Managers; Supervisors; Line Staff	Word processing; e-mail; internet; management info; payroll; tracking transfers; release dates; budgets; policies/procedures; interfacing	No	Yes	
YK	Administration; Managers; Supervisors; Line Staff	Word processing; e-mail; internet; management info; tracking transfers; release dates; staff scheduling; budgets	Yes	Yes	

Computer Usage in DOC Institutions

as of March 1999

	Access to Direct Use	Institutional Applications*[1]	LAN (Local Area Network) Usage	Unique Applications or General Comments
AL	Administration; Managers; supervisors: Line Staff (Limited)	a, b (limited), c, g, i (limited), j, k, n, o, p, r, t, v, w, dd, ee, ff, jj, nn, oo, pp, qq, uu, yy, zz, bbb, ccc, ddd, fff	Yes	
AK	Administration; Managers; Supervisors	a, b, c, d, e, f, g, i, j, r, ii, ll, yy, bbb, ccc,	Yes	
AR	Administration; Managers; Supervisors; Line Staff	b, c, d, f, g, i, l, m, r, t, y, z, dd, ee, ff, ii, jj, kk, ll, oo, qq, xx, w, zz, bbb	No	
CT	Administration; Managers; Supervisors; Line Staff (shared units per shifts)	a, b, c, d, e (pilot), f, g, h, i, j, m, n, o, p, r, s, t, u, v, w, x, y, aa, bb, cc, dd, ee, ff, gg, hh, ii, kk, mm, qq, ss, tt, uu, xx, zz, aaa, bbb, ccc, ddd, fff	Yes, but approximately 40% of department moved from SNA Network to WAN; remainder to be phased over within 18 months	Video conference inmate court appearances (a pilot project between the DOC and the Judicial Department)
DE	Administration; Managers; Supervisors; Line Staff	a, b, c, h, i, j, n, r, t, ii, zz	Yes	
FL	Administration; Managers; Supervisors	a, b, c, d, f, g, i, j, k, l, m, r, t, dd, ee, hh, ii, D, kk, ll, mm, nn, oo, pp, qq, zz, bbb, ccc, ddd eee, fff	Yes	
GA	Administration; Managers; Supervisors; Line (limited)	a, b c, d, e, f, g, h, i, j, m, n, o, p, r, t, v, w, y, z, dd, ee, ff, ii, kk, ll, mm, nn, oo, pp, qq, ww, yy, aaa, ccc, fff	Yes	
HI	Administration; Managers; Supervisors and Line Staff (Limited)	a, b, c, f, g, h, i, o, r, t, u, cc, ee, ff, hh, ii, jj, pp, qq, xx, bbb, ccc	Yes, within some facilities, but not between facilities	
ID	Administration; Managers; supervisors; Line Staff	a, b, c, d, f, h, i, j, k, l, m, n, o, p, r, s, t, u, v, w, x, y, z, aa, bb, cc, dd, ee, ff, gg, hh, ii, jj, kk, mm, nn, pp, qq, ss, K, uu, yy, zz, aaa, bbb, ccc, ddd, eee	Yes	
IA	Administration; Managers; Supervisors	a, b, c, d, e, g, h, i, j, k, n, o, p, r, t, u, v, w, x, bb, dd, ff, hh, jj, ll, mm, nn, pp, qq, ss, tt, uu, ww, w, zz bbb, ccc, ddd, eee, fff	No	
KS	Administration; Managers; Supervisors; Line Staff; and Parole Officers	b, c, f, g, h, i, j l, n, o, p, r, t, u, v, vv, x, dd, ee, ff, jj, kk, nn, pp, qq, uu, w, xx, yy, zz, bbb, ccc, ddd, eee	Yes	
KY	Administration; Managers; Supervisors; Line Staff	a, b, c, d, g, h, i, j, m, o, p, q, r, t, v, y, dd, ii, ll, qq, yy, zz, aaa, ccc, eee	Yes	
LA	Administration; Managers; Supervisors; Line Staff	a, b, c, d, f, g, h, i, j, k, l, m, n, o, p, q, r, s, t, y, z, dd, ee, ff, ii, jj, kk, ll, mm, nn, oo, pp, qq, tt, ww, xx, yy, zz, aaa, bbb, ccc, ddd, eee	Yes	Automated tracking of armory door opening/closing; interface between medical equipment and medical database for recording vital signs
ME	Administration; Managers; Supervisors; Line Staff (limited to availability)	a, b, c, d, g, h, i, j, k, n, o, p, r, s, t, w, dd, ee, ff, kk, nn, oo, pp, qq, n, xx, yy z, bbb, ccc, ddd, fff	Yes	
MD	Administration; Managers; Supervisors; Line Staff	a, b, c, d, g, h, i, j, r, t, dd, ii, kk, oo, pp, qq	No	
MO	Administration; Managers; Supervisors; Line Staff	a, b, c, d, g, h, i, j, m, n, o, p, r, t, u, v, x, y, dd, ee, ff, hh, ii, jj, kk, ll, mm, nn, pp, qq, tt, xx, yy, aaa, ccc, ddd, eee fff	No	
MT	Administration; Managers; Supervisors; Line Staff (in command posts)	a, b, c, d, f, g, h, i, j, m, n, o, p, q, r, s, dd, ee, ff, ii, kk, ll, mm, nn, oo, pp, qq, rr, xx, yy, bbb, ccc, ddd, eee	Yes, some (Industries program is a stand-alone system)	
NE	Administration; Managers; Supervisors; Line (limited)	a, b, c, d, e, f, g, h, i, j, k, l, m, n, o, p, q, r, s, t, u, v, w, x, y, z, aa, bb, cc, dd, ee, ff, gg, hh, ii, jj, kk, ll, mm, nn, oo, pp, qq, rr, ss, tt, uu, ww, xx, yy, zz, aaa, bbb, ccc, ddd, eee	Yes	
NJ	Administration; Managers; Supervisors; Line Staff	(Oct. '99) a, b, c, d, e, f, g, h, i, m, n, o, p, q, r, s, t, ii, jj, kk, ll, mm, nn, vv, bbb, ccc, ddd eee, fff	Yes	
NM	Administration; Managers; Supervisors; Line Staff	a, b c, d, e, g, h, i, j, k, m, n, o, p, r, dd, ff, kk, nn, pp, qq, xx, bbb, ccc, fff	Yes	

	Access to Direct Use	Institutional Applications*[1]	LAN (Local Area Network) Usage	Unique Applications or General Comments
NC	Administration; Managers; Supervisors; Line Staff	a, b, c, d, e, f, g, h, i, j, k, m, n, o, p, q, r, t, u, v, w, x, y, z, aa, bb, cc, dd, ee, ff, hh, ii, jj, kk, ll, mm, nn, pp, qq, w, ,w,, aaa, bbb, ccc, ddd, eee	Yes	
ND	Administration; Managers; Supervisors	a, b, c, d, g, i, j, n, r, t, ee, ff, ii, jj, ll, nn, pp, xx, zz, bbb, eee, fff	Yes	
OH	Administration; Managers; Supervisors; Line Staff	a, b, c, d, e, f, g, h, i, j, k, l, m, n, o, p, q, r, s, t, u, v, w, x, y, z, aa, bb, cc, dd, ee, ff, hh, ii, jj, kk, ll, mm, nn, oo, pp, ss, tt, uu, ww, xx, yy, zz aaa, bbb, ccc, ddd, eee, fff	Yes	
OK	Administration; Managers; Supervisors; Line Staff	a, b, c, d, e, f, g, h, i, j, l, m, n, o, p, r, t, u, bb, dd, gg hh, ii, jj, kk, ll, mm, nn, oo, pp, qq, ss, tt, uu, ww, xx, yy, zz, aaa, bbb, ccc, ddd, eee fff	Yes	
OR	Administration; Managers, Supervisors; Line Staff	a, b, c, d f, g, h, i, j, r, t, v, x, aa, bb, ee, ff, jj, ll, mm, nn, oo, pp, qq, tt, xx, zz, bbb, ccc, ddd, fff	Yes	
PA	Administration; Managers; Supervisors; Line Staff	a, b, c, d, e, g, h, i, j, k, l, n, o, p, r, s, t, u, v, w, x, y, bb, cc, dd, ee, ff, ii, jj, kk, mm, nn, pp, qq, tt, uu, xx, yy, zz, aaa, bbb, ccc, ddd, fff	Yes	
SD	Administration; Managers; Supervisors	a, b, c, d, g, h, i, m, n, o, p, r, v, w, x, dd, ii, kk, mm, nn, pp, qq, rr, xx, ,w,, zz, bbb, ccc, ddd, eee, m	Yes	
TN	Administration; Managers; Supervisors; Line Staff	a, b, c, d, f, g, i, j, k, l, n, o, p, r, t, u, v, w, x, bb, cc, dd, ff, ii, jj, kk, ll, mm, nn, pp, qq, ss, tt, uu, yy, zz, ccc, ddd, eee, fff	No	
TX	Administration; Managers	a, b, c, d, e, f, g, h, i, j, k, l, m, n, o, p, q, r, t, u, v, w, x, y, aa, bb, dd, ee, ff, gg, hh, ii, jj, kk, ll, mm, oo, pp, qq, tt, uu, w, ww, xx, yy, ccc, ddd, eee, fff	No	
VT	Administration; Managers; Supervisors; Some Line Staff	a, b, c, d, g, h, i, j, m, n, o, p, r, t, v, dd, ee, ff, kk, ll, mm, pp, xx, yy, zz, ccc, ddd	No (but through WAN)	
WA	Administration; Managers; Supervisors; Few Line Staff	b, c, d, f, g, h, i, j, m, n, o, p, r, u, v, w, x, dd, ee, ff, ii, kk, mm, pp, qq, ss, xx, yy, zz, bbb, ccc, eee	Yes (in some institutions)	
WV	Managers; Supervisors; Line Staff	a, b, c, d, a, f, g, h, i, j, m, n, o, p, r, t, u, v, x, dd, ee, ff, pp, yy	Yes	
WY	Administration; Managers, Supervisors; Line Staff	a, b, c, d, h, i, j, k, m, n, o, p, q, r, s, t, v, dd, ee, ff, pp, qq, xx, yy, zz, ccc, ddd, eee	Yes	
BC	Administration; Managers; Supervisors; Line Staff	b, c, d, f, g, h, i, j, m, n, o, p, r, s, u, v, w, x, y, aa, bb, dd, ee, ff, ii, kk, ll, pp, qq, ss, zz, bbb, ccc	Yes	
MB	Administration; Managers; Supervisors; Line Staff	a, b, c, d, f, g, h, i, j, k, n, o, p, r, u, x, aa, bb, ee, ff, pp, yy, zz, bbb, ccc	Yes	
NF	Administration; Managers; Supervisors; Line Staff	a, c, d, f, g, h, i, j, k, n, q, r, t, dd, ee, ff, jj, kk, nn, pp, xx, zz, bbb, ccc, ddd, eee, fff	No	
NS	Unavailable	a, b, c, d, g, h, i, j, n, o, p, t, ccc, ddd	Yes	
YK	Administration; Managers; Supervisors; Line Staff	a, b, c, d, f, g, i, j, m, n, o, p, r, u, v, bb, dd, ee, ff, jj, mm, bbb, ccc	Yes	

Note:

* APPLICATION CODE: a–Computerized Institutional Processing; b–E-Mail; c–Word Processing; d–Report Writing; e–Telemedicine; f–Digitized Photo/ID Cards; g–Classification; h–Sentence Computation; i–Records Management; j–Tracking Inmates/Staff; k–Drug Detection; l–ACA Accreditation Tracking; m–Housing Unit Logs; n–Case Management; o–Housing Unit Assignments; p–Inmate Movement; q–Inmate Equipment Issue; r–Inmate Financial Accounting; s–Mail Tracking; t–Commissary/Inventory and Issue; u–Security/CCTV; v–Perimeter Intrusion Detection; w–Fire Safety Monitoring; x–Security Door Operations, y–tool control; z–Chemical Accountability; aa–Audio Monitoring of Housing; bb–Video Monitoring of Housing; cc–Emergency Generator Testing; dd–Inmate Program Tracking; ee–Training Presentations; ff–Training Documentation; gg–Firearms Simulation Training; hh–Emergency Notification System; ii–Victim Witness Notification; jj–Personnel Monitoring; kk–Disciplinary Reporting and Documentation; ll–Pharmaceutical Issuance/Tracking; pp–Inmate Programming Tracking (GED, ABE, AA, etc.); qq–Approved Visitors; rr–Video Visitations; ss–Personal Alarm Monitoring; tt–Architectural Plans/Reviews/Modifications; uu–Communication Monitoring vv–Biometric ID (Hand and Facial Geometry); ww–Crisis Management; xx–Facility Maintenance; yy–Food Service (Menu/inventory); zz–Inmate Telephone Monitoring; aaa–Key Control/Tracking; bbb–Staff Scheduling; ccc–inmate Transfers; ddd–Security and Discipline; eee–Parole Reviews/Hearings; fff–Staff Training

Use of Force Definition and Policy Applications

as of April 1999

	Policy Adopted	Definition	Restraints (Ex., Chairs)	Force (Ex., Four-point)	Confinement (Ex., Strip Cells)	Non-lethal Methods	Control/Restraints Not Permitted	Video Taping Allowed
			POLICY APPLICATION INCLUSIONS					
AL	Over-time	Force: includes unwanted touching directed toward another	Yes	Yes	Yes	Yes	Choke holds	Yes
AK	1994	A continuum; only the minimal amount necessary may be used	Yes	Yes	No	Yes	Cradle position, choke holds, anything in excess of that necessary to gain/regain control	Yes
AZ	No Response							
AR	1996	A directed movement or overt action with or without weapons or devices, with the intention of restraining, regaining or maintaining control	No	No	No	Yes	N/A	Yes; extraction teams
CA	No Response							
CO	Unknown	Various types/amounts of force on a continuum	No	Yes	No; defined at specialized facilities	Yes; force continuum	Respiratory neck restraint, restraint chair,	Yes
CT	1993	Physical contact or contact through use of an armory item by staff in a confrontational situation to establish control or restore order	Yes	Yes	No	Yes	Body bags, wet sheet packs, strait jackets	Yes
DE	No Response							
DC	No Response							
FL	1974	Type and amount of force that reasonably appears necessary to accomplish the objective	Yes; Elections Restraint device, Stun Belt	Yes	No	Yes	No specific types	Yes
GA	Yes	Physical force to compel an inmate to take action against his/her will, or to prevent an inmate from taking action that would be damaging to himself/herself, other persons or property.	No	Yes, if special conditions are met in concurrence with medical staff	Yes	Yes	Restrained to fixed objects, such as cell doors or grill work hog tying	Yes
HI	Unknown	Use of hands, other parts of the body, objects, instruments, chemical devices, electric devices, firearms or other physical methods to restrain, subdue, intimidate, or to compel persons to act in a particular way, or to stop acting in a particular way.	No	Yes, but must be approved and assigned by Health Director	No; covered in general policy on "Inmate Segregation"	Yes	"SAP" gloves, blackjacks, "saps," metal knuckles	Yes, in all major incidents
ID	1996	Last alternative to resolve a situation with the minimal amount of force necessary	Yes	Yes	Yes	Yes	Corporal punishment, chokeholds	Yes

	Policy Adopted	Definition	POLICY APPLICATION INCLUSIONS				Control/Restraints Not Permitted	Video Taping Allowed
			Restraints (Ex., Chairs)	Force (Ex., Four-point)	Confinement (Ex., Strip Cells)	Non-lethal Methods		
IL	1972	Any physical contact used to coerce or prevent some action on the part of a committed person, and in the use of chemical agents	Yes (at Super-max)	Yes	Yes (Suicide/crisis watch)	Yes	Corporal punishment, hog tying	Yes
IN	1986 (revised 1998)	Any contact other than incidental body contact between staff and offender	Yes	Yes	Yes	Yes	Tasertron, C/S chemical agent	Yes
IA	1997	Any physical contact made by an employee with an inmate in a confrontational situation to control the inmate's behavior	Yes	Yes	Yes	Yes (chemical agents)	Not to be used as punishment, only control	Yes
KS	1984	The minimum amount of force required to control a situation	No	No	No	Yes	All methods not specifically approved	Yes
KY	No Response							
LA	1991 (revised 1999)	Bodily contact of some nature—either with or without the use of restraint, electrical device, chemical agent, less-than-lethal munition and device, or firearm—which causes someone either to act in a manner contrary to his intent or to change his behavior to the desired action	Yes	Yes	Yes	Yes	Stun guns and electrical devices, with exception of those listed on Weapons List	Yes
ME	No Response							
MD	1974	Act or action of one or more staff functioning individually, collectively or as a trained unit to apply force against an inmate(s) for the purpose of: self defense; defense of a third party; enforcing compliance with rules, orders or regulations; preventing an escape; preventing destruction of state property; or quelling a disturbance within a correctional facility.	Yes	No	Yes	Yes	Any technique deemed to be excessive force	Yes
MA	1991	Use of physical power; use of a weapon, a chemical agent or instrument of restraint to compel, restrain, or otherwise subdue a person	Yes	Yes	Yes	Yes	An employee shall not use or permit the use of excessive force or the use of force as punishment or discipline	Yes
MI	1984	Force which is reasonable in responding to a pre-defined situation, dependent upon the circumstances of the particular incident	Yes	Yes	Yes	Yes	Stun guns, choke holds	Yes
MN	1998	Force for the protection of persons or property, prevention of escape or restoring order; for maintaining custody, control or when enforcing rules	Yes	Yes	Yes (modified cells)	Yes (chemical irritants, riot control agents	Blackjacks (saps); not to be used as a punitive action	Yes
MS	1998	Utilized when and to the degree necessary to subdue an individual offender or restore order to a disruptive group of offenders; should only be employed as a last resort.	Yes	Yes	No	Yes	None	Yes

USE OF FORCE DEFINITION AND POLICY APPLICATIONS, *continued*

	Policy Adopted	Definition	POLICY APPLICATION INCLUSIONS				Control/Restraints Not Permitted	Video Taping Allowed
			Restraints (Ex., Chairs)	Force (Ex., Four-point)	Confinement (Ex., Strip Cells)	Non-lethal Methods		
MO	1980	Anything other than voluntary compliance, such as the placement of handcuffs; any use of hands, feet, chemical agents or other items to gain compliance.	Yes	Yes	Yes (dry cells)	Yes	Stun guns, electrical shock devices	Yes
MT	Unknown	Actions which staff may take in response to an emergency or situation which constitutes a serious threat to the safety of staff, offenders, others, property and facility security or order; limited to the minimum amount necessary to control a situation.	Yes	Yes (adults)	Yes	Yes	Depends upon the facility	Yes
NE	1984	Deadly force, physical force, use of chemical agents, emergency use of restraints, use of high pressure water	Yes (therapeutic 5-point bed restraint)	Yes	Yes	Yes	Choke holds, hog tying	Yes
NV	1982 (revised 1994)	Force, restricted to the minimum degree necessary to regain control or to repel attack by a resisting inmate.	Yes	Yes	No	Yes	Carotid restraints or lateral vascular neck restraints	Yes
NH	Yes	Force, restricted to instance of justifiable self-defense, protection of others, protection of property and prevention of escapes and then only as a last resort and in accordance with appropriate statutory authority.	Yes (stretcher restraint)	Yes	Yes	Yes	Stun guns	Yes
NJ	No Response							
NM	1984	The exercise of strength or application of physical force used to compel another to act or refrain from acting in a particular way.	Yes (medical restraints)	Yes (provides criteria for use of non-lethal/ lethal weapons)	No	Yes	Hog tying	Yes
NY	1993	An instance in which physical action is taken to resolve an incident; limited to body holds, but includes all instances where a baton, shield, chemical agents, mechanical restraints or firearms are used.	No	No	No	Yes	Choke holds, stun gun and/or stun shield, four-point restraints	Yes
NC	No Response							
ND	1982	A control measure when absolutely necessary based on the need for the application of force, the relationship between the need and the amount of force used, the extent of the injury, and whether applied in good faith or maliciously and sadistically.	Yes (restraint chair and restraint mattress)	Yes (restraint mattress)	No	Yes (empty hand control, chemical agents, water hoses)	Hog tying, four-point to bed (corner to corner)	Yes
OH	1984	Any violence, compulsion or constraint physically exerted by any means upon or against a person or thing.	No	Yes (immobili-zing restraints)	No	No		Yes (only planned use of force)

	Policy Adopted	Definition	POLICY APPLICATION INCLUSIONS Restraints (Ex., Chairs)	Force (Ex., Four-point)	Confinement (Ex., Strip Cells)	Non-lethal Methods	Control/Restraints Not Permitted	Video Taping Allowed
OK	No Response							
OR	1995 (revised in 1998)	Any situation in which an employee uses physical force against an inmate or other person, except those situations in which security restraints are used in a standard manner for arrest, escort or transport, or in which therapeutic restraints are used.	No	No (but therapeutic restraints can be used if ordered by a physician)	No (separate segregation rule applies)	No (covered in training)		Yes (only planned use of force)
PA	1992	Any action within the force continuum by a staff member intended to compel an inmate to act or to cease acting.	No (separate policy)	No (separate policy)	No (separate policy)	Yes	Anything not specifically addressed by policy	Yes
RI	No Response							
SC	Yes	Any physical contact with an inmate or the application of chemical agents to modify his/her behavior or anticipated behavior.	Yes	Yes	No (separate policy)	Yes	Four-point restraints are only used and permitted under specific, unique situations with the approval and oversight of medical staff	Yes (only planned use of force)
SD	1997	Force, to the degree that is reasonable and necessary to enforce obedience of rules, regulations, prohibited acts and directives; to provide for the safety of the public, staff and inmates; and to provide for the good order and disciplined operation of facilities.	No	Yes	Yes	Yes	Tasers or stun guns	Yes
TN	1997	Force, to be used in instances of justifiable self-defense, protection of others, protection of property, and prevention of escapes, to ensure compliance with lawful order and then only as a last resort and in accordance with procedures outlined in the policy.	Yes	Yes	Yes	Yes	Water hoses	Yes
TX	1985 (revised 1998)	A continuum; any physical contact in a confrontational situation with an offender by an Agency official, employee, or authorized agent, to control behavior or to enforce order.	No	Yes (medical purposes only)	Yes	Yes	Offensive tactics (punching, kicking, etc.)	Yes
UT	No Response							
VT	No Response							
VA	No Response							
WA	Yes	Physical use of any weapon, implement, or body movement to cause an offender to respond to staff orders.	Yes	Yes	No	Yes (based on five-tier model)	Carotid submission hold	Yes
WV	No Response							
WI	1978 (with regular updates)	Exercise of strength or power to overcome resistance or to compel another to act or refrain from acting in a particular way.	Yes	Yes	Yes	Yes (clearly defined force option continuum)	Excessive use of force; restraining to bed on stomach	Yes

USE OF FORCE DEFINITION AND POLICY APPLICATIONS, *continued*

	Policy Adopted	Definition	POLICY APPLICATION INCLUSIONS				Control/Restraints Not Permitted	Video Taping Allowed
			Restraints (Ex., Chairs)	Force (Ex., Four-point)	Confinement (Ex., Strip Cells)	Non-lethal Methods		
WY	1996	One-Plus-One concept; to use only the amount of force needed in controlling	Yes (four-point), weapons, defense techniques, chemical)	Yes	No	Yes	None	Yes
BC	1994	Physical constraint of inmates by means of: physical handling, restraint equipment, chemical agents, batons, water hoses, patrol dogs.	Yes (chair boards)	Yes	Yes (seg. And obs. but not strip cells)	Yes	Strikes/holds to head and neck; no firearms	Yes
MB	1989	Not defined; outlined for authority; training; criteria for use; and alternatives	Yes	Yes	Yes	No		No (cell extraction only)
NF	1982	To maintain a safe environment in the institution and to ensure the protection of the public by certain inmates through the use of minimum force when circumstances require.	Yes	No (but under review)	Yes	Yes (pepper spray)	Hog tying	No
ON	Yes	The degree of influence exerted over someone so they will respond to orders.	Yes (but not chairs or beds)	Yes	Yes (day cells with security clothing)	Yes	Certain types of handcuffing, carotid restraint, hog tying (i.e., not to a fixed object or an officer or any technique that interrupts blood flow to the brain)	No
CSC	Yes	Officer presence, verbal intervention, restraints, chemical agents, sprays, firearms, dogs, fire hoses, physical handling	Yes (four-point restraints and restraint chair)	Yes	Yes (suicidal/self-injurious inmates only)	Yes (batons, chemical agents)	Hog tying, bow position, or position where inmate cannot support his/her own weight)	Yes

Use of Force Equipment and Training

as of April 1999

	Policy Reviewed With Staff	Equipment Utilized	Formal Equipment Training	Formal Policy Training	Hours of Required Training	Self-defense Training	Crisis Intervention	Aggressive Inmates
AL	Annual training and after major incident	Chemical agents, shields, body armor, batons, firearms	Yes	Yes	94, basic; 10, annually	Pressure point tactics, restraint techniques, conflict resolution, firearms, stun devices, chemical agents	Same as for self-defense, with the addition of training given to five reactionary teams statewide	Self-defense, with the addition of training given to five reactionary teams statewide
AK	Annual training and after major incident	Chemical agents, shields, body armor, stun guns, firearms, batons, kinetic rounds o.c.	Yes	Yes	31-40	Restraint techniques, conflict resolution, firearms, chemical agents, pressure point tactics	Four-hour block; eight hours of "verbal judo"	Verbal judo, pressure point control tactics
AZ	No Response							
AR	Annual training	Chemical agents, shields, body armor, stun guns, firearms	Yes		11-20	Akido, restraint techniques, firearms, chemical agents	Interpersonal communications	Dealing with disturbed inmates
CA	No Response							
CO	Annual training, after major incident and special session	Chemical agents, shields, body armor, stun guns, firearms, various weaponry	Yes	Yes	31-40	Restraint techniques, conflict resolution, firearms, chemical agents	Twenty-four-hour crisis intervention	Forced cell entry, stun techniques, oc, emergency response, special ops, pressure point contacts, violent patient, emergency response team
CT	Annual training	Chemical agents, shields, body armor, firearms, batons	Yes	Yes	Unknown	Restraint techniques, conflict resolution, firearms, chemical agents	Critical incident team	Behavior management
DE	No Response							
DC	No Response							
FL	Annual training	Chemical agents, shields, body armor, stun guns, firearms	Yes	Yes	11-20	Restraint techniques, conflict resolution, firearms, chemical agents, defensive tactics	Intervention training and advanced course	Inmate manipulation, crisis intervention, on the job training
GA	Annual training	Chemical agents, shields, body armor, firearms	Yes	Yes	21-30	Akido, restraint techniques, conflict resolution, firearms, chemical agents	Interpersonal communications, mental health training	Self defense, interpersonal techniques, mental health training
HI	Annual training and when deemed appropriate	Chemical agents, shields, body armor, firearms, batons, restraints and water hoses	Yes	Yes	21-30	Restraint techniques, conflict resolution, firearms, chemical agents, pressure points control tactics	Prevention/intervention package program	Pressure points control tactics
ID	Annual training	Chemical agents, shields, body armor, firearms	Yes	Yes	1-10	Restraint techniques, conflict resolution, firearms, chemical agents	Critical incident stress debriefing	National Institute of Corrections prescribed program

USE OF FORCE EQUIPMENT AND TRAINING, *continued*

	Policy Reviewed With Staff	Equipment Utilized	Formal Equipment Training	Formal Policy Training	Hours of Required Training	Self-defense Training	Crisis Intervention	Aggressive Inmates
IL	Annual training	Chemical agents, shields, firearms, batons, handcuffs	Yes	Yes	11-20	Akido, restraint techniques, conflict resolution, firearms, chemical agents, pressure sensitive areas	Four-hour suicide training for cadets, 16-hour crisis intervention team course	Riot and baton squad training, control tactics, use of force continuum
IN	Annual training	Chemical agents, shields, body armor, stun guns, firearms	Yes	Yes	21-30	Akido, restraint techniques, firearms, chemical agents	Quick response team training	Personal protection, high security transport, quick response team
IA	Annual training	Chemical agents, shields, body armor, stun guns, firearms	Yes	Yes		Restraint techniques, conflict resolution, firearms, chemical agents		De-escalation techniques
KS	Annual training	Chemical agents, shields, body armor, stun guns, firearms, batons, water under pressure	Yes	Yes	1-10	Akido, restraint techniques, conflict resolution, firearms, chemical agents	Conflict resolution and interpersonal relations	Conflict resolution and interpersonal relations
KY	Annual training; special session	Chemical agents, shields, body armor, stun guns, firearms, batons. taser guns, taser shields	Yes	Yes	1-10	Akido, restraint techniques, conflict resolution, firearms, chemical agents, come-alongs	Non-violent crisis, emergency preparedness	Hostage, correcting inmate behavior
LA	Annual training; after major incident; special session; as needed	Chemical agents, shields, body armor, firearms, non-lethal weapons	Yes	Yes	11-20	Restraint techniques, conflict resolution, firearms, chemical agents	Conflict resolution, verbal communication skills	Control techniques, use of force
ME	Annual training	Chemical agents, shields, body armor firearms	Yes	Yes	1-10	Restraint techniques, firearms, chemical agents	Basic training	
MD	Annual training	Chemical agents, shields, body armor, firearms, restraint chair	Yes	Yes	1-10	Restraint techniques, firearms, chemical agents	None	Pressure point techniques
MA	Annual training	Chemical agents, shields, body armor, firearms	Yes	Yes	1-10	Restraint techniques, conflict resolution, firearms, chemical agents	Psychological self-defense; tactical inmate supervision	Forty hours of segregation training
MI	Annual training and after major incident	Chemical agents, shields, body armor, firearms	Yes	Yes		Akido, restraint techniques, conflict resolution, firearms, chemical agents	Forty-hour specialized program for managing prisoners, with 16-hour yearly update	Control techniques, use of force
MN	Annual training	Chemical agents, shields, body armor, firearms, batons	Yes	Yes	41-+, new officers; 11-20 thereafter	Conflict resolution, chemical agents, pressure point control techniques	Interpersonal communications, pressure point control techniques, conflict resolution	Use of force training, verbal judo, pepper spray, defensive tactics
MS	Unknown	Chemical agents, shields, body armor firearms, batons	Yes	Unknown	Unknown	Restraint techniques, firearms, chemical agents	Unknown	Unknown
MO	Annual training, after major incident and special session	Chemical agents, shields, body armor, firearms	Yes	Yes	11-20	Restraint techniques, conflict resolution, firearms, chemical agents	Hostage training, special tactical response, etc.	Use of force training, verbal judo, pepper spray, defensive tactics

	Policy Reviewed With Staff	Equipment Utilized	Formal Equipment Training	Formal Policy Training	Hours of Required Training	Self-defense Training	Crisis Intervention	Aggressive Inmates
MT	Annual training and special session	Chemical agents, shields, body armor, firearms, cuffs/shackles	Yes	Yes	Depends on job duties[1]	Restraint techniques, conflict resolution, firearms, chemical agents, pressure point control techniques, CPI, IPC	Crisis intervention, emergency response, Interpersonal communications, OC, cell extraction	Use of restraints, cell extraction, OC, pressure point control techniques
NE	Annual training	Chemical agents, shields, body armor, firearms, batons, video camera	Yes	Yes	21-30	Restraint techniques, conflict resolution, firearms, chemical agents, pressure point control techniques	Emergency preparedness	Correctional communication, pressure point control techniques, cell extraction
NV	Annual training, after major incident, and as required by shift supervisor	Chemical agents, shields, body armor, firearms, taser, batons, K-9's	Yes	Yes	11-20	Akido, restraint techniques, conflict resolution, firearms, chemical agents	Interpersonal communications, suicide prevention, inmate grievance process, drug addiction awareness, management of disruptive groups and high profile inmates	Supervision of inmates, use of force policy, emergency response
NH	Annual training and after major incident	Chemical agents, shields, body armor, firearms, OC, PR-24 sert team	Yes	Yes	31-40, pre-service; 1-10, annual	Restraint techniques, firearms, chemical agents	Verbal judo, cognitive problem solving	Aggression management training
NJ	No Response							
NM	Annual training	Chemical agents, shields, body armor, firearms, stun guns, riot sticks/batons, dogs, water	Yes	Yes	31-40	Akido, restraint techniques, conflict resolution, firearms, chemical agents	Class and role playing	
NY	Annual training	Chemical agents, shields, body armor, firearms	Yes	Yes	41-+, recruits; 11-20 in-service	Restraint techniques, conflict resolution, firearms, chemical agents, unarmed defensive tactics	Crisis intervention unit (120 hours in-service and 4 hours/month thereafter)	Recognizing and controlling aggressive behavior (24 hours plus 8-hour refresher)
NC	No Response							
ND	Annual training	Chemical agents, stun guns, firearms, water hoses, batons	Yes	Yes	1-10	Restraint techniques, firearms, chemical agents, pressure point control techniques	None	Force cell move training
OH	Annual training	Chemical agents, shields, body armor, firearms, stun shield	Yes	Yes	1-10 (annual)	Akido, restraint techniques, firearms, chemical agents	Interpersonal communication skills	Interpersonal communication skills and other specific training

USE OF FORCE EQUIPMENT AND TRAINING, *continued*

	Policy Reviewed With Staff	Equipment Utilized	Formal Equipment Training	Formal Policy Training	Hours of Required Training	Self-defense Training	Crisis Intervention	Aggressive Inmates
OK	No Response							
OR	Annual training	Chemical agents, shields, body armor, stun guns, firearms, batons water force, security restraints	Yes	Yes	1-10	Restraint techniques, conflict resolution, firearms, chemical agents	Emergency preparedness, use-of-force training, inmate mental health issues, suicide prevention, interpersonal communications, non-violent crisis intervention, hostage negotiation training and employee assistance	Basic security practices, use of force, cell extraction, basic firearms, searches/restraints, interpersonal communication and electronic immobilizing devices
PA	Annual training and after major incident	Chemical agents, shields, body armor, stun guns, firearms, batons	Yes	Yes	11-20	Restraint techniques, conflict resolution, firearms, chemical agents	Interpersonal communications, conflict management, suicide prevention, control of aggressive behavior, emotionally disturbed inmates and special behavioral problems	
RI	No Response							
SC	Annual training	Chemical agents, shields, body armor, stun guns, firearms, PR-24 sert teams, batons	Yes	Yes	11-20	Restraint techniques, conflict resolution, firearms, chemical agents, self defense	Suicide intervention, hostage negotiation, emergency preparedness and barricaded inmate negotiations	Crisis intervention, communication skills, hostage negotiation
SD	Annual training	Chemical agents, shields, body armor, firearms, mechanical restraints, batons, rubber pellets, bean bag slugs, soft restraints	Yes	Yes	11-20	Restraint techniques, conflict resolution, firearms, chemical agents, pressure point control techniques	Non-violent crisis intervention	Pressure point control techniques, non-violent crisis intervention, internally developed lesson plan
TN	Annual training, after major incident and as needed	Chemical agents, shields, body armor, stun guns, firearms	Yes	Yes	Pre-service, 28.5; in-service, 11	Restraint techniques, conflict resolution, firearms, chemical agents	Cert teams and negotiation management	
TX	Annual training	Chemical agents, shields, body armor, firearms	Yes	Yes	11-20	Restraint techniques, conflict resolution, firearms, chemical agents	Non-violent intervention techniques, interpersonal communications	Use of force, restraint tactics, defensive tactics, riot baton
UT	No Response							

	Policy Reviewed With Staff	Equipment Utilized	Formal Equipment Training	Formal Policy Training	Hours of Required Training	Self-defense Training	Crisis Intervention	Aggressive Inmates
VT	No Response							
VA	No Response							
WA	Annual training; special team training	Chemical agents, shields, body armor, stun guns, firearms, helmets, gas masks, elbow and knee pads	Yes	Yes	1-10	Restraint techniques, conflict resolution, firearms chemical agents	Tactical verbal skills	Small team tactics, cell extraction, ERT and SERT team training
WV	No Response							
WI	Annual training	Chemical agents, shields, body armor, stun guns, firearms	Yes	Yes	1-10	Restraint techniques, conflict resolution, firearms, chemical agents	Principles of subject control	
WY	Annual training and after major incident	Chemical agents, shields, body armor, stun guns, firearms	Yes	Yes	80	Restraint techniques, conflict resolution, firearms, chemical agents, self-defense	Very little and only verbally	Restraining/take downs
BC	Special session and initial training	Chemical agents, shields, body armor, batons, OC, CN, ASP	Yes	Yes	21-30	Restraint techniques, conflict resolution, chemical agents, Hapido	In-house program adapted from Crisis Prevention Institute and Justice Institute	Justice Institute of British Columbia
MB	Annual training and periodic audits	Chemical agents, shields, body armor, riot batons, distraction devices	Yes	Yes	1-10	Akido, restraint techniques, conflict resolution, chemical agents	Non-violent intervention and riot/hostage taking training	Physical crisis intervention techniques
NF	After major incident	Shields, firearms, pepper spray	No (under review)	No (under review)	None	Pepper spray	Under review	Minimal training in restraint chair
ON	Special session	Chemical agents, shields, body armor, handcuffs, leg irons, batons, fire hose and strait jackets	Yes (except fire hose and strait jackets)	Yes	11-20	Akido, restraint techniques, conflict resolution, chemical agents, batons	Tactical team, crisis negotiator, hostage awareness, non-violent intervention, diffusion of hostility, disturbances, prior safety training	Diffusion of hostility, restraints, self defense, emotionally disturbed inmates
CSC	Annual training	Chemical agents, shields, firearms	Yes	Yes	41-+	Akido, restraint techniques, conflict resolution, firearms, chemical agents	Crisis negotiation and crisis management	Interpersonal communication and crisis management

Note:
1. MONTANA: Support staff, 1-10; some COs and support staff, 21-30; specialized response teams, 41-+

Use of Force Incidents and Review Process

as of April 1999

	Policy Review Schedule in Department	Written Report mandatory	Administrative Review Process in Place	All Incidents Subject to Review	Criteria for Review	Title of Reviewer	Administrative Levels of Reviewers	Witnesses Included in Review
AL	Annual training or as necessary	Yes	Yes	Yes	N/A	N/A	Central office investigators and legal counsel	Yes
AK	Annual training, after major incident, special session, or as needed	Yes	Yes	Yes	All on paper; most serious, on-site; interviews, etc.	Director of Institutions	Shift commander, superintendents, Central Office staff	May be
AZ	No Response							
AR	Annual review of policies	Yes	Yes	Yes	Seriousness; injuries and additional information coming forth	Wardens and assistant deputy director managers, internal affairs	Shift commander, superintendents, central office staff,	
CA	No Response							
CO	Annually	Yes	Yes	Yes	All are reviewed	Deputy Director of Institutions, Inspector General, commanders, shift commanders	Shift commander, superintendents and central office staff	No
CT	During regular policy revision cycle	Yes	Yes	Yes	All are reviewed	Dependent upon the level of force used; at minimum the unit administrator	Dependent upon the level of force used; Shift commander, superintendents, central office staff, managers, regional staff	Yes—witnesses file reports
DE	No Response							
DC	No Response							
FL	Annual training	Yes	Yes	Yes	All are reviewed and defined by the use of force policy	Shift commander and higher authority, assistant superintendent, superintendent, etc.	Shift commander, superintendents, central office staff, managers, regional staff	Yes
GA	Annual training	Yes	Yes	Yes	All are reviewed and defined by the use of force policy	N/A	Shift commander, superintendents, central office staff, managers, regional staff	Yes
HI	As needed; currently being revised	Yes	Yes	No	Physical injury, death, discharge of firearms, chemical agents	Review goes up the chain of command to the Director	Shift commander, superintendents, central office staff, managers, attorney general	Yes
ID	Annual training	Yes	Yes	Yes	All are reviewed	Deputy warden, warden, prison administrator	Shift commander, superintendents, central office staff	Yes
IL	Annual training	Yes	Yes	Yes	All are reviewed	Each CAO is responsible for review	Shift commander, superintendents, central office staff	Yes
IN	Annual training	Yes	Yes	Yes	All are reviewed	Field specialist, captain	Shift commander, central office staff	Yes
IA	Periodically as needed	Yes	Yes	Yes	All are reviewed	Deputy director	Shift commander, superintendents, central office staff	

	Policy Review Schedule in Department	Written Report mandatory	Administrative Review Process in Place	All Incidents Subject to Review	Criteria for Review	Title of Reviewer	Administrative Levels of Reviewers	Witnesses Included in Review
KS	Annual training	Yes	Yes	Yes	All are reviewed	Risk management coordinator	Shift commander, superintendents, central office staff, managers, legal staff	Yes
KY	**Annually per ACA standard**	**Yes**	**Yes**	**Yes**	**All are reviewed**	**Shift commander, superintendents, central office staff**	**Yes—staff office reports**	
LA	**Annual training, after major incident, as needed**	**Yes**	**Yes**	**Yes**	**All are reviewed**	**Various**	**Shift commander, superintendents, central office staff, managers, investigators**	**Yes**
ME	Annual training	Yes	Yes	Yes	All are reviewed	Shift commander, major, chief of security	Shift commander, major, chief of security	Sometimes
MD	Annual	Yes	Yes	Yes	All are reviewed	Shift commander, chief of security, warden, director of security operations, internal investigation unit	Shift commander, superintendents, central office staff, chief of security	Yes
MA	Annual training	Yes	Yes	Yes	All are reviewed	Superintendent or his designee, special unit director or his designee	Shift commander, superintendents, central office staff, managers, director of operations/security	Yes
MI	Annual training, after major incident	Yes	Yes	Yes	Agency critical incident policy	Deputy warden, warden, regulation administrator, deputy director	Shift commander, superintendents, central office staff, managers, regional staff, post incident review committee	Yes
MN	Annual training, after major incident	Yes	Yes	Yes	All are reviewed	Warden or designee	Superintendents, managers, associate wardens, security directors	Yes—through written incident reports
MS	Unknown	Yes	Yes	Yes	All are reviewed	Superintendent, warden, community service director or designee	Superintendents, warden	Unknown
MO	Annual training, after major incident, as needed	Yes	Yes	Yes	All are reviewed	Superintendent of institution, chief of custody, DOC chief of security coordinator	Shift commander, superintendents, central office staff, security coordinator	Yes
MT	Quarterly policy reviews, as needed	Yes	Yes	Yes		Warden, superintendent, director, legal unit	Shift commander, superintendents, central office staff, managers, wardens, legal	
NE	Annual administrative review	Yes	Yes	Yes	All are reviewed	Security administrator, warden, department security coordinator, assistant director	Shift commander, superintendents, central office staff	Yes

USE OF FORCE INCIDENTS AND REVIEW PROCESS, *continued*

	Policy Review Schedule in Department	Written Report mandatory	Admin- istrative Review Process in Place	All Incidents Subject to Review	Criteria for Review	Title of Reviewer	Administrative Levels of Reviewers	Witnesses Included in Review
NV	Annual training, after major incident, special session, and to be updated as required by the director	Yes	Yes	Yes	All are reviewed	Shift commander, warden, inspector general	Shift commander, superintendents, central office staff, managers	Yes
NH	Annual training, after major incident, PPD revised annually	Yes	Yes	Yes	All are reviewed	Wardens, superintendents, assistant commissioner	Superintendents, central office staff	Yes
NJ	No Response							
NM	Annual training	Yes	Yes	Yes		Director of adult prisons	Shift commander, superintendents, central office staff	Yes
NY	Ongoing basis with annual review	Yes	Yes	Yes	All are reviewed	Superintendent or acting super- intendent	Shift commander, superintendents	No
ND	Annual	Yes	Yes	Yes	All are reviewed	Chief of security	Shift commander, managers	No
OH	Policy being revised	Yes	Yes	Yes		Appointed by the warden	Shift commander, superintendents, central office staff regional staff	Yes
OK	No Response							
OR	Annual, as needed	Yes	Yes	Yes	All are reviewed	Officer in charge, security manager, superintendent, central office chief of security, inspector general	Shift commander, superintendents, central office staff, managers, chief of security, inspector general	May be
PA	Annual training	Yes	Yes	Yes	All are reviewed	Facility manager, regional deputy secretary, secretary of corrections, central office security division	Superintendents, central office staff, managers, regional staff	Yes
RI	No Response							
SC	Annual	Yes	Yes	Yes	All are reviewed	Supervisors, deputy director of operations	Shift commander, office staff wardens	Upon request
SD	Annual training	Yes	Yes	Yes	All are reviewed	Officer of special security, secretary of corrections, division of criminal investigation	Shift commander, superintendents, central office staff, managers	Yes
TN	Annual training, after major incident, as needed	Yes	Yes	Yes	All are reviewed	Warden	Determined by warden	Yes
TX	Continuous	Yes	Yes	Yes	All are reviewed	Various	Shift commander, superintendents, central office staff, managers, regional staff, internal affairs division	Yes
UT	No Response							
VT	No Response							
VA	No Response							

	Policy Review Schedule in Department	Written Report mandatory	Administrative Review Process in Place	All Incidents Subject to Review	Criteria for Review	Title of Reviewer	Administrative Levels of Reviewers	Witnesses Included in Review
WA	After major incident, every three years	Yes	Yes	Yes	All are reviewed	Superintendent	Shift commander, superintendents, managers	Yes
WV	No Response							
WI	Annually, as needed	Yes	Yes	Yes	All are reviewed	Security director	Shift commander, superintendents, central office staff	Yes, on occasion
WY	Annual training	Yes	Yes	Yes	All are reviewed	Security manager, warden, division of prison administrator	Shift commander, superintendents, central office staff, managers	Yes
BC	After major incident, special session, initial training	Yes	Yes	Yes	All are reviewed	Director of operations	Shift commander, central office staff, managers	Yes
MB	Annual training	Yes	Yes	Yes	All are reviewed	Superintendent or deputy superintendent	Shift commander, managers	Yes
NF	Presently under review	Yes	Yes	Yes	All are reviewed	Internal review officer	Shift commander, superintendents	Yes
ON	Annual training, after major incident, special session	Yes	Yes	Yes	If injuries result or allegations are made by the inmate	Superintendent or delegate, ministry's investigation unit	Superintendents, managers, regional staff	Yes
CSC	Special session	Yes	Yes	Yes	All are reviewed	Various	Shift commander, superintendents, central office staff, regional staff	

Prison Industries: Participation

As of January 2000

	POPULATION		NO. ELIGIBLE		NO. EMPLOYED		WAITING LIST		Death Row Eligible	Eligibility Requirements	Remedial Help Offered
	Male	Female	Male	Female	Male	Female	Male	Female			
AL	23,137	1,651	All but life without parole and death row		1,900	100	None	None	No	Institution job board review on case-by-case basis	Counseling, GED courses, assignment to in-house institutional support position
AK	4,011	314	1,264	186	148	10	NA	NA	NA	Job availability determination; based on custody level and past behavior; location of offender	Educational courses, etc., if prerequisite requirements are designated
AZ	23,893	2,078	20,296	1,765	1,378	237	471	150	No	Varies according to location; must be discipline-free	Counseling by the institution
AR	9,999	744	5,000	14	570	14	NA	4	No	Medium security or above; minimum of 60 days on initial job assignment; desire to learn from experience; prior experience helpful	No Answer
CA	150,479	11,326	19,300	700	6,000	600	NA	NA	No	Discipline free for 6 months and general population inmate	NA
CO	12,400	826	7,357	733	1,168	40	Unknown		No	GED or high school diploma; no disciplinary action for last 30–90 days; job-specific requirements	Many shops work with vocational programs to hire inmates as they complete vocational training
CT	16,010	1,235	7,200	800	300	60	None kept		No	Level 3 or 4 facility with an industry program, willingness to follow rules and policies of program, meet skill or aptitude requirements of position	Vocational help is generally available through the education department
DC	1,900	0	1,800	0	200	0	100	0	No	Completion of mandatory adult basic education	ABE, GED and college programs
DE	4,664	367	4,664	367	206	5	250	50	No	Clean disciplinary record; completion of court ordered programming; 7-hour daily availability (M-F)	Program availability, counseling services
FL	65,449	3,790	Varies	Varies	2,460	140	NA	NA	No	Preferably between 1–5 years prior to release date; program performance in classes recommended by staff; noninterference with set time for mandatory literacy/education classes; satisfactory general record	Counseling; academic education, self-improvement program, etc.
GA	No Response										
HI	3,170	399	2,190	200	430	20	Unknown		NA	Clearance from social worker and medically approved	None
ID	4,234	372	Not available		382	19	Unknown	NA	No	Good behavior, infraction-free for 6 months	None
IL	42,116	2,855	1,498	159	1,437	145	NA	NA	No	Openings are posted and copies sent to an assignment committee. Special efforts are made, and documented, to conform to affirmative action requirements	Inmate goes before assignment committee for further consideration
IN	17,987	1,227	6,650	699	1,445	91	None kept		Yes, only in their cell house	Application and interview for posted openings, job-specific skills	Does not hire

	POPULATION		NO. ELIGIBLE		NO. EMPLOYED		WAITING LIST		DEATH ROW	Eligibility Requirements	Remedial Help Offered
	Male	Female	Male	Female	Male	Female	Male	Female	Eligible		
IA	6,723	539	2,500	100	350	25	NA	NA	No	Able; willing; position available	Iowa Prison Industries hires all inmates for whom work is available
KS	8,006	574	4,598	271	424	10	NA	NA	No	Assigned to Incentive Level 2 or 3; no disciplinary reports for 120 days	None
KY	No Response										
LA	18,191	940	16,362	785	695	68	100	10	No	Proper duty status	Initial training provided by vocational instructors
ME	1,643	61	1,150	45	101	10	200	34	NA	Free of disciplinary actions; time of sentence remaining; medical clearance; drug-free; work history	Determined on individual basis
MD	21,866	1,115	12,162	773	1,124	185	Unknown		No	11th grade education or GED or specific skills, infraction-free for last 90 days, assigned by institution classification team, comply with all rules and regulations of assigned plant/service center	GED equivalent
MA	9,165	637	8,000	400	468	20	435	50	NA	High school diploma or equivalent up to specific experience	Inmate education and training division programs
MI	42,667	1,787	5,120 est.	214 est.	1,299	63	Unknown		Not applicable	Inmate interest; no disciplinary problems; completion of recommended school programs and medical clearance	Counseling
MN	5,581	328	5,023	295	765	91	0	0	No death penalty	Able to perform the work; available for assignment; participating in literacy classes, if applicable	Literacy classes provided through institution education programming
MS	16,960	1,414	3,000	300	720	90	50	15	No	Good behavior; willingness to learn skill/work; meets and exceeds classification guidelines	Counseling
MO	24,167	1,992	13,552	1,101	1,245	117	Not available		Yes	High school education or GED, must apply and interview	GED classes for those not meeting educational requirements
MT	1,343	71	402.9	17.75	258	9	None maintained		No	GED or high school diploma, appropriate custody level	High school diploma/GED assistance; items to decrease custody
NB	3,333	246	1,350	115	526	53	NA	NA	No	Open, depending on position	Pre-employment training
NV	8,942	754	5,750	475	390	9	200	10	No	6 months without a major violation; 6 months incarceration; no minimum security	None—NA
NH	2,074	160	1,311	95	286	13	NA	NA	NA	Open enrollment for those who remain discipline-free; some positions require certain educational and/or skills level	Work closely with education and vocational training programs to provide inmates with necessary tools
NJ	29,084	1,734	Unknown		1,522	276	None kept		No	Inmates assigned by the Industrial Classification Committee with representation by the Bureau of State Use Industries/DEPTCOR, no specific requirements, no educational requirements	Inmates may enroll in the education program on their own
NM	4,703	448	3,703	420	293	50	Inmates apply as positions become available		No	Reviewed on a case-by-case basis, but GED is a minimum requirement	GED classes; adult basic education

PRISON INDUSTRIES: PARTICIPATION, *continued*

	POPULATION		NO. ELIGIBLE		NO. EMPLOYED		WAITING LIST		Death Row Eligible	Eligibility Requirements	Remedial Help Offered
	Male	Female	Male	Female	Male	Female	Male	Female			
NY	68,305	3,500	68,305	3,500	2,517	85	Unknown		No	Must have high school diploma or equivalent and good institutional record	GED programs
NC	29,696	1,889	29,225	1,860	2,027	57	Unknown		No	No Response	No Response
ND	879	66	615	45	122	5	15	0	NA	Must be in compliance with all treatment recommendations; no major infraction reports in past six months; must have worked at least 60 days within the institution; high school diploma or GED	All remedial help is provided through the inmate's case manager at the penitentiary
OH	43,800	2,800	Unknown		2,864 avg.	105 avg.	List not centrally monitored—maintained at appropriate institutions		No	GED or high school diploma, industry-specific skills, good attendance record—which excludes those in disciplinary control	Adult basic education, GED preparation
OK	13,725	1,263	5,000 est.	400 est.	1,200 avg.	100 avg.	None kept		No	Clear conduct record, other qualifications are dependent on position and facility limitations	Training and entry level positions are available in most areas
OR	No Response										
PA	34,870	1,514	12,156	838	1,790	41	4,294	50	No	Minimum 5th grade reading level; no misconduct citations in last 12 months; 18 months remaining on sentence	Reading classes for those below 5th grade level
RI	2,858	201	2,096	196	320	5	150	NA	NA	Good disciplinary record	
SC	19,521	1,388	Dependent on institutional adjustment and skills		1,744	173	1,715	169	No	In PIE programs, no disciplinary problems for 6 months and have GED; in other programs, ability to perform required tasks	Inmates unable to perform certain job requirements are offered alternate jobs such as material handlers
SD	2,313	188	NA	NA	157	25	NA	NA	No	Physically and mentally able to perform required duties; meet job-specific custody requirements	
TN	15,969	857	9,084	424	837	69	699	6	Yes	High school diploma or GED; position-specific requirements	Vocational programs
TX	136,873	11,188	6,750	250	6,627	246	NA	NA	No	No physical limitations; related vocational training; prior industry experience a plus	Jobs in other departments, i.e., food service, laundry, etc.
UT	4,751	320	3,124	40	843	11	Unknown		No	Medium or minimum security inmates who are allowed to move about the institution	No
VT	1,521	72	Theoretically all are eligible		100		Varies due to programming and education needs		NA	Basic safety course, basic literacy, participation in programming/education per case plan	Cooperative counseling/support, safety training, education, OJT used to promote employees to higher levels responsibility/participation
VA	25,012	1,727	Unknown		1,205 average in fiscal year		Unknown		No	No Response	No Response
WA	12,466	756	11,115	756	1,786	138	NA	NA	No	8th grade equivalency; additional job-specific requirements	Education
WV	2,736	154	NA	NA	264	7	NA	NA	NA	High school diploma or equivalency	Enrollment in GED program

	POPULATION		NO. ELIGIBLE		NO. EMPLOYED		WAITING LIST		Death Row Eligible	Eligibility Requirements	Remedial Help Offered
	Male	Female	Male	Female	Male	Female	Male	Female			
WI	18,504	1,331	2,820	180	629	77	620	80	No death penalty	6th grade level M reading and math scores under the TABE tests or an 8th grade level under the ABLE test; related vocational training depending upon the industry; exceptions may be granted	Education programs
WY[1]	1,435	140	669	96	91	26	0	0	No	Females: read, write, keyboard; any classification close or below. Males: no history of escape; no physical limitations as required by job; close custody or below	Females: education assistance. Males: none
FBP	113,836	8,605	79,876	7,634	18,865	1,423	Unknown[2]		No	All are eligible except those medically ineligible, pretrial or under order of deportation/removal. Inmates are hired from waiting lists, in order, unless they possess special skills which are needed	All newly hired inmates go through pre-industrial or on-the-job training
BC	2,583	157	1,115	123	NA	NA	NA	NA	NA	Usually, sentenced inmates	NA
NB	No provincial prison industries										
MB	1,337	59	767	22	125	0	Unknown		NA	Sentenced inmates only; generally, most work industries accessed by lower-risk population	None available unless on a case by case exceptional basis only
NF	Yes		39		39		0		NA	All inmates admitted to Salmonier CI participate in prison industries	NA
ON	7,245	444	3,000	0	300	0	NA	NA	NA	Relevant security levels; sentenced and have no outstanding charges; good health and attitude	NA
SK	1,048	62	763	49	70	13	109	7	NA	Appropriate security rating; identified programming need	NA
YK	No provincial prison industries										
CSC	12,547	351	Not available		1,831	29	103	0	No death penalty	Must have 10th grade education or GED	Educational requirement may be gained through prison school's programs

Notes:
1. WYOMING: formal program was established by the Legislature in 1999 to expand correctional industries and currently is pending appointment of an advisory board and hiring for two positions.
2. FEDERAL BUREAU OF PRISONS: With 100 factories at 68 institutions, actual numbers cannot be provided.

Prison Industries: Financial and Wages

as of January 2000

	Current Budget	Financing Options	Basis for Inmate Pay	Inmate Pay Range	Distribution of Wages if Garnished
AL	$18,000,000	Self-sustaining revolving fund	Hourly rate	$1.76/day	None
AK	$3,914,500	General funds, self-sustaining revolving fund, PIE cooperative ventures	Hourly rate	$37.50/week	Room/board, inmate family support, fines/cost imposed by court, savings, victim restitution
AZ	$19,323,800	Self-sustaining revolving fund	Hourly rate	$.40 to $5.15/hour	Room/board, inmate family support, fines/cost imposed by court, savings, victim restitution
AR		Self-sustaining revolving fund	No pay	NA	NA
CA	$150,000,000	Self-sustaining revolving fund	Hourly rate	$.56/hour	Victim restitution
CO	$33,000,000	Self-sustaining revolving fund	Hourly rate; production incentive	Non-PIE $.50/hour	Room/board, inmate family support, savings, victim restitution
CT	$6,943,000	Self-sustaining revolving fund	Hourly rate; production incentive	$.50/hour	Room/board, inmate family support, fines/cost imposed by court, victim restitution
DC	$5,659,792	Self-sustaining revolving fund	Hourly rate	$1.34/hour to $140.00/month	NA
DE	$4,179,600	Self-sustaining revolving fund	Hourly rate	$.25 to $1.30/hr	Inmate family support, fines/costs imposed by court, victim restitution
FL	No budget	Managed and operated by a self-supporting not-for-profit organization called PRIDE Enterprises Inc.	Hourly rate; production incentive	$.20 to $.55/hour	PIE program wages only: room/board, inmate family support, fines/costs imposed by court, savings, victim restitution, taxes
GA	No Response				
HI	$7,000,000	Self-sustaining revolving fund	Hourly rate	$.48 to $7.50/hour	Room/board, inmate family support, fines/costs imposed by court, savings, victim restitution
ID	$6,700,000	Self-sustaining revolving fund	Flat daily rate; hourly rate	$.80	Room/board, inmate family support, fines/cost imposed by court, savings, victim restitution
IL	$53,821,000	Self-sustaining revolving fund	Production incentive	$135.00/month average	3% of monthly inmate compensation returned to DOC for costs of incarceration
IN	$28,300,000	Self-sustaining revolving fund	Hourly rate	$.30/hour	Room/board, inmate family support, savings, victim restitution
IA	$13,000,000	Self-sustaining revolving fund	Hourly rate	$.41 to $.90/hour	Room/board, inmate family support, victim restitution
KS	$10,693,892	Self-sustaining revolving fund	Hourly rate	$.25 to $.60/hour	Fines/costs imposed by court
KY	No response				
LA	$27,844,237	Self-sustaining revolving fund	Hourly rate	$.14/hour	Room/board, savings, victim restitution
ME	$1,192,000	Self-sustaining revolving fund	Hourly rate	$.50/hour	Inmate family support, fines/costs imposed by court, savings, victim restitution
MD	$37,000,000	Self-sustaining revolving fund	Base pay plus incentive; paid overtime	$4.41/day	Not applicable
MA	$11,350,000	Self-sustaining revolving fund	Hourly rate	$.75/hour avg.	Savings
MI	$12,700,000	Self-sustaining revolving fund	Hourly rate; production incentive	$6.30/day	
MN	$25,073,000	10% general fund appropriation, 90% self-sustaining revolving fund	Hourly rate	Non-interstate, $.83/hour; interstate, $6.33/hour	Room/board, inmate family support, fines/costs imposed by court, savings, victim restitution

	Current Budget	Financing Options	Basis for Inmate Pay	Inmate Pay Range	Distribution of Wages if Garnished
MS	$4,200,000	Nonprofit corporation—stand alone agency—receives no government funds	Hourly rate; production incentive	$.25/hour	
MO	$35,701,000	Self-sustaining revolving fund	Flat daily rate; hourly rate	$.55/hour	Fines/costs imposed by court, victim restitution
MT	$7,509,451	Self-sustaining revolving fund, general fund-license plates and vocational education	Flat daily rate; hourly rate	$4.90/day; $.50 to $5.15/hour	Room/board, inmate family support, victim restitution
NE	$6,400,000	General fund appropriation	Flat daily rate; hourly rate; production incentive (quarterly bonus)	$125.61/month	Inmate family support, fines/costs imposed by court, 5% mandatory savings, federal court filing fees, restitution
NV	$6,592,824	Self-sustaining revolving fund	Flat daily rate; hourly rate; production incentive	Farm $7.00/day, non-farm $3.89/hour	Room/board, fines/costs imposed by court, savings, victim restitution
NH	$2,300,000	Self-sustaining revolving fund	Flat daily rate; production incentive	$1.50/day up to $3.50 bonus	Room/board
NJ	$18,142,000	Self-sustaining revolving fund	Hourly rate; production incentive	$.48/hour to $.88/hour	Not controlled by prison industries
NM	No general funds available, self-supporting	Self-sustaining revolving fund	Hourly rate	$.70/hour average	Inmate family support, fines/costs imposed by court, victim restitution
NY	$72,000,000	Internal service fund	Hourly rate	$.50/hour	Fines/costs imposed by court
NC	$69,000,000	Self-sustaining revolving fund	Flat daily rate; hourly rate; production incentive	$.26/hour (highest wage)	
ND	$7,522,000 for 99-01 biennium	Self-sustaining revolving fund	Hourly rate	Traditional $192/month, PIE $5.15/hour	Inmate family support, fines/costs imposed by court, savings, payments for damages incurred
OH	$45,000,000	Self-sustaining revolving fund	Hourly rate; longevity incentive	$.47/hour average	Room/board, inmate family support, victim restitution
OK	$19,000,000 projected	Self-sustaining revolving fund	Hourly rate; production incentive	$.45/hour average	Room/board, inmate family support, fines/costs imposed by court, savings, victim restitution, inmate welfare fund
OR					
PA	$40,650,000	Self-sustaining revolving fund	Hourly rate; production incentive	$100/month approximately	Whatever is owed by the inmate to the Commonwealth
RI	Based on a rotary account	Self-sustaining revolving fund	Flat daily rate	$3.00/day	Savings
SC	$20,444,229	Self-sustaining revolving fund	Flat daily rate; hourly rate; production incentive; no pay	Traditional $0 to $.60/hour; service industry $.35 to $1.00/hour; PIE $5.25 to $6.50/hour	Room/board, inmate family support, fines/costs imposed by court, savings, victim restitution
SD	No specific budget; based on whatever spending authority is approved	Self-sustaining revolving fund	Hourly rate	Traditional $.40 to $1.00/hour, private sector industry comparable to similar work in surrounding community	Room/board, inmate family support savings, victim restitution
TN	$25,300,000	Self-sustaining revolving fund	Hourly rate, production incentive	$1.00	Fines/costs imposed by court, Criminal Injuries Compensation Fund, medical co-payments, room/board, mandatory savings, victim restitution
TX	$21,000,000	Self-sustaining revolving fund	No pay-inmates are paid in time (credit on time served)	NA	NA

PRISON INDUSTRIES: FINANCIAL AND WAGES, *continued*

	Current Budget	Financing Options	Basis for Inmate Pay	Inmate Pay Range	Distribution of Wages if Garnished
UT	$12,500,000	Self-sustaining revolving fund	Hourly rate	Traditional $.60-$1.05/hour, private sector $8.00/hour	Fines/costs imposed by court, savings, victim restitution, supervision fees
VT	$2,807,500	Self-sustaining revolving fund	Hourly rate; production incentive	$.25-$1.50/hour	Room/board, inmate family support, fines/costs imposed by court, victim restitution
VA	$32,770,130	Self-sustaining revolving fund	Hourly rate	$.65/hour	Inmate family support and victim restitution (if working in PIE program); fines/costs imposed by court
WA	$36,450,000	General fund appropriation; self-sustaining revolving fund	Production incentive	$.35 to $1.10/hour	Room/board, inmate family support, fines/costs imposed by court, savings, victim restitution
WV	$7,750,000	Self-sustaining revolving fund	Hourly rate	$.77/hour	Mandatory 10% savings
WI	$ 22,949,000	Self-sustaining revolving fund	Hourly rate	Traditional $.75/hour, PIE $6.76/hour	Room/board, inmate family support victim restitution
WY	$ 1,475,499 (for mares)	General fund appropriation	Hourly rate end production incentive (females)	$30 to $90/month (males)	Room/board, inmate family support, fines/costs imposed by court, victim restitution
FBP		Self-sustaining revolving fund	Hourly rate	$.23 to $1.15/hour	Inmate family support, fines/costs imposed by court, victim restitution, child support (through Inmate Financial Responsibility Program)
BC	$ 1,600,000	Self-sustaining revolving fund	Flat daily rate; hourly rate	NA	Fines/costs imposed by court, victim restitution
MB	No specific budget	General fund appropriation, combination of self-sustaining and budget financed	Flat daily rate	$5.00/day	Fines/costs imposed by court, victim restitution, inmate welfare fund institutional disciplinary board
NB	No provincial prison industries				
NF	$ 150,000,000	General fund appropriation	No pay	NA	
ON	Must operate within revenues generated	General fund appropriation	No pay	NA	NA
SK	$ 1,253,000	Revolving fund with subsidy	Flat daily rate; production incentive	$11.46/day average	
YK	No provincial prison industries				
CSC	$ 17,500,000 appropriation, $ 56,500,000 sales	General fund appropriation, self-sustaining revolving fund	Flat daily rate; production incentive	Flat daily $5.25-$6.90, incentive $3.55/day average	Room/board, fines/costs imposed by court, savings, inmate welfare fund

Types of Prison Industries

as of January 2000

Industries / Products / Services	Overall Sales	Profit Status	Sell to Private Sector	Private Partnership in Place	Most Profitable Industries	Targeted for Expansion	Least Profitable Industries	Targeted for Change or Elimination
AL Printing, data entry, furniture restoration, vehicle repair, renovation, construction and remodeling, inmate clothing, janitorial chemicals, furniture and seating, office modular systems, paint, boxes, institutional furniture, license plates, metal fabrication, custom furniture	$16,000,000	Profitable	No	No	Janitorial supplies, clothing, construction and remodeling	Yes, construction and janitorial supplies	Boxes and paint	Restructuring to reduce overhead
AK Wood furniture, office panels, open desk systems, ergonomic chairs, slaughter house/meat processing, metal fabrication, auto body repair, commercial/hospital laundry, garment/flat goods	$3,337,442	Profitable	Yes	Yes, PIE-certified operation	Commercial laundry, furniture, auto body repair	No, due to building space constraints	Slaughter house and meat operation	Privatization is under consideration
AZ Agricultural commodities, bakery, bindery, data processing/fulfillment, decals, flat goods, furniture, garments, license plates, mattresses, metal products, printing, refurbishing, signs, telephone services, upholstery	$16,898,580	Profitable	Yes	Yes, for farm and agricultural products, aluminum screened windows, customized doors, inmate labor	Baked goods, inmate clothing, flat goods, copy service, chair kit manufacturing, and private sector partnerships, including inmate labor	Yes, prison industry//private sector and prison industry/governmental partnerships	Furniture, agriculture and data fulfillment	None anticipated
AR Printing, vinyl products, garments, vehicle refurbishing, janitorial products		Profitable	No	No	Printing, vinyl product, garments	Yes	Vehicle refurbishing, janitorial products	Not at this time
CA Bedding, clothing/textiles, detention equipment, detergents, flags, food products, food service equipment, wood and metal furniture, systems furniture, accessories, shoes, books, gloves, signs, stationery products	$154,000,000	Profitable	No	No	Special services	No	Agriculture	No
CO Garments, dairy, wild horse program, office furniture and chairs, farm, printing, heavy equipment, panel systems, ranch, metal products, greenhouse, recycling, institutional furniture, furniture refurbishing, license plate and validation tags, vegetable processing, service station, CAD/GIS, leather products manufacturing, graphic design/signage, computer manufacturing, surplus property, forms management, artifacts restoration, general services/light construction	$29,000,000	Profitable	Yes	No	NA	NA	NA	NA
CT Laundry, printing, clothing, mattresses, woodworking, dental, optical, office systems, metal fabrications, markers, graphic arts, mailing services, DATA CON (data entry), optical imaging (to be operational 6/30100)	$6,279,000		No	One—produces baseball type caps for a variety of markets	Marker, textile, optical	Sheet metal fabrication	Furniture	None

TYPES OF PRISON INDUSTRIES, *continued*

	Industries / Products / Services	Overall Sales	Profit Status	Sell to Private Sector	Private Partnership in Place	Most Profitable Industries	Targeted for Expansion	Least Profitable Industries	Targeted for Change or Elimination
DC	Construction crews, concrete/precast products, metal fabrication, wood shop, upholstery picture framing, silk screening, auto body and paint, printing small appliance repair, vehicle maintenance, grain farming, swine, furniture refurbishing, garment manufacturing	$1,431,059	Loss	Yes	Americorps 'Computers for Classrooms' program	Printing	printing concrete/precast products	Vehicle maintenance, furniture refurbishing, furniture manufacturing	Swine program eliminated and farm operations restructured
DE	Printing, metal fabrication, industrial laundry metal and wood furniture repair, upholstery, metro (cushions for buses and subways)	$4,005,472	Profitable	No	No	License plates, printing upholstery	No	Laundry	All prison industries to be closed along with all Lorton base's institutions
FL	Printing, textiles, metal and wood furniture, boxes, brooms and brushes, cattle, citrus, sugar cane, cleaning chemicals, digital Information services dairy, dental prosthetics, poultry eyewear, fire apparatus renovation, footwear	$78,400,000	Profitable	Yes	Eyewear, trailer components, produce processing	NA	NA	NA	NA
GA	No Response								
HI	Agriculture, beef cattle, bindery construction, furniture, garments, laundry, metal products, printing, refurbishing signs, upholstery, computers, interactive media designs, full-color plotting, CD-Rom duplications, large-scale scanning, A+ computer servicing	$6,200,000	Profitable	Yes	Sewing, furniture and agriculture	Printing and furniture	High-tech products and services	Garments	No
ID	Signs, metal products, office furniture, license plates, microfilm, decals, printing, labor services, agricultural	$6,800,000	Profitable	Yes	Potato producer	License plates	No	Signs	No
IL	Asbestos abatement, bakery, belts, boxes, brooms and wax, call center, central distribution, data entry, dry cleaning, farms furniture and furniture refinishing, garments, knitwear, laundry, mattresses, meat processing, metal furniture, milk processing, optical, modular furniture installation, re-refined oil, recycling, sewing, signs, silk screening and embroidery, soap, tires, vehicle servicing warehouse, waste removal	$ 53,085,489	Profitable	Yes, agricultural Products	No	Food products	Breadmaking	Tire recycling and dry cleaning	Yes, dry cleaning
IN	Metal cabinets, offender garments, license plates, office furniture, mattresses, wood remanufacturing, laundry, CAD, park and patio furniture, mops and brooms, highway signs, GIS, electronic component assembly, printing, boxes, janitorial/hygiene products, laundry chemicals, validation stickers, food products, farming, remanufactured automotive parts	$29,373,000	Profitable	Yes	Electronic component assembly, activation device assembly, remanufactured automotive parts	License plates, validation stickers, laundry	Laundry, food processing, PIE programs	Office furniture, highway signs, GIS	None
IA	Metal stamping, sign, graphic arts, Braille, housekeeping/laundry, metal furniture, custom wood, auto body, furniture, textile tourism, dry cleaning, surplus property, moving and installation, printing, CD Rom	$13,239,954	Profitable	No	No	Metal works	Yes	Braille, automotive	None
KS	Furniture, signs, clothing, paint, janitorial products, farming, microfilm service, data entry, telephone answering, vehicle refurbishing, furniture refurbishing, surplus property service	$10,537,650	Profitable	No	No	Office systems and chairs	Office systems and chairs	Farm products	Combining paint janitorial supply factories and vehicle/furniture refurbishing will change to metal fabrication

	Industries / Products / Services	Overall Sales	Profit Status	Sell to Private Sector	Private Partnership in Place	Most Profitable Industries	Targeted for Expansion	Least Profitable Industries	Targeted for Change or Elimination
KY	No Response								
LA	Furniture/restoration, license plates, mattresses, brooms, mops, metal fabricating, silk screening, sign shop, food distribution, printing, transportation, heavy equipment operations, garments, soaps, detergents, solvents, janitorial services, food processing, office chairs	$21,061,190	Profitable	No	Limited protective garments	Bags, soap, garments, office chairs	Garments, furniture	Printing, silk screening, signs	
ME	Upholstery, garment, compost, printed items, wood products, lumber	$ 750,000 est.	Profitable	Yes	Wood products, garment	Garments, upholstery wood products	Yes, to be determined	Printed items, compost	Yes, to be determined
MD	Furniture restoration, graphics, textiles, metal furniture, brush and carton, upholstery meat, construction, heavy equipment operations, sewing/nags, telemarketing, data entry picture frames, partitions, wood and furniture assembly, license plate tags, signs, mattresses, uniforms, warehousing, reselection, aquaculture, recycling, agriculture	$35,750,429	Profitable	No	Handmade cloth items, metal switchgear components	Meat processing, upholstery modular office systems	Meat processing, modular office systems	Wood, agriculture, recycling, aquaculture	None
MA	Binders, clothing, embroidery, flags, furniture, janitorial supplies, mattresses, milk processing, optical, printing refinishing, signs, silk screening	$11,764,821	Profitable	Yes	No	Optical	Optical, printing	Milk processing	Milk processing
MI	Laundry, optical, data entry, geographical information, restoration/refinishing, dental, shoes, underwear, clothing, textiles, license plates, vinyl products, dimensional lumber, mattress linens, chairs, meat, milk, metal and wood furniture, signs and cartons	$ 31,889,564	Profitable	No	No	License plates, janitorial products, cut and sew	Janitorial products	Data entry, wood furniture, food processing	Yes
MN	Wood furniture, systems furniture, seating products, printing, license plates, vehicle refurbishing, sewn products, paper products, three ring binders, mattresses, laundry, jail furniture, data entry telemarketing, subcontract services, farm machinery, docks and piers, park and patio products	$18,451,541	Profitable	Yes	Subcontracts, including packaging, bird feeders, data entry telemarketing, metal fabrication, systems furniture, laundry	License plates, metal manufacturing, subcontracting	Yes, all are growth industries	Paper products, furniture, vehicle refurbishing, laundry	Yes, all for possible restructuring
MS	Garment/clothing, bedding and linens, office furniture, detention furniture, metal fabrication, janitorial products bookbinding, printing, signs and silk screening, recreational products, equine tack, wood products, holiday decorations, assembling and packaging processing, painting	$4,100,000	Profitable	Yes, within state restrictions	Equine tack, chicken processing	Textiles, metal fabrication	Yes	Printing, bookbinding, equine tack, office furniture	Yes, realignment
MO	Laundry, dry cleaning, metal products, signs, data entry cartridge recycling, printing, clothing and mattress, chair frame and tube bending, graphic arts and engraving, tire recycling, chairs, shoes, furniture, office systems, chemicals, license plates	$31,203,432	Profitable	No	No	Office systems, furniture, chairs	Clothing	Tire recycling	None
MT	Ranching, upholstery, furniture, print, sign, telemarketing, garments, vocational training, vocational education classroom, food bank, motor vehicle maintenance, license plates	$4,967,225	Profitable	Yes	Telemarketing	Ranching	Industries-PIE programs	Print, sign, motor vehicle maintenance, garden, logging	None; Garden and logging closed 10/99

TYPES OF PRISON INDUSTRIES, *continued*

Industries / Products / Services	Overall Sales	Profit Status	Sell to Private Sector	Private Partnership in Place	Most Profitable Industries	Targeted for Expansion	Least Profitable Industries	Targeted for Change or Elimination
NE Wood/metal furniture, furniture reconditioning, paints/stains, painting metal products, Braille transcription, tourism operations, sewn products, modular office systems, clerical, data entry, warehousing/distribution, janitorial products, assembly/ packaging, telemarketing, signs/decals, microfilming, engraving, chairs, large letter printing, work detail crews	$6,700,000	Profitable	Yes, Private Sector Prison Industries	Private Sector Prison Industries	Metal products	Work detail crews, Braille transcribing, Private Venture operations	Wood furniture and chairs	No
NV Printing, bookbinding, linen, mattresses, detergent, license plates, furniture, metal products, agricultural products, wild horses, draperies, auto repair/restoration, stained glass, waterbeds, fiberglass auto bodies, wiring harnesses	$3,290,955	Profitable	Yes	Auto bodies, wiring harnesses, auto restoration, stained glass, waterbeds, card sorting, repackaging	Metal products	Drapery, mattresses, furniture	Drapery	Not at this Time
NH License plates, signs, engraving, indoor signage, printing, stickers, desktop publishing, camera work, custom remanufactured wood products, vegetables, hay, computer recycling, picnic tables, relocation services, forest management, cordwood and campfire wood, bulk mailing, data entry, software development, web page design, hardware integration and networking, computer refurbishing for "Computers for Schools" program, sheeting and towels, metal furniture, light bulb assembly and repair	$2,500,000	Profitable	Yes	No	Farm/cordwood	Information technology	Tailor shop/sheeting and towels	No
NJ Clothing, metal products, printing, knit, furniture, teleresponse, mattress/pillow, sign, data entry, sewing machine repair, brush/mop, auto tag, bakery, concrete and shed	$17,197,000	Not available	No	No	Bakery, auto tag, clothing	No	Data entry, concrete and shed	Concrete and shed was recently taken over from institution operation and is being considered for restructuring
NM Inmate shoes and uniforms, feedlot, dairy, warehousing and transportation, printing, telemarketing, data entry micrographics, boxer shorts, sheets and pillow cases	$5,018,170	Profitable	No	No, but currently in process of establishing two programs	Furniture	Not at this time	Farming	Farming
NY Garments, beds and bedding, furniture, asbestos abatement, soap products, modular housing, printing, signage, eyewear, teleresponse, custom steel fabrication, institutional furnishings, license plates	$72,000,000	Profitable	No	No	Soap, license plates, selected furniture products	All	Garments	Not at this time
NC License tags, sewing items, food processing, paint, janitorial products, farming, printing, laundry, signs, eyewear, wood/metal products, manpower services	$75,000,000	Profitable	No	No, but in formative stage	NA	All industries	NA	None
ND Signs, furniture, upholstery, metal containers, license plates, labor services, specialty sports exercise belts	$2,900,000	Profitable	Yes, with restrictions	Upholstered products for electric cars, specialty sports exercise belts	Furniture, upholstery	Furniture, PIE program	Signs, metal products	None

	Industries / Products / Services	Overall Sales	Profit Status	Sell to Private Sector	Private Partnership in Place	Most Profitable Industries	Targeted for Expansion	Least Profitable Industries	Targeted for Change or Elimination
OH	Furniture, health-tech, institutional, business, automotive products and services, highway signs, flags, refurbishing, auto tags and stickers	$38,500,000	Profitable	Yes	No	As a matter of policy, not available			
OK	Office furniture, ringbinders, printing, traffic control signage, wood and upholstery renovation, metal fabrication, garments, janitorial supplies, chemical products, mattresses, boxes, record conversion, customer services	$15,415,000	Profitable	No	Telemarketing, computer graphics	Modular systems, furniture products	Chemical, janitorial, garments, furniture upholstered products	Printing, chemical, janitorial	
OR	No Response								
PA	Vehicle restoration, optical shop, signs/tags, license plates, cell furniture, inmate clothing, wood/metal furniture, correctional officer uniforms, printing, soap/detergent products, laundry, freight, modular office systems, cartons, shoes	$34,392,914	Profitable	No	No	Garments	Yes	Dairies	Discontinued
RI	Auto body repair, systems furniture, metal fabrication, license plates, janitorial products, paint, garments/flat goods, printing, signs/decals, wood furniture, work detail crews, moving/painting/furniture installation crews	Not provided	Profitable	No	No	Systems furniture and license plates	Systems/office furniture	Auto body	No
SC	Apparel, upholstery, travel reservations, laundry, signs, seating, case goods, packaging, janitorial products, textile recycling, metal products, wire harnesses, mattresses, pillows, tire retread, transmission repair, printing, picture framing, office modular systems, license tags, glove packaging	$20,244,229	Profitable	Yes, through PIE program and service contracts	Hardwood flooring, apparel, faucet handles, wire harnesses, furniture	Laundry, apparel, office modular systems, janitorial products, license tags, wire harnesses, printing, tire retread, glove	All are expanding	Travel reservations, picture framing	
SD	Furniture, upholstery, printing, decals, bookbinding, signs, Braille transcription unit, license plates, machine shop, garment, date entry, eyeglass repair, wheelchair repair, contract welding, machine tool work, woodworking and assembly, electronic assembly, inspection and packaging of automotive parts	$2,001,054	Profitable	Yes	Yes	License plates		Bookbinding	
TN	License plates and decals, security staff and inmate clothing, bedding, metal file cabinets, in-cell furniture, open office landscape systems, furniture refurbishing, office furniture, student desks, dormitory furniture, highway signs and interior signage, highway paint printing, data entry janitorial product packaging, achievement test distribution, draperies and bedspreads, Tenncare/telephone services, laser toner cartridge recycling, sports ball packaging, milk, eggs, tea, fruit drinks, pallets, livestock, crops, firewood	$22,500,000	Profitable	Yes	PIE programs and joint venture partnerships	License plates, business services	Business services	Wood refurbishing	
TX	Garments/textiles, graphics, furniture, metal, chemicals, detergents, computer, GIS, refurbishing computers	$83,000,000	Profitable	No	No	Metal products, textiles	All areas are expected to grow	Wood furniture	

TYPES OF PRISON INDUSTRIES, *continued*

Industries / Products / Services	Overall Sales	Profit Status	Sell to Private Sector	Private Partnership in Place	Most Profitable Industries	Targeted for Expansion	Least Profitable Industries	Targeted for Change or Elimination
UT Asbestos abatement, telephone call center, laser cartridge recycling, community work crews, computers for schools, asphalt crack resealing, construction, data entry textiles, license plates, meat processing, metal fabrication, micrographics, milk processing, commercial sewing, printing, roofing, private telemarketing, seating, signs, tire shredding, document scanning, waste recycling	$12,500,000	Small loss for first time since 1985	Yes, under PIE only	Five PIE programs in operation	License plates, printing, signs	All are currently under evaluation for possible expansion	Furniture	
VT Wood office, institutional and case goods, lumber and timbers, printing, packing, warehousing, shipping, signs, highway signs and silk screen design, license plates	$2,698,800	Loss	No	"PIE manpower model" with capacitor manufacturer	Signs, pack and ship, printing	Pack and ship	Furniture, sawmill	
VA Clothing, license tags, office systems, wood/metal furniture, shoes, vinyl binders, silk screening, laundry, dental, microfilm	$34,000,000	Profitable	Yes	PIE program	Clothing and assembling BBQ grills	Office systems license tags	Wood products	No
WA Asbestos abatement, printing/engraving, bindery, dairy, field crops, flat goods, food factory, furniture, garments, herds, Individual Personal Protection packs, laundry, license plates/ tags, farm vehicle maintenance, mattresses, meat cooking, metal products, office systems/chairs, optical lab, panel installation, ProCAD, drafting, quality/warranty control, signs, recycling, socks, table assembly, underground storage tank	$36,500,000	Profitable	No	No	License plates/tags, optical lab	Optical lab	Field crops, bindery (file folders), net goods	Field crops
WV Validation stickers, janitorial supplies, license plates, printing, signs, Braille books, furniture manufacturing/refinishing, welding, upholstery, linens, seating, mattresses, engraving, inmate undergarments	$5,705,683	Profitable	No	No	License plates, printing, seating	Sign production	Upholstery and inmate under-garments	Incorporating inmate clothing into the undergarment shop
WI Data entry, wood furniture, metal furniture, upholstery, screen printing, systems furniture, computer repair and recycling, textiles, laundry, printing, metal shop and signage	$20,245,000	Profitable	Yes, only under PIE program	Furniture, signage	Metal stamp, sign, wood furniture, upholstery, systems furniture	Sign, wood products, upholstery	Data entry, screen printing	
WY Females: game and fish licenses/data entry, state parks camping permits/data entry. Males: laundry, license plates, printing, garment factory, sign shop	$73,244	Not set up as pro- fit/loss venture	No	No	Data entry and license plates	No	Not determined	None
FBP Apparel, pajamas, knitwear, linens, undergarments, surgical clothing drapes, parachutes, work clothing, general purpose trunks, protective clothing, sweat outfits, metal, shelving/ lockers and cabinets, steel doors and frames, wire cable assemblies, circuit boards, Kevlar products, radio mounts, interactive kiosks, lawn and garden equipment, plaques, decals, data entry, signs, printing laundry, remanufactured laser toner cartridges, household furniture (dormitory and quarters), office furniture (modular systems/Ergo), miscellaneous furniture	$534,279,000	Profitable	No	Yes, for lawn and garden equipment and component parts of inter- active kiosks	Textiles and systems/metal furniture	No	Graphic services and electronics	No

	Industries / Products / Services	Overall Sales	Profit Status	Sell to Private Sector	Private Partnership in Place	Most Profitable Industries	Targeted for Expansion	Least Profitable Industries	Targeted for Change or Elimination
BC	Forestry, silviculture work, campground cleanup, recycling, tailor shops, flowers, firehose repair and drying, fish hatchery	NA	Slight profit	Yes	No	Recycling, specialized services for other government agencies	No	Forestry	No
MB	Call center operation, office furniture manufacturing/repair, specialty items (carpentry), tailor shop, garden/work detail crews	$325,000	Loss	Limited to nonprofit Agencies	Call center, with private TV network; office furniture	Garden/work detail crews	No	Carpentry	Prison industries currently under review by Department of Finance
NB	No provincial prison industries								
NF	Eggs, beef, pork, milk	$150,000,000	Breaking even	Yes	Eggs, beef, pork, milk	Milk	No	Pork	
ON	License plates, laundry, signs, mattresses, grounds maintenance, metal fabrication, tailor shop, textiles	$10,000,000 (Canadian)	Profitable	No	Mattresses	License plates, grounds maintenance, mattresses, linens	Recently expanded tailor shops	Signs	
SK	Custom manufacturing of wood, metal, and fabric products; auto repair	$933,000	Loss	Yes	No	Metal and wood manufacturing	Metal manufacturing	Auto repair	
YK	No provincial prison industries								
CSC	Wood and metal furniture, upholstery, metal lockers/storage, clothing/textiles data collection, telemarketing, laundry, beef, dairy, field crops, construction	$56,500,000	Loss	Yes	Produce parts under contract, produce and sell products under license	Furniture products, metal storage products, laundry	No significant expansions planned at this time	Textiles, agribusiness	

Probation/Parole/Aftercare Service Providers

as of September 30, 1998

	Number Board Members*	Adult Paroling Authorities	Adult Parole Services	Adult Probation Services	Juvenile Parole/Aftercare Services	Juvenile Probation Services
AL	3	Bd Pardons & Paroles	Bd Pardons & Paroles	Bd Pardons & Paroles	Co Courts	Dept Youth Svs ($# only) & Co Cts
AK	5 (PT)	Bd Parole	Dept Corrections	Dept Corrections	No parole/aftercare	DHSS/Div Family & Youth Svcs**
AZ	5	Bd Exec Clemency	Bd Exec Clemency	State Courts	DYTR/Parole Admin	States Courts
AR	7	Post-Prison Transfer Board	Bd C&Cmty Pun/Dept Cmty Pun**	Bd C&Cmty Pun/Dept Cmty Pun**	Courts/DHS/ Youth Svcs Bd	Courts/DHS/Youth Svcs Bd
CA	9	Bd Prison Terms	YAC/DOC/Par & Cmty Svcs Div	Co Courts	YAC/DYA/Parole Svcs & Cmty Corr	Co Courts
CO	7	Bd Parole	DOC/Div Adult Parole Supv	Judicial Dept	DHS/Div Youth Svcs	Judicial Dept
CT	13 (PT)[1]	Bd Parole	DOC/Div Op/Cmty Svcs	Office Adult prob	Dept Children & Families	Superior Court Juv Matters/ Family Div
DE	5 (PT)[1]	Parole Bd	DOC/Div Cmty Svcs	DOC/Div Cmty Svcs	DSCYF/Div Youth Rehab/ Cmty Svcs**	DSCYF/Div Youth Rehab/ Cmty Svcs**
DC	5	Bd Parole	Bd Parole	DC Superior Ct/ Social Svcs Div	DHS/YS Admin/Bu of Ct & Cmty Svcs	DC Superior Ct/ Social Svcs Div
FL	3	Parole Cmsn	DOC/Prob & Parole Svcs**	DOC/Prob & Parole Svcs**	DHRS/Juvenile Justice	DHRS/Juvenile Justice
GA	5	Bd Pardons & Paroles	Bd Pardons & Paroles**	DOC/Cmty Corr Div	DHR/Dept Ch Youth Svcs & Co Courts	DHR/Dept Ch Youth Svcs & Co Courts
HI	3 (PT)[1]	Paroling Authority	Paroling Authority/ Field Svcs	State Judiciary/Prob Ofc	DHS/OYS/Yth Corr Facil/ Cmty Svcs	State Judiciary/Family Courts
ID	5 (PT)	Cmsn for Pardons & Parole	DOC/Div Field & Cmty Svcs	DOC/Div Field & Cmty Svcs	DHW/Bur of Juv Justice	DHW/Bur of Juv Justice/ Co Courts
IL	12	Prisoner Review Bd	DOC/Cmty Svcs Div	Judicial Circuits/Prob Div	DOC/Juv Div/Juv Field Svcs	Judicial Circuits/Prob Div
IN	5	Parole Bd	DOC/Parole Svcs Section	Judicial/County Courts	DOC/Parole Svcs Section	Judicial/County Courts
IA	5 (PT)[1]	Bd Parole	DOC/Div Cmty Corr Svcs	DOC/Div Cmty Corr Svcs	DHS/Div Adult, Children & Family Svcs	Judicial Districts
KS	4	Parole Bd	DOC/Cmty Field Svcs**	Judicial Districts/ Ct Svcs Div	Juvenile Justice Authority	Judicial Districts/Ct Svcs Div
KY	7	Parole Bd	DOC/Cmty Svcs & Facil/ Div PP	DOC/Cmty Svcs & Facil/ Div PP	Dept Juvenile Justice	Dept Juvenile Justice
LA	7	Bd Parole	DPSC/Div Prob & Parole**	DPSC/Div Prob & Parole**	DPSC/Ofc Youth Development	DPSC/Ofc Youth Development
ME	5 (PT)	Parole Bd[2]	DOC/Div Prob & Parole	DOC/Div Prob & Parole	DOC/Div Prob & Parole	DOC/Div Prob & Parole
MD	8	Parole Cmsn	DPSCS/Div Parole & Prob	DPSCS/Div Parole & Prob	Dept Juv Svcs	Dept Juv Svcs
MA	8	Parold Bd	Parole Bd	Office of Cmsnr Prob/Courts	DYS/Bur Cmty Svcs	Office of Cmsnr of Prob/ Courts
MI	10	Parole Bd	DOC/Field Op Admin	DOC/Field Op Admin & Dist Cts	DSS/Office Delinq Svcs/ Co Cts	DSS/Office Delinq Svcs/ Co Cts
MN	4 (PT)[3]	DOC/Office Adult Release**	DOC/Prob Par Supv Rel**/Co Cts or Cca	DOC/Prob Par Supv Rel**/Co Cts or CCA	DOC/Prob Par Supv Rel**/Co Cts or CCA	DOC/Prob Par Supv Rel**/ Co Cts or CCA
MS	5	Parole Bd	DOC/Cmty Svcs Div	DOC/Cmty Svcs Div	DHS/DYS/Cmty Svcs Div	DHS/DYS/Cmty Svcs Div
MO	5	Bd Prob & Parole	DOC/Bd Prob & Parole	DOC/Bd Prob & Parole	DSS/Div Youth Svcs & Jud Circuits	Judicial Circuits
MT	3 (PT)	Bd Pardons & Parole	DCHS/CD/Prob & Parole Bureau	DCHS/CD/Prob & Parole Bureau	Dept Family Svcs/ Corr Div	Judicial Districts
NE	5	Bd Parole	DCS/Adult Parole Admin**	NE Prob System	DJS/Juv Parole Admin**	NE Prob System
NV	7	Bd Parole Cmsnrs	DMV/Div Parole & Prob	DMV/Div Parole & Prob	DHR/YCS/Youth Parole Bureau	District Courts
NH	7 (PT)	BD Parole	DOC/Div Field Svcs**	DOC/Div Field Svcs**	DHHS/DCYS/ Bur Children	DHHS/DCYS/Bur Children

	Number Board Members*	Adult Paroling Authorities	Adult Parole Services	Adult Probation Services	Juvenile Parole/Aftercare Services	Juvenile Probation Services
NJ	9	Parole Bd	DOC/Bureau Parole	The Judiciary/Prob Div	DLPS/Juvenile Justice Cmsn	DLPS/Juvenile Justice Cmsn
NM	4	Adult Parole Bd	CD/Prob & Parole Div**	CD/Prob & Parole Div**	CYFD/Cmty Svcs Div	CYFD/Cmty Svcs Div
NY	19	Bd Parole	Div Parole	Div Prob & Corr Alt/ Co Courts	Exec Dept/Div for Youth/ Div Parole**	Exec Dept/Div Prob & Corr Alt/Courts
NC	5[4]	Parole Cmsn	DOC/Div Adult Prob & Parole	DOC/Div Adult Prob & Parole	Admin Office Courts/ Juv Svcs Div	Admin Office Courts/ Juv Svcs Div
ND	3 (PT)	Parole Bd	DCR/Div Parole & Prob	DCR/Div Parole & Prob	DCR/Div Juv Svcs**	DCR/Div Juv Svcs**/Supr Cts
OH	12[5]	DRC/Prob & Parole Field Svcs/Ad Parole Auth & Parole Bd**	DRC/Prob & Parole Field Svcs**	DRC/Prob & Parole Field Svcs** & Co Courts	DYS/Div Courts, Par, & Cmty Svcs**	Co Court
OK	5 (PT)	Pardon & Parole Bd	DOC/Prob & Parole Svcs**	DOC/Prob & Parole Svcs**	DHS/OJA/Juvenile Svcs Unit**	DHS/OHH/Juvenile Svcs Unit**
OR	3	Bd Parole & Post Prison Supv	DOC/Cmty Corrections	DOC/Cmty Corrections	OR Youth Authority	OR Youth Authority
PA	5[6]	Bd Prob & Parole & Co Cts.[6]	Bd Prob & Parole & Co Cts	Bd of Prob & Parole** & Co Cts	Co Courts	Co Courts
RI	6 (PT)	Parole Bd	DOC/Div Rehab Svcs	DOC/Div Rehab Svcs	DCYF/Div Juv Corr Svcs	DCYF/Div Juv Corr Svcs
SC	7 (PT)	Bd Paroles & Pardons	Dept Prob, Parole & Prdn Svcs	Dept Prob, Parole &, Prdn Svcs	Dept Juv Justice/ Cmty Div	Dept Juv Justice/Cmty Div
SD	6 (PT)	Bd Pardons & Paroles	DOC	Unified Judicial Sys/ Ct Svcs Dept	Unified Judicial Sys/ Ct Svcs Dept	Unified Judicial Sys/ Ct Svcs Dept
TN	7	Bd Paroles	BP/Parole Field Svcs**	DOC/Adult Field Svcs**	DCS/Juv Corr Div**	DCS/Juv Corr Div**
TX	18	Bd Pardons & Paroles	TDCJ/PPD/Parole Supv	TDCJ/Cmty Jus Asist Div/ Dist Cts	TYC/Cmty Svcs Div/ Ofc Par Supv**	Co Courts
UT	5	Bd Pardons	DOC/Div Field Operations	DOC/Div Field Operations	DHS/Div Youth Corr	Juv Courts
VT	5 (PT)	Bd Parole	AHS/DOC	AHS/DOC	AHS/DSRS[7]	DSRS/Div Social Svcs
VA	5	Parole Bd	DOC/Div Cmty Corr	DOC/Div Cmty Corr	Dept Youth & Fam Svcs**	Dept Youth & Fam Svcs**
WA	3	Indeterminate Sent Review Bd	DOC/Div Cmty Corr	DOC/Div Cmty Corr & Co Cts	DSHS/Juv Rehab Admin	Co Courts
WV	5	Parole Board	DPS/Div Corrections	DPS/DOC & Judicial Circuits	DMAPS/DJS (Compact) and courts	DMAPS/DJS (Compact), Jud Circuits[8]
WI	5	Parole Cmsn	DOC/Div Prob & Parole	DOC/Div Prob & Parole	DOC/Co Soc Svcs Depts	Co Social Svcs Depts
WY	7 (PT)	Bd Parole	DOC/Div Field Svcs	DOC/Div Field Services	Dept Family Svcs	Dept Family Svcs/ Co Munic Depts
US	9	Parole Cmsn**	Admin Ofc of US Courts	Admin Ofc of US Courts/Div of Prob		

Notes:

*   All members serve full-time unless coded "PT."
**   Accredited by Commission on Accreditation for Corrections.
1.   Chairman serves full-time; members part-time.
2.   ME—Parole Board hears pre-1976 cases of parole. Flat sentences with no parole under criminal code effective 5/1/76.
3.   MN—Executive Officer & three Deputy Executive Officers (CCA Cmty Corr Act.)
4.   NC—commissioners
5.   OH—Plus 19 hearing officers.
6.   PA—The Board of Probation and Parole administers adult services when sentence is over 2 yrs; county courts when sentence is 2 yrs or less. 3 members are part-time.
7.   VT—No functional juvenile parole system. Children in custody go into placement and eventually return to community under supervision of caseworker.
8.   WV—Under state statute, juv release is judicially, rather than administratively, determined and is considered probation.
The following states have one or more independent county, municipal or city departments: CO, GA, IN, KS, KY, LA, MO, NE, NY, OK, TN, WY.
All Boards are independent except MD, MI, MN, OH, TX.

Community Corrections: Administration
as of June 1999

	Budget Allocation	Category Considerations	Oversight Responsibility	Eligibility Determination	Assignments
AL	1% approximately	Alternative to prison	Local governments	Left to department or courts by state law[1]	Courts
AK	Unknown	Alternative to prison; enhanced probation/parole for violators	Department of corrections	Nonviolent offenders; probation/parole violators; department of corrections	Department of corrections
AZ	1.5%	Transition, post-incarceration	Department of corrections	All offenders released to community under supervision	Department of corrections; statutory releases; Board of Executive Clemency
AR	Department of Community Punishment established as separate state agency	Alternative to prison; transition, post-incarceration	Department of Community Punishment	Nonviolent offenders; first-time offenders; probation/parole basic and violators	Courts; Post Prison Transfer Board
CA	4.463% approximately	Relieve overcrowding, mandated by state legislature	Department of corrections, custody; local government, housing and supervision (peace officer); private company, housing and super vision (nonpeace officer)	All inmates and parole violators who meet criteria for placement in CCF facility	Department of corrections
CO	No Response				
CT	3.92%	Transition, post-incarceration	Department of corrections[2]	Nonviolent offenders	Department of corrections
DE	15.8%	Alternative to prison; transition, post-incarceration	State department of corrections	Nonviolent offenders; first-time offenders; probation/parole violators	Courts
DC	3% approximately	Alternative to prison (one center); transition, post-incarceration (four contract houses)	Local governments	Nonviolent offenders; first-time offenders; probation/parole violators; violent offenders; mandatory releases; and considered by department or courts	Courts; department of corrections
FL	13.9%	Alternative to prison	Department of corrections	Department of corrections	Courts; Parole Commission
GA	No Response				
HI	No Response				
ID	No Response				
IL	4.3%	Transition, post-incarceration	Department of corrections	Nonviolent offenders; first-time offenders; probation/parole violators	Department of corrections
IN	No Response				
IA	23.6%	Alternative to prison; transition, post-incarceration; pretrial release	Department of corrections[3]	All offenders are potential participants, including pretrial release	Department of corrections
KS	7%	Alternative to prison	Local governments, with funding and oversight by department of corrections	Determined by Sentencing Guidelines; parole violators through contracts with KDOC	Courts; department of corrections

	Budget Allocation	Category Considerations	Oversight Responsibility	Eligibility Determination	Assignments
KY	.25%	Alternative to prison	State department of corrections	Nonviolent offenders; first-time offenders; probation/parole violators	Courts
LA	1%	Alternative to prison (probation); transition, post-incarceration (parole); work release	All offenders by statute	Department of corrections (including probation and parole)	Courts; department of corrections
ME	Less than 9%	New program; concept of post-release services into community supervision	Department of corrections	Courts	Courts (probation); department of corrections (prerelease and supervised community confinement)
MD	No Response				Department of corrections
MA	11%	Transition, post-incarceration	Department of corrections	Department of corrections or courts	Courts; department of corrections
MI	2%, plus 7% for probation, parole and electronic monitoring functions	Alternative to prison	Department of corrections; probation/parole; local governments	Nonviolent offenders; probation/parole violators; some offenders convicted of assaultive offenses (depending on behavior pattern)	
MN	No Response				
MS	9.5%	Alternative to prison; transition, post-incarceration	Department of corrections	Nonviolent offenders; first-time offenders; probation/parole violators; considered by department or courts	Courts; department of corrections
MO	4%	Alternative to prison; transition, post-incarceration; supervision option	Department of corrections	Department of corrections or courts	Courts; department of corrections; probation/parole officers
MT	33%	Alternative to prison; transition, post-incarceration; pre-release, probation/parole	Department of corrections	All offenders, with no restrictions	Courts; boards of pardons/paroles
NE	.6%	Alternative to prison; transition, post-incarceration	Department of corrections	Nonviolent offenders; first-time offenders, nonhabituals	Courts
NV	1% (not including inmate payments for room and board)	Community trustee housing with work release	Department of corrections	Department of corrections or courts	Department of corrections
NH	2.35%	Transition, post-incarceration	State department of corrections	Nonviolent offenders; first-time offenders; probation/parole violators, or courts	Department of corrections
NJ	5%	Transition, post-incarceration	Department of corrections	Department of corrections or courts	Department of corrections
NM	16%	Alternative to prison; transition, post-incarceration	Department of corrections; probation and parole division	Nonviolent offenders; first-time offenders; probation/parole violators; department of corrections or courts and parole board	Courts; department of corrections (jointly approved by courts for probationers or parole board for parolees)
NY					

¹Community corrections is not included in the mandates of the state's department of corrections

COMMUNITY CORRECTIONS: ADMINISTRATION, continued

	Budget Allocation	Category Considerations	Oversight Responsibility	Eligibility Determination	Assignments
NC	14%	Alternative to prison; transition, post-incarceration	Department of corrections	Nonviolent offenders; first-time offenders; probation/parole violators	Courts; department of corrections
ND	16%	Alternative to prison; transition, post-incarceration	Department of corrections	Nonviolent offenders; first-time offenders; probation/parole violators; department of corrections; courts	Courts; department of corrections
OH	13.6%	Transition, post-incarceration; also provide grant funds to local justice systems for alternative sanctions to jail and prison	Department of corrections; grant funds to local justice systems for most probation oversight	Nonviolent offenders; first-time offenders; probation/parole violators; department of corrections; courts	Courts, department of corrections
OK	5%	Transition, post-incarceration	Department of corrections; probation/parole division	Nonviolent offenders	Department of corrections
OR	No Response				
PA	4.5% approximately	Transition, post-incarceration	Department of corrections; probation/parole staff assist with residents	Nonviolent offenders; first-time offenders; probation/parole violators; prerelease[4]	Department of corrections referrals from parole board
RI	6% (includes those sentenced, those awaiting trial and community corrections)	Alternative to prison; transition, post-incarceration	Department of corrections	All adult offenders; specific guidelines for some programs apply	Courts; department of corrections; parole board
SC	100% (probation and parole)	Alternative to prison; transition, post-incarceration	Probation/parole	Nonviolent offenders; first-time offenders; probation/parole violators; department of corrections, courts	Courts; parole board
SD	Not a separate budget but included in institutional and parole aftercare	Transition, post-incarceration	Department of corrections	Nonviolent offenders (for work release and classified to minimum custody)	Department of corrections
TN	2%	Alternative to prison	Probation/parole	Nonviolent offenders; first-time offenders; courts	Courts
TX	7%, parole; 10%, probation (not including indirect administration)	Transition, post-incarceration (parole)	Probation/parole (probation jointly designed, funded and monitored by local and state entities)	Department of corrections or courts	Courts for probation; board of pardons for parole
UT	19%	Alternative to prison; transition, post-incarceration; sentencing option	Department of corrections	Nonviolent offenders; first-time offenders; probation/parole violators; or as determined by parole board or courts	Courts, parole board
VT	No percentage allotted	A continuum of risk management and other services for offenders, victims and communities	Department of corrections	All offenders participate in community corrections programs	Department of corrections
VA	36.6%	Alternative to prison	Department of corrections; probation/parole	Nonviolent offenders; first-time offenders; probation/parole violators	Courts

	Budget Allocation	Category Considerations	Oversight Responsibility	Eligibility Determination	Assignments
WA	21%	Transition, post-incarceration (from jail)	Department of corrections	Nonviolent offenders (certain programs); first-time offenders; violators; department of corrections or courts	Courts; department of corrections
WV	3%	Transition, post-incarceration	Department of corrections	Nonviolent offenders; first-time offenders	Department of corrections
WI	23.5%	Transition, post-incarceration; sentencing alternative	Department of corrections; probation/parole	Nonviolent offenders; first-time offenders; probation/parole violators	Courts
WY	7.5%	Alternative to prison; transition, post-incarceration	Department of corrections	Nonviolent offenders; first-time offenders; probation/parole violators; department of corrections or courts; parole board, statutory guidelines	Courts; department of corrections; parole board
BC	18.4%	Alternative to prison; transition, post-incarceration; court-ordered supervision; direct placement (probation)	Provincial Ministry of Attorney General	Nonviolent offenders; first-time offenders; probation/parole violators; courts (supervision); specialized program participants (wife assaulters, sex offenders), etc.	Courts
MB	25% approximately	Alternative to prisons; transition, post-incarceration	Provincial department of corrections	Nonviolent offenders; first-time offenders; probation/parole violators; those sentenced to community supervision	Department of corrections
NB	15% approximately (based on 1997-98 budget)	Alternative to prison; transition, post-incarceration	Probation/parole; private company	Nonviolent offenders; first-time offenders; department of corrections or courts	Courts; department of corrections
NF	16% approximately	Court-ordered supervision (probation)	Provincial department of corrections	Court-ordered supervision (probation)	Courts
ON	14.4%	Alternative to prison, transition, post-incarceration	Provincial department of corrections; probation/parole	Nonviolent offenders; first-time offenders; probation/parole violators; department of corrections or courts; offence specific, such as male batterer, anti-shoplifting, etc.	Courts; department of corrections
SK	19%	Alternative to prison; transition, post-incarceration	Provincial department of corrections; probation/parole	Department of corrections or courts; defined on basis of risk/needs and availability of appropriate interventions	Courts; department of corrections
YK	A Community Corrections unit operates within the Community and Correctional Services Branch, providing all probation services				

Notes:

1. ALABAMA: Felons must meet a minimum 10-point total for the state to reimburse county authority for contract amount. No violent or first-degree sex offenders are reimbursed by state funds.
2. CONNECTICUT: Program responses are specific to department of corrections' Community Enforcement program, halfway houses and transitional supervision program. Judicial branch has AIC programs and Board of Parole has parole supervision.
3. IOWA: State department of corrections provides funding, program direction and oversight; however, each of the eight districts has a board consisting of county supervisors and local interested persons who hire a director and govern local operations.
4. PENNSYLVANIA: Prerelease qualified inmates must be within 1 year of their minimum sentence dates, have served half of their minimum sentences and been incarcerated in a state correctional institution for at least 9 months.

Community Corrections: Programs and Services

as of June 1999

	Program Components	Program Services	Use of Volunteers	Interagency Involvements
AL	Electronic monitoring, house arrest, residential living, day reporting centers, full-time treatment, community service, restitution	Substance abuse counseling, GED, job training, cognitive skills, housing, job search	No	Sometimes
AK	Electronic monitoring, residential living, community service, restitution	Substance abuse counseling, GED, cognitive skills, job search, transportation	No	Yes for substance abuse, cognitive skills, education, etc.
AZ	Electronic monitoring, house arrest, community service, restitution, community supervision and referral to treatment (state offsets cost)	Job search by staff; substance abuse counseling, GED, job training, parenting skills and health care, each by referral to community agencies	Yes, to assist parole officers	Yes, as noted in the listing of program services
AR	Electronic monitoring, house arrest, residential living, full-time treatment, community service, restitution; day reporting centers in planning stage	Substance abuse counseling, GED, job training, cognitive skills, housing (Transitional Living), job search, mental health treatment, behavioral modification, therapeutic community	Yes, AA/NA sponsors, chaplaincy, college interns, and for special programming	Yes, to provide necessary services for the offenders
CA	System operates community corrections centers that provide community service through supervised inmate work crews; one CCF facility accepts civil narcotic addicts assigned to full-time substance abuse programs	Substance abuse counseling, GED, cognitive skills, parenting skills, health care (minimal on site services), computer classes and culinary training (at some CCF facilities)	Yes, AA/NA sponsors	Sometimes, as outside consultants
CO	No Response			
CT	Electronic monitoring, residential living, day reporting centers, full-time treatment, community service, restitution	Substance abuse counseling, GED, job training, cognitive skills, housing, job search, transportation, parenting skills, health care	Yes, as mentors, transportation, AA/NA sponsors	Yes, private, nonprofit residential and nonresidential programs
DE	Electronic monitoring, house arrest, residential living, day reporting centers, full-time treatment, community service, restitution	Substance abuse counseling, GED, job training, housing, job search, transportation, parenting skills	Yes	Yes
DC	Residential living	Substance abuse counseling, GED, job training, housing, job search, transportation, parenting skills, health care	Yes, as mentors for academic tutoring and bible study, conducting AA/NA meetings; proposal pending for additional use	Yes, for food and medical services
FL	Electronic monitoring, house arrest, residential living, full-time treatment, community service, restitution	All services are contracted to private vendors	Yes, as mentors and to provide assistance to probation officers in their offices	Yes, drug counseling, Global Positioning System, electronic monitoring
GA	No Response			
HI	No Response			
ID	No Response			
IL	Electronic monitoring, residential living, day reporting centers, full-time treatment	Substance abuse, GED, job training, cognitive skills, housing, job search, transportation, parenting skills	Yes, AA/NA sponsors	Yes, substance abuse counseling

	Program Components	Program Services	Use of Volunteers	Interagency Involvements
IN	No Response			
IA	Electronic monitoring, house arrest, residential living, day reporting centers, full-time treatment, community service, restitution, Violator Program[1]	None as a direct provider but in some cases will help access services	Yes, as mentors, AA/NA sponsors, education and community service	Yes, but varies by district and program
KS	Electronic monitoring, house arrest, residential living (in two populous counties), day reporting centers, full-time treatment, community service, restitution	Substance abuse counseling, GED, job training, cognitive skills, housing, job search, transportation, child care, parenting skills	Yes, in a variety of tasks related to offender supervision	Yes, substance abuse treatment, sex offender treatment, mental health counseling
KY	Electronic monitoring, house arrest, community service, restitution, drug court	Substance abuse counseling, GED, job training, cognitive skills, job search, transportation, parenting skills, drug testing	No	No, but grantees may contract
LA	Electronic monitoring (parole), house arrest (probation), community service, restitution	Job search; division makes referrals for other services to community agencies	Yes, as mentors, support staff and to assist in investigations	Sometimes, drug testing for training purposes (work release)
ME	Electronic monitoring, house arrest, community service, restitution	Substance abuse counseling, GED, job training, health care	Yes, transportation and AA/NA sponsors	Yes, with Volunteers of America (prerelease)
MD	No Response			
MA	Electronic monitoring, full-time treatment, community service, restitution (if court ordered), maintenance of minimum and prerelease institutions designed to responsibly reintegrate offenders	Substance abuse counseling, GED, job training, cognitive skills, job search, transportation, parenting skills, health care	Yes, as mentors, AA/NA sponsors, and program facilitators inside for AA/NA, Violence Reduction, etc.	Yes, operating two Community Resource Centers that provide basic education, cognitive skill programming and job training/placement
MI	Electronic monitoring, house arrest, residential living, day reporting centers, full-time treatment, community service, restitution	Substance abuse counseling, GED, job training, cognitive skills, job search, parenting skills	Yes, as mentors and AA/NA sponsors	Yes[2]
MN	No Response			
MS	Electronic monitoring, house arrest, community service, restitution, field officers	Substance abuse counseling, GED, cognitive skills, job search, transportation, parenting skills, health care	No	No
MO	Electronic monitoring, residential living, day reporting centers, full-time treatment, community service, restitution	Substance abuse counseling, GED, job training, cognitive skills, housing, job search, transportation	Yes, probation and parole officers	Yes, electronic monitoring, housing, substance abuse treatment
MT	Electronic monitoring, day reporting centers, community service, restitution	Variety of programs are offered through transition centers	No	Sometimes
NE	Unknown as this is the first year of program implementation	Unknown as this is the first year of program implementation	Yes, whatever communities desire	No
NV	Restitution	Housing, job search, health care	No	No
NH	Residential living	Cognitive skills, housing, job search, goal seeking, budgeting	Yes, as mentors and AA/NA sponsors	No
NJ	Electronic monitoring, residential living, day reporting centers, full-time treatment, community service, restitution	Substance abuse counseling, GED, job training, cognitive skills, housing, job search, parenting skills, health care	Yes, as AA/NA sponsors	Yes, with agencies for residential, community release programs

COMMUNITY CORRECTIONS: PROGRAMS AND SERVICES, *continued*

	Program Components	Program Services	Use of Volunteers	Interagency Involvements
NM	Electronic monitoring and house arrest (if appropriate to community risk), residential living (limited), day reporting centers, full-time treatment, community service, restitution (if court-ordered)	Substance abuse counseling, GED, job training, cognitive skills, housing (2-month assistance), job search, parenting skills, social skills/anger management, special needs counseling	Yes, as AA/NA sponsors and with literacy and GED programs	Yes, treatment and monitoring services and for specific supervision
NY	Community corrections is not included in the mandates of the state's department of corrections			
NC	Electronic monitoring, house arrest, day reporting centers, full-time treatment, community service, restitution	Substance abuse counseling, GED, job training, cognitive skills, job search, transportation, parenting skills	Yes, as mentors and AA/NA sponsors	Yes, with local and state agencies such as community colleges and mental health centers
ND	Electronic monitoring, house arrest, residential living, day reporting centers, full-time treatment, community service, restitution	Substance abuse counseling, GED, job training, cognitive skills, housing, job search, parenting skills	Yes, as mentors and for life skills training	Yes, for all noted services
OH	Electronic monitoring, house arrest, residential living, day reporting centers, full-time treatment, community service (probation only), restitution (probation only)	Substance abuse counseling, GED (by referral), job training, housing (by referral), job search, parenting skills, sex offender groups and mental health counseling	Yes, to provide life skills and program options under supervision	Yes, for sex offender, mental health and substance abuse services
OK	Electronic monitoring, residential living, day reporting centers, full-time treatment, community service, restitution	Substance abuse counseling, GED, job training, cognitive skills, housing, job search, transportation, parenting skills, health care	Yes, as mentors, AA/NA sponsors and for transportation	Sometimes
PA	Residential living, full-time treatment (in some cases), community service, restitution	Substance abuse counseling, housing, job search and maintaining in the community, parenting skills, and a variety of support services within the community	Yes, AA/NA sponsors	Yes, approximately 75% of participants for housing
RI	Electronic monitoring (also for parole), house arrest, full-time treatment (substance abuse/parole), community service, restitution, sex offender treatment, domestic violence program	Substance abuse counseling, job training, batterers and sex offender treatment intervention	Yes, AA sponsors and for court coverage	Yes, substance abuse and sex offender treatment
SC	Electronic monitoring, house arrest, residential living, community service, restitution	Substance abuse counseling, GED, job training, cognitive skills, parenting skills (each by referral), housing, job search	Yes, AA/NA sponsors	Sometimes
SD	Residential living, community service, restitution	Substance abuse counseling, GED, job training, housing, job search, transportation, parenting skills, health care	No	Yes, for halfway houses
TN	Electronic monitoring, residential living, day reporting centers, full-time treatment, community service, restitution	Substance abuse counseling, GED, job training, cognitive skills, job search	Yes, AA/NA sponsors	No
TX	Electronic monitoring, residential living (probation only), day reporting centers, full-time treatment (parole only), community service, restitution[3]	Substance abuse counseling, GED, job training (probation only), cognitive skills (parole only), job search, parenting skills (parole only)[4]	Yes, as mentors and for AA/NA sponsors (probation only); conducting specialized classes (parole only)	Yes, parole with halfway houses and probation for residential services
UT	Electronic monitoring, residential living, day reporting centers, full-time treatment, community service, restitution, probation and parole supervision, halfway houses	Substance abuse counseling, GED, job training, cognitive skills, housing, job search, parenting skills	Yes, mentors, AA/NA sponsors, office aides	Yes, mental health agencies

	Program Components	Program Services	Use of Volunteers	Interagency Involvements
VT	Restorative casework, day treatment, intensive supervision	Substance abuse counseling, high school, job training, cognitive skills, housing, job search, child care, parenting skills, health care	Yes	Yes
VA	Electronic monitoring, house arrest, residential living, day reporting centers, full-time treatment, community service, restitution, intensive supervision	Substance abuse counseling, GED, job training, cognitive skills, housing, job search, parenting skills, health care (limited, in residential centers)	Yes, mentors; also, variety of tasks done by student interns	Yes, with public mental health and substance abuse agencies
WA	Electronic monitoring, day reporting centers, community service, restitution, general supervision if court-ordered	Substance Abuse counseling, cognitive skills	Yes, AA/NA sponsors	No
WV	Day reporting centers, full-time treatment, community service, restitution	Substance abuse counseling, GED, job training, cognitive skills, housing, job search, transportation, health care	No	Sometimes
WI	Electronic monitoring, residential living, day reporting centers, part- and full-time treatment, community service, restitution	Substance abuse counseling, GED (by referral), job training, cognitive skills, housing, job search, transportation, child care and parenting skills (both by referral), sex offender, domestic violence and anger management	No	Yes, for specific programs, statewide and area
WY	House arrest, residential living, community service, restitution	Substance abuse counseling, job training, cognitive skills, housing, job search, transportation	Yes, mentors, transportation and as AA/NA sponsors	Yes, via private contracts with local correctional boards
BC	Electronic monitoring, community service, restitution, general supervision if court-ordered (probation)	Substance abuse counseling, planning to establish GED, job training and cognitive skills	No	Yes, in most programs, such as sex offender treatment and spousal assault
MB	Community service, restitution	Substance abuse counseling, job training, cognitive skills, job search, transportation	Yes, as mentors	Sometimes, in domestic violence intervention program
NB	House arrest, community service, restitution, community-based treatment	Substance abuse counseling, cognitive skills, job search, anger management, spousal abuse treatment	Yes, AA/NA sponsors	Yes, all community-based programs
NS	House arrest, community service, restitution (each is for probation)	Probation enforcement and supervision	Yes, for supervision	Sometimes, in treatment and assessment
ON	Electronic monitoring, residential living, day reporting centers, part-time treatment, community service	Substance abuse counseling, job training, cognitive skills, job search, parenting skills, literacy, restitution, domestic violence prevention, anger management, sexual abuse counseling, anti-shoplifting	Yes, mentors, AA/NA sponsors, literacy efforts and supervision	Yes (fee-for-service contracts)
SK	Electronic monitoring, residential living, day reporting centers, community service, restitution	Substance abuse counseling, cognitive skills, housing, job search, parenting skills, sex offenders, spousal abuse, spiritual healing	Yes, mentors and AA/NA sponsors	Yes, some educational programs targeted at criminogenic needs
YK	The Department of Justice currently is developing alternative measures framework and protocol (post-incarceration)			Yes, via Department of Justice within six communities for supervision

Notes:
1. IOWA: The Violator Program is a prison-based, short-term program that allows offenders to maintain probation/parole status.
2. MICHIGAN: state contracts with local governments for implementation of local comprehensive corrections plans; local governments, in turn, use funds to purchase services per contractual terms and conditions.
3. TEXAS: Probation and parole also participate in intensive supervision, surveillance and specialized caseloads. Additionally, parole contracts with halfway houses for special needs offenders.
4. TEXAS: Probation provides nonacademic education classes, victim services and a battering intervention and prevention project. Parole offers sex offender treatment, mentally retarded/impaired and special needs programs, as well as family support groups.

Community Corrections: Participation

as of June 1999

	PRE-INCARCERATION		WORK RELEASE		EDUCATIONAL RELEASE		OTHER SERVICES		Effect on Prison Population
	Men/Women	Completions	Men/Women	Completions	Men/Women	Completions	Men/Women	Completions	
AL	503 / 109	Not available	NA	NA	NA	NA	NA	NA	Fewer coming to prison
AK	Not available	Not available	Not available	Not available	Not available	Not available	Not available	Not available	Fewer coming to prison
AZ	NA	NA	55 total	Not available	NA	NA	0 / 30 approx.	Not available	NA
AR	24,391 / 9,192	12%	0	NA	0	NA	0	NA	Fewer coming to prison
CA	NA	NA	NA	NA	NA	NA	NA	NA	Hasn't stopped increases
CO	No Response								
CT	NA	NA	395 / 38 (community enforcement program)	94%	NA	NA	778 / 125[1]	73.5%	NA
DE	NA	NA	NA	NA	NA	NA	NA	NA	NA
DC	240 / 45	57%	275 / 53	65%	3 / 0	1%	185 / 8	64%	Hasn't stopped increases
FL	111,954 / 32,880	57.6%	1,374 / 180	91%	NA	NA	112,540 / 32,917	NA	Fewer coming to prison
GA	No Response								
HI	No Response								
ID	No Response								
IL	NA	NA	1,231 / 121	73.3%	NA	NA	550 / 123	71.1%	NA
IN	No Response								
IA	987 / 252[2]	94.5%	NA	NA	NA	NA	NA	NA	Fewer coming to prison
KS	4,386 combined	NA	121 combined	NA	NA	NA	NA	NA	Hasn't stopped increases
KY	Not available	Not available	Not available	Not available	Not available	Not available	Not available	Not available	Fewer coming to prison
LA	Not available	Not available	657 / 40	Not available	NA	NA	NA	NA	NA
ME	7,300 / 300	12%	100 / 0	NA	NA	NA	10 / 0	NA	NA
MD	No Response								
MA	NA	NA	324 / 24	Not available [3]	25 / 0 [3]	Not available [3]	1,657 / 112	60% approx.	NA
MI									Fewer coming to prison but population increased because length of stay has increased
MN	No Response								
MS	NA		Based in restitution centers	Not available	NA	NA	NA	NA	NA
MO	1,000 / 100	Not available	NA	NA	NA	NA	Not available	60%	Fewer coming to prison
MT	NA	NA	NA	NA	NA	NA	22 / 3	Not available	Fewer coming to prison, but female increase is noted

	PRE-INCARCERATION		WORK RELEASE		EDUCATIONAL RELEASE		OTHER SERVICES		Effect on Prison Population
	Men/Women	Completions	Men/Women	Completions	Men/Women	Completions	Men/Women	Completions	
NE	NA	NA	NA	NA	NA	NA	NA	NA	Program too new to determine
NV	NA	NA	117 / 20	85%	NA	NA	NA	NA	NA (not used for pre incarceration)
NH	NA	NA	132 115	90%	NA	NA	NA	NA	Fewer coming to prison
NJ	NA	NA	NA	NA	NA	NA	NA	NA	NA
NM	309 / 104	42% (probationers)	NA	NA	NA	NA	253 / 49	31% (parole)	Hasn't stopped increases
NY	[4]								
NC	84,456 / 22,853	Not available	NA	NA	NA	NA	NA	NA	Fewer coming to prison
ND	2,650 / 250	75%	NA	NA	NA	NA	28 / 2	75%	Fewer coming to prison
OH	11,500	Not available	NA	NA	NA	NA	294 / 55	Not available	Fewer coming to prison
OK	NA	NA	230 / 109[5]	95%	NA	NA	56 / 5	96%	NA
OR	No Response		NA	NA	NA	NA	2,105 / 106	Not available	NA
PA	NA	NA	NA	NA	NA	NA	NA	NA	Not available
RI	23,000 (probation and community)	92% (probation)	81 / 35	NA	NA	NA	NA	NA	Not available
SC	NA	NA	NA	NA	0 / 0	NA	180 / 24	NA	NA
SD	NA	NA	54 / 12	73%	0 / 0	NA	0 / 0	NA	NA
TN	4,544 combined	NA	0 / 0	NA	0 / 0	NA	0 / 0	NA	Fewer coming to prison
TX	355,847 approx. / 75,483 approx.	Not available	NA	NA	NA	NA	NA	NA	Not available, but developing a system for determining
UT	11,098 / 2,537	NA	0 / 0	NA	0 / 0	NA	156 / 0	NA	Fewer coming to prison, but population increasing
VT	7,000 / 2,000	NA	NA	NA	NA	NA	440 / 50	NA	Fewer coming to prison
VA	245 / 80	70% approx.	NA	NA	NA	NA	974 combined	70% approx.	Fewer coming to prison
WA	0 / 0	NA	63 / 40	50%	0 / 0	NA	0 / 0	NA	NA
WV	NA	NA	93 / 21	95%	Not available	Not available	NA	NA	NA
WI	0 / 0	NA	1,726 / 0	Not available	NA	NA	0 / 0	NA	Programs are alternatives to revocation
WY	147 combined	Not available	NA	NA	NA	NA	103.73	Not available	Fewer coming to prison

COMMUNITY CORRECTIONS: PARTICIPATION, *continued*

	PRE-INCARCERATION		WORK RELEASE		EDUCATIONAL RELEASE		OTHER SERVICES		Effect on Prison Population
	Men/Women	Completions	Men/Women	Completions	Men/Women	Completions	Men/Women	Completions	
BC	NA	NA	NA	NA	NA	NA	NA	NA	NA
MB	9,000 approx.	Not available	0 / 0	NA	0 / 0	NA	0 / 0	NA	Hasn't stopped increases
NB	171 / 90	Not available	NA	NA	NA	NA	850 combined	71%	Fewer coming to prison
NS	67300 combined	Not available	NA	NA	NA	NA	NA	NA	NA
ON	Not available	NA	Not available	NA	Not available	NA	Not available	NA	Fewer coming to prison
SK	3,748 / 873	75%	68 / 0[6]	80 %	88 / 8	80%	88 / 8	80%	Fewer coming to prison
YK	NA	NA	NA	NA	NA	NA	NA	7	NA

Notes:
1. CONNECTICUT: Program additionally has 226 men and 101 women in drug and alcohol treatment residential facilities.
2. IOWA: RWS (Release With Service) is a pretrial program for those not yet adjudicated by the court.
3. MICHIGAN: Work release or school release programs are not promoted or encouraged in the jails; rather, use of alternative forms of supervision are used for those already working or participating in educational programs outside the jails. Estimates are 60-80% successful.
4. NEW YORK: Community corrections is not included in the mandates of the state's department of corrections.
5. OHIO: Transitional control program enables offenders to be placed in halfway houses for last 180 days of their prison terms or parole eligibility with opportunity to seek services (housing, employment, etc.) before release.
6. SASKATCHEWAN: Community residential programs include mixed work, educational and transitional programs. The figures noted in those categories are not cumulative.
7. YUKON TERRITORY: Department of Justice currently is in the process of developing an alternative measures framework and protocol for post release programs.

PERSONNEL

Personnel in Adult and Juvenile Corrections

as of June 30, 1998

	ADULT CORRECTIONS								JUVENILE CORRECTIONS								
	Employees Total	White M	White F	Black M	Black F	Hispanic M	Hispanic F	All Others M	All Others F	Employees Total	White M	White F	Black M	Black F	Hispanic M	Hispanic F	All Others M	All Others F
AL	3,231	1,138	337	1,135	594	—	—	22	5	701	98	96	325	179	0	1	0	2
AK	1,256	—	—	—	—	—	—	—	—	376								
AZ	8,495	3,939	1,883	334	181	1,328	601	137	92									
AR	1,967	603	159	625	580	—	—	—	—									
CA	44,586	16,737	7,777	3,640	2,577	6,847	3,330	2,439	1,239	2,028	632	164	387	174	428	122	94	27
CO*	3,817	2,004	907	141	59	443	185	57	21	637	235	161	69	47	77	42	4	2
CT	6,331	3,319	1,072	930	413	435	112	33	17									
DE*	963	485	63	299	101	5	0	10	0									
FL	25,919	11,728	6,630	2,694	3,202	788	415	306	156									
GA	14,397	5,046	2,910	3,511	2,721	77	20	70	42									
HI	2,067	257	116	62	13	—	—	1,195	424	77	2	4	4	1	2	0	46	18
ID	1,321	835	380	11	6	44	19	18	8	208	124	75			2	4	2	1
IL	15,072	9,354	2,964	1,560	786	230	60	76	42									
IN	7,769	4,232	2,153	584	584	55	19	82	60									
IA	2,669	1,781	753	48	12	35	10	16	14	200	137	58	3	0	1	0	1	0
KS	2,852	1,856	708	124	48	54	12	31	19	528	—	—	—	—	—	—	—	—
KY	1,860	1,405	328	84	33	8	0	2	0	1,075	503	416	102	46	3	0	3	2
LA	4,829	2,719	401	1,169	524	16	0	0	0									
ME																		
MD	6,617*	2,741*	686*	1,750*	1,423*	4*	1*	7*	5*	1,481	344	295	378	434	10	6	4	10
MA	5,453	3,945	923	282	111	123	24	38	7									
MI	17,368	9,830	4,041	1,309	1,442	233	111	291	111	1,222	—	—	—	—	—	—	—	—
MN	3,710	2,085	1,360	79	41	24	17	71	33									
MS	3,538	710	455	1,041	1,317	4	0	4	2	474	59	113	155	147	—	—	—	—
MO	8,216	5,137	2,491	325	167	41	15	27	13	1,125*	363*	456*	150*	137*	6*	7*	5*	1*
MT	—	—	—															
NE	1,611	1,072	539	66	38	39	17	967	484	—								
NV*	2,020	1,226	456	107	62	82	18	52	17	256	135	108	10	0	1	0	2	0
NH*	885	682	192	2	1	4	0	2	2									
NJ	9,501	4,590	1,226	2,063	1,037	447	121	73	24	373	200	11	108	24	26	2	1	1
NM	2,017	523	228	56	5	912	249	34	10									
NY	21,857	17,696	969	1,550	722	661	106	136	17	3,539*	1,254*	813*	858*	376*	153*	54*	21*	10*
NC	17,594	7,602	3,336	3,578	2,613	96	33	231	105	1,259	277	206	471	291	6	1	3	4
ND	572	330	221	2	0	1	0	12	6									
OH	13,239	7,333	3,087	1,527	1,043	104	21	91	33	2,415	737	652	564	408	9	8	9	10
OK	5,201	2,694	1,412	268	251	50	32	337	157									
OR	2,617*	1,509*	680*	55*	19*	82*	27*	170*	75*	516	308	132	22	7	26	4	11	6
PA	12,675	9,004	2,430	761	317	85	29	32	17	1,094	570	245	173	98	4	2	2	0
RI	1,512	1,065	297	70	26	32	11	9	2									
SC	6,770	1,820	1,085	2,127	1,650	—	—	54	34									
SD	854	549	265	9	3	4	1	17	6									
TN	4,994	2,629	1,216	543	490	35	3	41	37	2,858	703	1,281	279	566	—	—	11	18
TX	27,283	11,173	4,012	3,625	3,509	3,664	1,062	168	70	4,400	1,059	987	747	801	491	275	25	15
UT*	850	699	96	11	3	22	7	9	3	1,186	536	381	80	14	41	23	85	26
VT*	925	667	258															
VA	11,934	4,435	2,208	2,739	2,424	70	19	32	7	2,240	504	571	612	517	19	15	2	0
WA	2,943	1,917	525	191	48	105	15	98	44	1,413	1,133[1]		137[1]		61[1]		82[1]	
WV*	1,150	810	319	10	8	3	0	0	0									
WI	8,151	4,305	3,071	261	187	104	75	87	61	300*	189*	26*	35*	35*	4*	5*	6*	
WY	336	203	85	2	0	26	12	6	2	160	88	52	—	—	12	7	1	—
Total	331,951	165,596	64,056	38,986	29,517	16,766	9,571	7,283	3,400	23,209	6,873	4,930	4,086	3,259	1,087	447	290	103
FBP	30,432	15,328	5,086	3,871	2,050	2,387	696	749	265									
Cook	2,996	—	—	—	—	—	—	—	—	507*	3*	18*	340*	140*	3*	3*		
NYC	13,111[1]	2,279*	133*	3,431*	3,170*	1,534*	380*	382*	92*	671	19	11	304	203	74	48	6	6
PHL	1,975	377	150	684	629	94	27	11	3									
MB	555	—	—	—	—	—	—	1	1									
VI	53	1	1	14	35	0	0	1	1	62*	0*	0*	39*	17*	5*	1*	0*	0*

Notes:
— Not available
* Data as of 6/30/97
1. Combines male and female

Correctional Officers in Adult Systems

as of June 30, 1998

		ETHNIC GROUP								RANK				Training Level		Ratio 1 CO Per No. of Inmates	Turn-over Rate
		White		Black		Hispanic		Other		Supervisory		Non-Supervisory					
	Total	M	F	M	F	M	F	M	F	M	F	M	F	M	F		
AL	2,268	811	61	994	386	—	—	16	—	257	62	1,564	385	—	—	8.8	—
AK	688	—	—	—	—	—	—	—	—	107*		581*		—	—	5.12	12
AZ	5,175	2,706	699	228	76	1,082	253	88	43	649	124	3,455	947	—	—	4.8	25.5
AR	1,942	591	153	619	579	—	—	—	—	398	32	812	700	—	—	5.6	39.8
CA	21,096	9,529	1,714	2,737	871	4,431	965	1,170	185	2,676	482	14,685	3,193	—	—	8	—
CO†	2,242	1,268	356	106	33	343	94	42		842	165	917	318			4.1	10
CT	4,393	2,462	353	820	283	377	67	25	6	359	65	3,300	642	25	2	3.71	5
DC	—	—	—	—	—	—	—	—	—	—	—	—	—	—	—	—	—
DE†	948	471	63	299	99	5	0	10	1	70	20	682	132	33	11	5.72	6
FL	15,134	8,127	2,413	2,051	1,680	551	106	167	39	3,695	946	7,201	3,292	—	—	4.38	30.3
GA	8,642	3,129	827	2,904	1,640	63	11	45	23	762	116	5,379	2,385	—	—	—	—
HI	1,138	159	33	40	9	—	—	768	129	223	32	744	139	—	—	3.24	—
ID	706	547	99	10	4	28	4	12	2	86	11	511	98	—	—	5.7	25.8
IL	8,969	6,641	884	890	327	134	30	51	12	1,316	118	6,400	1,135	—	—	5	5.2
IN	—	—	—	—	—	—	—	—	—	—	—	—	—	—	—	4	18
IA	1,604	1,263	253	25	9	30	8	11	5	128	27	1,201	248	—	—	4.59	9.38
KS	1,811	1,331	290	86	35	37	5	21	6	359	59	1,055	255	61	22	4.5	22.47
KY	1,821	1,375	323	80	33	8	0	2	0	295	40	1,170	316	—	—	—	22
LA	4,046	1,863	481	1,049	638	10	0	5	0	469	54	2,458	1,065	—	—	3	29
ME	—	—	—	—	—	—	—	—	—	—	—	—	—	—	—	—	—
MD†	4,923	2,282	240	1,470	922	2	0	6	1	935	203	2,824	960			4.01	17
MA	3,827	3,067	318	228	72	100	12	29	1	681	83	2,737	319	6	1	—	5
MI	10,268	6,889	1,370	829	688	182	54	205	51	1,095	235	7,010	1,928	—	—	4.3	4.2
MN	1,624	1,118	375	41	21	18	7	35	9	99	27	1,113	385	—	—	3.4	5.9
MS	2,433	326	154	904	1,043	3	0	2	1	325	112	815	947	95	139	5	—
MO	4,936	3,532	1,017	220	93	41	10	17	6	681	104	3,129	1,022	—	—	—	17.4
MT	386	—	—	—	—	—	—	—	—	56*	—	330*	—	—	—	—	—
NE	711	502	137	26	8	23	4	11	0	89	16	473	133	—	—	5.01	22.09
NV†	1,312	913	172	77	30	64	8	38	10	83	9	842	48	167	48	3.6	8.2
NH†	493	437	50	0	0	4	0	2	0	71	12	70	38	2		4.1	12.9
NJ	6,243	3,270	263	1,718	553	345	48	44	2	794	51	4,583	815	—	—	3.9	4.4
NM	1,047	281	41	36	1	638	40	10	0	302	18	663	64	—	—	3	18.9
NY	21,796	17,660	965	1,537	718	657	106	136	17	1,822	72	17,372	1,562	796	172	3.25	3.8
NC	10,204	4,723	876	2,756	1,535	75	26	160	53	1,364	249	6,350	2,241	—	—	2.989	20.2
ND	194	143	44	0	0	0	0	6	1	16	3	133	42	—	—	5	6
OH	8,428	5,223	1,252	1,185	602	83	10	60	13	785	126	5,766	1,751	—	—	6.5	15
OK	2,062	1,356	239	131	51	31	14	194	46	887	111	825	239	—	—	10	14.4
OR†	1,540	1,034	230	37	10	69	16	118	26	189	35	1,039	247			5	7
PA	7,312	6,095	419	563	138	65	11	16	5	1,341	104	4,753	367	645	102	4.9	4.3
RI	922	757	63	53	14	24	6	5	0	83	4	753	77	3	2	—	3.3
SC	4,474	987	348	1,756	1,129	0	0	37	17	841	278	1,912	1,199	27	17	4.91	22.5
SD	369	268	81	3	2	2	1	7	4	38	7	243	81	—	—	6.54	28
TN	2,726	1,716	357	370	198	28	23	28	6	579	80	1,563	504	—	—	4.6	34
TX	27,199	11,124	4,000	3,619	3,504	3,653	1,062	167	70	2,511	351	16,052	8,285	—	—	5.3	17.42
UT																	
VT†	416	371	45							43		328	45			3.13	12.5
VA	7,088	2,692	571	2,215	1,546	45	5	14	0	813	121	4,153	2,001	—	—	3.72	16.53
WA	2,927	1,908	520	191	47	105	15	97	44	362	75	1,574	395	365	156	4.62	—
WV†	705	588	100	12	5	0	0	0	0	61		539	105			3	10
WI	3,203	2,396	549	98	23	67	16	44	10	159	27	2,446	571	—	—	5	—
WY	263	163	53	2	0	25	12	6	2	32	6	162	61	2	0	5.6	21.6
Total	210,105	116,730	22,595	31,014	18,556	12,961	2,931	3,711	808	27,534	4,428	135,426	39,787	2,025	613	4.80	15.32
		139,325		49,597		15,892		4,519		31,962		175,213		2,638		(avg)	(avg)
FBP	12,918	7,310	750	2,393	643	1,356	152	273	30	1,898	300	9,434	1,275			8	9.53
Cook	2,828	—	—	—	—	—	—	—	—	292*	—	2,446*	—	90*	—	4	
NYC	11,408*	2,188†	125†	3,348†	3,109†	1,510†	371†	379†	9†	855†	200†	6,560†	3,490†	10†	5†	1.73†	4.9†
PHL	1,658	276	78	616	573	87	18	8	2	166	57	821	614	0	0	3.76	7.7
CSC†	12,355	7,704	4,651							211	16	3,963	1,064	15	4	2.86	2.6
AB†		735								8						2.7	
BC†	1,531																
MB	461	—	—	—	—	—	—	—	—	99*	—	362*	—			—	—
NF†	199	187	12							28	2	159	10			2.17	
PEI†	60	50	10													2.05	
VI	167	—	—	111	46	8	—	—	—	24	3	95	41	—	4	4	0.2

Notes:
— Not available
* Combines males and females
† Data as of 6/30/97

Jail and Detention Facility Staff

as of June 30, 1999

(Excludes States with Combined Jail/Prison Systems)

	ALL JAILS		SMALL		MEDIUM		LARGE		MEGA	
	Payroll	CO[1]	Payroll	CO	Payroll	CO	Payroll	CO	Payroll	CO
Alabama	985	706	67	30	343	278	399	256	176	142
Arizona	821	703	11	20	178	160	186	163	446	360
Arkansas	540	381	268	172	190	142	82	67	0[2]	0
California	12,724	7,080	21	19	731	512	10,100	5,556	1,872	993
Colorado	2,135	1,654	147	106	373	303	830	626	785	619
Florida	14,232	10,258	31	29	679	612	4,261	2,947	9,261	6,670
Georgia	3,926	2,368	102	73	1,074	867	893	657	1,857	771
Idaho	342	281	61	43	145	107	136	131	0	0
Illinois	1,533	1,237	107	96	663	547	763	594	0	0
Indiana	1,142	795	85	53	638	408	419	334	0	0
Iowa	804	613	460	374	78	65	266	174	0	0
Kansas	945	571	317	171	189	160	439	240	0	0
Kentucky	978	816	80	81	334	318	564	417	0	0
Louisiana	1,557	1,144	31	4	489	357	684	589	353	194
Maine	457	455	160	144	145	200	152	111	0	0
Maryland	1,753	1,301	0	0	269	196	1,009	769	475	336
Massachusetts	2,990	1,579	0	0	375	290	1,864	1,289	751	0
Michigan	3,528	2,459	159	117	591	512	839	648	1,939	1,182
Minnesota	1,368	1,095	322	307	530	421	516	367	0	0
Mississippi	499	353	185	104	242	184	72	65	0	0
Missouri	1,465	928	229	156	437	314	799	458	0	0
Montana	221	186	132	116	29	28	60	42	0	0
Nebraska	615	547	181	166	108	88	326	293	0	0
Nevada	599	842	42	43	163	108	223	160	171	531
New Hampshire	477	379	0	0	221	179	256	200	0	0
New Jersey	4,395	3,755	17	15	763	559	1,742	1,394	1,873	1,787
New Mexico	1,499	1,067	64	25	408	389	587	343	440	310
New York	15,415	4,563	76	84	1,288	797	3,633	1,804	10,418	1,878
North Carolina	2,112	1,794	159	136	832	708	884	768	237	182
North Dakota	184	164	126	113	58	51	0	0	0	0
Ohio	2,186	2,126	209	216	1,106	904	464	634	407	372
Oklahoma	928	780	159	95	203	141	237	221	329	323
Oregon	1,938	1,173	70	46	577	400	1,291	727	0	0
Pennsylvania	5,017	3,945	54	59	1,076	870	2,202	1,675	1,685	1,341
South Carolina	1,958	1,527	121	103	534	398	1,303	1,026	0	0
South Dakota	207	176	103	82	32	45	72	49	0	0
Tennesee	3,628	2,534	191	53	886	658	710	489	1,841	1,334
Texas	6,289	4,008	405	287	1,177	848	1,670	1,364	3,037	1,509
Utah	373	269	13	20	201	116	159	133	0	0
Virginia	5,241	3,598	282	204	1,758	1,389	3,201	2,005	0	0
Washington	2,231	1,626	81	42	321	179	672	529	1,157	876
West Virginia	328	280	26	38	116	92	186	150	0	0
Wisconsin	2,470	1,839	152	107	596	579	1,187	749	535	404
Wyoming	284	226	120	115	164	111	0	0	0	0
Total	113,319	74,181	5,626	4,264	21,310	16,590	46,338	31,213	40,045	22,114

Notes:
1. Not all correctional officers are reported within "total staff."
2. "0" entries mean either that there are no facilities in this category OR that the facility(ies) did not report staff figures.

Personnel in Juvenile Detention Facilities by Sex and Race

As of March 31, 1997

	TOTAL POPULATION			WHITE Not of Hispanic Origin		BLACK Not of Hispanic Origin		HISPANIC White and Black		ALL OTHERS	
	Total	Male	Female	M	F	M	F	M	F	M	F
AL	342	193	149	70	79	121	95	2	1		
AK	188	134	54	104	42	15	6	4	1	9	7
AZ	400	216	184	111	108	36	20	66	50	4	5
AR	155	78	77	64	55	14	20				2
CA	3,341	1,926	1,415	806	601	765	497	600	489	113	124
CO	14	10	4	4	2			6	2		
CT	119	76	43	39	21	29	18	8	4		
DE	108	71	37	26	16	44	21	1			
DC											
FL	509	329	180	81	57	226	133	21	2	1	1
GA	1,184	759	425	241	149	514	274	2		2	2
HI											
ID	122	72	50	70	47	1		1	3		
IL	987	582	405	208	149	338	142	24	12	10	3
IN	659	351	308	260	254	84	52	6	1	1	1
IA	178	90	88	65	80	23	7	1	1	1	
KS	553	289	264	206	209	70	44	15	9	3	1
KY	219	123	96	85	60	38	36				
LA	810	389	421	97	111	290	261	32	18		1
ME	63	44	19	42	19	1		1			
MD	140	63	77	13	21	50	56				
MA	139	109	30	59	25	27	3	21	1	2	1
MI	1,042	597	435	281	223	294	207	19	9	3	6
MN	572	331	241	297	225	26	14	2		6	2
MS	156	82	74	31	38	49	38				
MO	399	196	203	89	104	105	98	2	1		
MT	112	55	57	51	54	3		1			3
NE	151	79	72	49	58	24	12	5	2	1	
NV	130	89	41	49	34	31	5	7	3	1	
NH											
NJ	721	408	313	172	117	199	178	35	15	2	3
NM	257	142	115	47	43	12	6	80	60	3	6
NY	211	114	97	80	74	28	21	6	2		
NC	150	92	58	29	29	61	29	1		1	
ND	49	11	38	8	35					3	3
OH	1,241	701	540	396	334	289	198	11	4	5	4
OK	258	153	105	73	68	73	33	2	1	5	3
OR	616	421	195	350	161	28	12	25	9	18	13
PA	1,353	870	483	306	234	549	238	12	11	3	
RI	14	12	2	9	2	3					
SC	424	247	177	201	114	44	61	3			1
SD	174	90	84	82	83	5		1		2	1
TN	232	130	102	62	49	67	53			1	
TX	1,047	580	467	183	169	162	107	233	185	1	4
UT	89	52	37	46	34	2		1	1	3	2
VT	17	10	7	10	7						
VA	565	352	213	154	114	190	99	6	1	2	
WA	597	304	293	208	240	53	34	28	11	15	8
WV	109	65	44	43	41	13	2				
WI	148	80	68	66	59	10	4	1	4	3	1
WY	74	47	27	46	27	1					
Total	21,012	12,129	8,873	6,050	4,864	4,942	3,104	1,291	913	224	208

Note: Totals for above tables may not add up because of unavailable breakdowns for personnel.

1999 Salary Ranges in Adult Corrections for Selected Positions and Union/Association Affiliations

as of January 1999

Position	Starting Wage	Top Range	Median	Union Participation	Association Affiliation
AL				Union Local 1370; Laborers' International Union of North America	Alabama State Employees' Association Alabama State Correctional Association
Chief Administrator	79,000	Set by Governor			
CO at Entry	740 bi-weekly	1,305 bi-weekly	972 bi-weekly		
CO after 1 year	858 bi-weekly	1,305 bi-weekly	972 bi-weekly		
CO Captain or above	1,183 bi-weekly	1,792 bi-weekly	1,438 bi-weekly		
Industries Director	1,665 bi-weekly	2,537 bi-weekly	2,028 bi-weekly		
Warden/Superintendent	1,438 bi-weekly	2,731 bi-weekly	2,417 bi-weekly		
AK No Response					
AZ				AFSCME	Arizona Probation, Parole and Corrections Association American Correctional Association
Chief Administrator	80,000	120,000	120,000		
CO at Entry	20 604	20,604	20,604		
CO after l year	21 639	30,214	26,810		
CO Captain or Above	34,676	47,273	NA		
Industries Director	55,179	80,771	80,771		
Warden/Superintendent	48,627	73,882	73,882		
AR				Local 100; Self-Help Union; Arkansas Law Enforcement Union	Arkansas State Employees Association
Chief Administrator	102,280	102,280			
CO at Entry	18,860	35,614	25,593		
CO after 1st year	18 860	NA			
CO Captain or Above	25 856	48,872	35,067		
Industries Director	65,352	65,352			
Warden/Superintendent	35,387	66,837	48,038		
CA				California Corrections Peace Officers Association and 20 other unions	
Chief Administrator	5,972/mo.	6,584/mo.	6,271/mo.		
CO at Entry	7.04/hr.	NA	NA		
CO after 1st year	2,473/mo.	2,861/mo.	2,662/mo.		
CO Captain or Above	5,560/mo.	6,130/mo.	5,838/mo.		
Industries Director	7,052/mo.	7,627/mo.	7,405/mo.		
Warden/Superintendent	7,188/mo.	7,774/mo.	7,547/mo.		
CO No Response					
CT				AFSCME, CSEA, CEUI, A & R, New England Health Care	Connecticut Criminal Justice Association; American Correctional Association
Chief Administrator	Legislative Determination	NA			
CO at Entry	26,727				
CO after l year	29,696 (after 10 weeks)	38,652			
CO Captain or Above	48,853	62,666			
Industries Director	65,539	84,070			
Warden/Superintendent	60,580	106,377			
DE				AFSCME Local 247	Delaware Correctional Officers Association
Chief Administrator	69 600	NA	NA		
CO at Entry	22 241 + 1,560 hazard	NA	NA		
CO after 1 year	22,241 + 1,560 hazard	NA	NA		
CO Captain or Above	38,214	57,321	47,767		
Industries Director	43,88	65,829	54,857		
Warden/Superintendent	57,351	112,764	82,074		
DC No Response					

1999 SALARY RANGES IN ADULT CORRECTIONS FOR SELECTED POSITIONS, *continued*

Position	Starting Wage	Top Range	Median	Union Participation	Association Affiliation
FL					
Chief Administrator	No Equivalent Position	NA	NA	Florida Police Benevolent Association (PBA)	
CO at Entry	23,024	34,283	23,594		
CO after 1 year	Legislative determination	NA	NA		
CO Captain or above	28,598	43,806	38,103		
Industries Director	No Equivalent Position	NA	NA		
Warden/Superintendent	59,408 (1) 65,561 (11)	65,561 (1) 81,353 (11)	59,408 (1) 65,561 (11)		
GA	No Response				
HI				United Public Workers (uniform staff); Hawaii Government Employee's Association (professional and other staff)	Hawaii Criminal Justice Association; American Correctional Association
Chief Administrator	85,302 by statute				
CO at Entry	23,676	28,956	25,620		
CO after 1 year	25,620	31,416	27,756		
CO Captain or Above	35,652	44,232	38,856		
Industries Director	83,400 by statute				
Warden/Superintendent	52,380	78,948	60,000 approx.		
ID				AFL-CIO (but may not be currently in effect)	
Chief Administrator	29.57/hr.	43.48/hr.	34.78/hr.		
CO at Entry	10.97/hr.	16.13/hr.	12.91/hr.		
CO after 1st year	Legislative Determination	NA	NA		
CO Captain or Above	20.47/hr.	30.11/hr.	2.08/hr.		
Industries Director	25.57/hr.	37.60/hr.	30.08/hr.		
Warden/Superintendent	23.63-27.72/hr.	34.75-40.77/hr	27.80-32.62/hr.		
IL				AFSCME	INA (Illinois Nurses Association), ISEA (Illinois State Employees Association) Illinois Correctional Association; American Correctional Association
Chief Administrator	3,599/mo.	8,457/mo.	6,028/mo.		
CO at Entry	2,200 (trainee)-2,398/mo.	2,398/mo.	NA		
CO after 1st year	2,494/mo.	2,942/mo.	2,689/mo.		
CO Captain or above	2,612/mo.	5,709/mo.	4,161/mo.		
Industries Director	3,599/mo.	8,457/mo.	6,028/mo.		
Warden/Superintendent	3,599/mo.	8,457/mo.	6,028/mo.		
IN				AFSCME; Unity Team	Indiana Correctional Association; American Correctional Association
Chief Administrator	60,814	99,658			
CO at Entry	18,850	30,758			
CO after 1 year	18,850	30,758			
CO Captain or Above	23,556	36,062			
Industries Director	45,968	74,802			
Warden/Superintendent	33,956	82,342			
IA				AFSCME; Iowa United Professionals	State of Iowa Employees
Chief Administrator	68,700	96,800	82,750		
CO at Entry	27,165	28,558	NA		
CO after 1st year	28,558	33,862	31,210		
CO Captain or Above	36,733	46,425	41,579		
Industries Director	64,500	81,536	73,018		
Warden/Superintendent	67,641	85,446	76,544		
KS				AFSCME; KAPE (Kansas Association of Public Employees	American Correctional Association; Kansas Correctional Association
Chief Administrator	46,238	65,062	51,002		
CO at Entry	20,176	28,413	22,256		
CO after 1 year	21,774	NA	NA		
CO Captain or Above	31,283	44,034	34,507		
Industries Director	51,002	71,760	56,202		
Warden/Superintendent	53,539	58,989	5,3797		

	Position	Starting Wage	Top Range	Median	Union Participation	Association Affiliation
KY	Chief Administrator	5,750/mo.	11,500/mo.	8,625/mo.	NA	
	CO at Entry	1,438/mo.	2,607/mo. (can exceed)	1,981/mo.		
	CO after 1 year	1,510/mo.	Same	Same		
	CO Captain or Above	1,820/mo.	3,500/mo.	2,660/mo.		
	Industries Director	3,590/mo.	6,494/mo.	5,274/mo.		
	Warden/Superintendent	3,949/mo.	6,663/mo.	5,772/mo.		
LA	Chief Administrator	Set by Legislature	6,250/mo.	Set by Legislature	AFL-CIO; AFSCME; Local 969 of New Orleans; Louisiana Association of Educators; Probation and Parole Officers Association	Louisiana Council on Criminal Justice; American Correctional Association
	CO at Entry	1,277/mo.	2,109/mo.	1,693/mo.		
	CO after 1 year	1,423/mo.	2,257/mo.	1,812/mo.		
	CO Captain or Above	1,791/mo.	2,958/mo.	2,375/mo.		
	Industries Director (incl. farming operation)	3,771/mo.	6,227/mo.	4,999/mo.		
	Warden/Superintendent	3,293-4,942/mo.	5,439-8,162/mo.	4,366-6,552/mo.		
ME	Chief Administrator	55,120	81,037	66,789	AFSCME "93"	
	CO at Entry	20,354	25,503	22,255	SEIU, Maine State Employees Union	
	CO after 1 year	21415	NA	NA		
	CO Captain or Above	27061	37,128	30,867		
	Industries Director	29,786	41,246	34,050		
	Warden/Superintendent	50,523	70,637	58,282		
MD	Chief Administrator	77,860	95,466	90,060	AFSCME-Teamsters; AFSCME: AFT of AFL-CIO	Maryland Criminal Justice Association; American Correctional Association
	CO at Entry	23,279	29,917	23,279		
	CO after 1 year	26,258	32,123	29,244		
	CO Captain or Above	32,906	42,821	38,949		
	Industries Director	57,568	70,509	66,535		
	Warden/Superintendent	62,073	76,049	71,756		
MA	No Response					
MI	Chief Administrator	32.65/hr.	46.93/hr.	43.45/hr.	MSEA; MCO; MPES; LOCAL 31-UAW; AFSCME; OPEIU; MAGE	Michigan Correctional Association; American Correctional Association
	CO at Entry	12.13/hr.	17.29/hr.	15.02/hr.		
	CO after 1st year	14.53/hr.	18.05/hr.	16.11/hr.		
	CO Captain or Above	17.39/hr.	24.28/hr.	21.06/hr.		
	Industries Director	32.65/hr.	46.93/hr.	43.45/hr.		
	Warden/Superintendent	29.97/hr.	44.01/hr.	40.75/hr.		
MN	Unable to respond at this time					
MS	Chief Administrator	Legislative Determination	NA	NA		Miss. Association of State Employees; State Employees Alliance of Miss. (voluntary membership)
	CO at Entry	1,409/mo.	1,423/mo.	1,409/mo.		
	CO after 1st year	1,473/mo.	1,858/mo.	1,497/mo.		
	CO Captain or Above	2,207/mo.	3,272/mo.	2,463/mo.		
	Industries Director	Separated by State Statute	NA	NA		
	Warden/Superintendent	3,858-4,877/mo.	4,733-5,778/mo.	4,122-5,664/mo.		
MO	Chief Administrator	7,377/mo.	Unclassed/no range	NA	AFSCME; SEIU (Service Employees Int'l Union)	Missouri Correctional Association; American Correctional Association
	CO at Entry	1,647/mo.	2,312/mo.			
	CO after 1 year	1,708/mo.	3,206/mo.			
	CO Captain or Above	2,139/mo.	4,942/mo.			
	Industries Director	3,074/mo.	NA			
	Warden/Superintendent	2,719-3,489/mo.	4,329-5,778/mo.			

1999 SALARY RANGES IN ADULT CORRECTIONS FOR SELECTED POSITIONS, *continued*

	Position	Starting Wage	Top Range	Median	Union Participation	Association Affiliation
MT	Chief Administrator	52,670	77,702	60,004	Montana Federation of Women's Prison Employees Local 4699; MFTE Local 4700	
	CO at Entry	16,796	23,484	18,722		
	CO after 1 year	18,219	25,575	21,504		
	CO Captain or Above	23,343	33,177	28,147		
	Industries Director	33,025	47,723	40,000		
	Warden/Superintendent	36,137	77,702	55,072		
NE	Chief Administrator	Negotiable	NA	NA	NAPE (Nebraska association of Public Employees)	Nebraska Correctional Association; American Correctional Association
	CO at Entry	21,858	29,144	24,981\		
	CO after 1st year	23,497	29,144	24,981		
	CO Captain or Above	33,248	46,547	39,898		
	Industries Director	44,403	62,164	53,284		
	Warden/Superintendent	41,305	57,827	49,566		
NV	Chief Administrator	Unavailable	Unavailable	80,919	AFSCME; SNEA	Nevada Correctional Association
	CO at Entry	25,797	34,486	29,163		
	CO after 1 year	27,993	37,566	31,693		
	CO Captain or Above	42,794	58,502	48,881		
	Industries Director	55,901	77,051	64,090		
	Warden/Superintendent	53,441	73,567	61,224		
NH	Chief Administrator	62,519	78,686			
	CO at Entry	22,142	25,678			
	CO after 1 year	23,806	27,674			
	CO Captain or Above	33,894	39,863			
	Industries Director	43,690	51,865			
	Warden/Superintendent	56,044	72,206			
NJ	Chief Administrator	NA	115,000	NA	Policemen's Benevolent Association	New Jersey Chapter Association; American Correctional Association
	CO at Entry	34 070	NA	NA		
	CO after 1st year	37,478	52,126	44,802		
	CO Captain or Above	56,637	78,963	67,800		
	Industries Director	NA	72,719	NA		
	Warden/Superintendent	77,500	88,108	82,804		
NM	Chief Administrator	75,642	NA	NA	AFSCME	New Mexico Correctional Association American Correctional Association
	CO at Entry	17,727	24,708	20,590		
	CO after 1 year	18,348	24,708	20,590		
	CO Captain or Above					
	Industries Director	52,273	83,775	68,024		
	Warden/Superintendent	45,614	68,423	57,019		
NY	Chief Administrator	NA	NA		Council 82 (security personnel); CSEA (Civil Service Employees' Association); PEF (Public Employees' Federation)	New York Corrections and Youth Services Association; American Correctional Association
	CO at Entry	25,029 (1st 6 most)	26,436 (2nd 6 most)			
	CO after 1 year	30,570	39,680			
	CO Captain or Above	50,513	54,020			
	Industries Director	76,687	97,061			
	Warden/Superintendent	62,324-80,332 2	78930- 109,861			
NC	Chief Administrator	20,744	33,265		None	American Correctional Association; North Carolina Correctional Association
	CO at Entry					
	CO after 1 year					
	CO Captain or Above	26,508	43,489			
	Industries Director					
	Warden/Superintendent	31,640	72,134			

	Position	Starting Wage	Top Range	Median	Union Participation	Association Affiliation
ND	Chief Administrator	Negotiable	NA	NA	None	
	CO at Entry	1,443/mo.	2,338/mo.	1,891/mo.		
	CO after 1 year	1,718/mo.	2,801/mo.	2,260/mo.		
	CO Captain or Above	2,266/mo.	3,516/mo.	2,837/mo.		
	Industries Director	2,721/mo.	4,434/mo.	3,578/mo.		
	Warden/Superintendent	3,603/mo.	5,874/mo.	4,739/mo.		
OH	Chief Administrator	NA	NA	NA	AFSCME; AFL-CIO; Ohio Civil Service Employees Association	Ohio Corrections and Court Services Association; American Correctional Association
	CO at Entry	25,979	31,554	28,122		
	CO after 1 year	27 331	31,554	28,122		
	CO Captain or Above	33155	41,434	37,128		
	Industries Director	NA	NA	NA		
	Warden/Superintendent	59,530	78 208	64,293		
OK	Chief Administrator	80,000	80 000	80,000	None	Oklahoma Public Employees Association; Oklahoma Correctional Association; American Correctional Association
	CO at Entry	16,672	21,780			
	CO after 1 year	17,805	23,299			
	CO Captain or Above	26,013	34,305			
	Industries Director	56,392	56,392	56,392		
	Warden/Superintendent	50,923	59,923	59,923		
OR	Chief Administrator	5,551/mo.	7,806/mo	6,678	AFSCME; OPEN (Oregon Public Employees Union)	AOCE (Association of Correctional Employees)
	CO at Entry3	2,175-2,220/mo.	NA	NA		
	CO after 1 year	2,283-2,331/mo.	2,866-2,923/mo			
	CO Captain or Above	2,664/mo.	3,570	3,117		
	Industries Director	4,563/mo.	7,806	6,184		
	Warden/Superintendent	4,141/mo.	9,491	6,972		
PA	Chief Administrator	105,000	105,000	105,000	AFSCME: PSSU: CIVEA: SEIU: FOSCEP: PASMHP: PNA	
	CO at Entry 1st year	22,304	22,304	22,304		
	CO after 1 year	23 618	44,503	35,886		
	CO Captain or Above	39,516	66,368	50,616		
	Industries Director	55,766	84,773	67 991		
	Warden/Superintendent	72,646	99,482	84 773		
RI	Chief Administrator	73,423 (Asst. Dir.)	82,751	78 087	RI Brotherhood of correctional Officers, Howard Union of Teachers RI Probation and Parole Association AFSCME, IBPO	
	CO at Entry	25,808	36,606	31,207		
	CO after 1 year	26,704	36,606	31,665		
	CO Captain or Above	35,828	50,299	43,064		
	Industries Director	45,134	51,164	48,149		
	Warden/Superintendent	72,455	NA	NA		
SC	Chief Administrator	122,404	NA	NA	None	South Carolina Correctional Association; American Correctional Association
	CO at Entry	18,706	30,767	25,112		
	CO after 1 year	20,233	30,767	25,112		
	CO Captain or Above	32,403	51,271	41,837		
	Industries Director	47,968	75,908	61,938		
	Warden/Superintendent	46,120	73,008	59,564		
SD	Chief Administrator	Set by the Governor	NA	NA	None	
	CO at Entry	8.17/hr	12.25/hr	10.21/hr		
	CO after 1 year	5% salary increase	NA	NA		
	CO Captain or Above	1,147/bi-weekly	1,720/bi-weekly	1,434/bi-weekly		
	Industries Director	1,434/bi-weekly	2,151/bi-weekly	1,793/bi-weekly		
	Warden/Superintendent	2,128/bi-weekly	3,192/bi-weekly	2,660/bi-weekly		

1999 SALARY RANGES IN ADULT CORRECTIONS FOR SELECTED POSITIONS, *continued*

	Position	Starting Wage	Top Range	Median	Union Participation	Association Affiliation
TN	Chief Administrator	7,045/mo.	7,045/mo.	7,045/mo.	AFSCME (At Brushy Mountain Correctional Complex only)	Tennessee State Employees Association
	CO at Entry	1,442/mo.	2,309/mo.	1,876/mo.		
	CO after 1 year	Admin. policy determined	NA	NA		
	CO Captain or Above	2,095/mo.	3,348/mo.	2,722/mo.		
	Industries Director	TRICOR board policy	NA	NA		
	Warden/Superintendent	3,817/mo.	6,116/mo.	4,967/mo.		
TX	Chief Administrator	NA	127,000 (Legis.)	NA	AFSCME; CEC (Correctional Employees Council #7)	American Correctional Association; Texas Correctional Association; SSCA; ASCA; TPEA; TSCA; TIFA (Texas Inmate Families Assoc.)
	CO at Entry	17,724	22,548	20,544		
	CO after 1st year	23,976	25,524	NA		
	CO Captain or Above	28,032	36,132	32,082		
	Industries Director	NA	61,217	NA		
	Warden/Superintendent	46,200	60,165	53,352		
UT	No Response					
VT	Dir., Correctional Svce	25.02/hr	39.82/hr		VSEA (Vermont State Employees Association)	
	CO at Entry	10.37/hr COI	16.41/hr			
	CO after 1 year	10.95/hr COII	17.33/hr			
	CO Captain or Above	13.72/hr	21.75/hr			
	Industries Director	19.80/hr	31.45/hr			
	Warden/Superintendent	19.80/hr	31.45/hr			
VA	No Response					
WA	Chief Administrator	Governor Appointment	93,000 approx.		Teamsters; Marine Masters and Mates; Federation of State Employees	Washington Correctional Association; American Correctional Association
	CO at Entry	23,976	30,264	26,928		
	CO after 1 year	25,116	NA	NA		
	CO Captain or Above	47,916	58,572	53,244		
	Industries Director	63,408	81,180	71,724		
	Warden/Superintendent	58,872	75,372	66,612		
WV	Chief Administrator	NA	55,000	NA	AFSCME; Communication Workers of America	W. Virginia Association of Corrections Employees
	CO at Entry	18,120	26,256	21,192		
	CO after 1st year	18,129	26,256	21,192		
	CO Captain or Above	24,648	36,852	28,772		
	Industries Director	29,712	48,336	39,072		
	Warden/Superintendent	34,032	55,344	44,748		
WI	Chief Administrator	46,487	Set by Governor		WSEU (Wisconsin State Employment Union), except crafts, nurses, engineers, fiscal and staff services	Wisconsin Correctional Association; American Correctional Association
	CO at Entry	10.21/hr.	14.188/hr.			
	CO after 1 year	10.84/hr	Service length basis			
	CO Captain or Above	16.87/hr	26.268/hr.			
	Industries Director	23,700	47,400			
	Warden/Superintendent	23,700	47,400			
WY	Chief Administrator	5,416/mo	6,000/mo	NA		
	CO at Entry	1,535/mo	2,566/mo	1,803/mo		
	CO after 1st year	1,635/mo	2,566/mo	1,803/mo		
	CO Captain or Above	2,115/mo	3,913/mo	2,731 /mo		
	Industries Director	1,837/mo	3,398/mo	2,478/mo		
	Warden/Superintendent	4,233/mo	5,400/mo	NA		
FBP	Unable to respond at this time					

	Position	Starting Wage	Top Range	Median	Union Participation	Association Affiliation
MB	Chief Administrator	67,273	80,380	73,450	MGEV represents the correctional work force, excluding management positions	
	CO at Entry	26,149	NA	NA		
	CO after 1st year	31,826	36,187	33,333		
	CO Captain or Above	37,335	44,535	40,727		
	Industries Director	43,008	52,029	47,225		
	Warden/Superintendent	47,022	68,200	61,306		
NB	Chief Administrator	62,712	70,330	66,482	Canadian Union of Public Employees; New Brunswick Nurses Union	New Brunswick Public Employees Association
	CO at Entry	27,144	29,816	28,275		
	CO after 1 year	28,275	32,019	28,993		
	CO Captain or Above	31,863	37,577	34,574		
	Industries Director					
	Warden/Superintendent	39,702	59,930	49,816		
NF	Chief Administrator				NAPE (Newfoundland Association of Public Employees); Newfoundland and Labrador Nurses Union	Newfoundland Correctional Officers, maintenance and operations, general service, and nurses
	CO at Entry	23,945	26,606			
	CO after 1 year	31,207	38,701			
	CO Captain or Above		51,866			
	Industries Director					
	Warden/Superintendent					
NS	Chief Administrator				Nova Scotia Government Employees Union	
	CO at Entry	30,929	36,272	33,508		
	CO after 1 year	32,613	39,982	35,393		
	CO Captain or Above	37,070	43,662	40,273		
	Industries Director					
	Warden/Superintendent	35,064	60,324	47,694		
ON	Chief Administrator	88,230 (District Admin.)	98,610		OPSEU (Ontario Public Service Employees Union)	Association of Management; AMAPCEO (Administrative and Professional Crown Employees of Ontario)
	CO at Entry	17.39/hr	18.87/hr			
	CO after 1 year	18.72/hr	21.39/hr	20.22/hr		
	CO Captain or Above	44,637	52,276			
	Industries Director	55,025	67,882			
	Warden/Superintendent	61,143	72,038			
SK	Unable to participate at this time					
YK	Chief Administrator	NA	NA		Public Service Alliance of Canada; Yukon Employees Union	
	CO at Entry	41,266	47,513	44,387		
	CO after 1 year	42,916				
	CO Captain or Above	49,817	57,514	53,665		
	Industries Director					
	Warden/Superintendent	65,220	84,698	74,959		

Notes:
1. ARKANSAS: After successful completion of BCOT class, an additional 5.5% hazardous duty pay is added, plus an additional 11% if working in maximum security area.
2. NEW YORK: Starting Wages and Top Wages for wardens/supervisors are factored on number of inmates supervised. 3 OREGON: Wages for Entry Level Correctional Officers and for those after one year vary, based on participation with the AFSCME or AOCE unions.

1999 Fringe Benefits Offered in Adult Corrections

as of January 1999

	Cost of Living	Merit Increase	Leaves of Absence	Holidays	Vacation	Retirement Plans	Percent State Paid
AL	Legislature determines, last, 8% October, 1998	2 1/2 step; 2 steps can be dictated by annual evaluation	na	13 (after 90 days)	13	State, SS and Deferred (deferred is employee's choice)	3.1 1; changes yearly
AK	No Response						
AZ	Legislature determines	Up to 5%, depending on amount allocated to agencies	NA	10	12-21, depending on years of service	State, SS and Deferred	5%, DOC only
AR	Legislature determines	None	None	11 plus 1 1	12 plus 7 hours/mo. over 20 years	State, SS and Deferred	10%
CA	Varies by bargaining unit and excluded employee status	Varies by bargaining unit and excluded employee status	Varies by bargaining unit and excluded employee status	12	Varies by bargaining unit and excluded employee status	State, SS and Deferred	Varies by bargaining unit and excluded employee status
CO	No Response						
CT	Based on contracts and legislative actions classification	Based on contracts and legislative actions	Based on contracts and legislative actions	12	12-20, depending on years of service and	State, SS and Deferred	Dependent on plan
DE	3% (general increase)	Flat $400	NA	11 plus 2 (if elections)	15-21, depending on years of service	State Plan only	Varies, based on highest 3-year compensation and length of State service
DC	No Response						
FL	Legislature determines annually	NA	FMLA (Family and Medical Leave Act of 1993)	10	15-21, depending on years of service and classification	State and SS; deferred compensation is optional	27.10%
GA	No Response						
HI	None	None	21 (sick leave only)	13	21	State Plan and SS (deferred available at employee's expense)	100%
ID	None	Based solely on legislative decision	3.7 hours per pay period for sickness	10	96-169 hours, depending on years of service	State, with options for deferred compensation and 401 K	61% gross, regular; 85% if classified as law enforcement
IL	3% through AFSCME contract	0-5%, reviewed annually	1 day/month, accumulated indefinitely in case of illness	12; 13 in election years	10-25 depending on services	State, SS and Deferred	9.528%
IN	4-8%, depending on annual salary	None since 1988	3 personal; 9 sick per year	13	12 plus 3-13 bonus days depending on years of service	State Plan and SS (deferred available at employee's expense)	3% plus additional amount to composite pension fund
IA	3%	5%	365 days, barring extensions	9	10-25, depending on years of service	State, SS and Deferred	3.8%

	Cost of Living	Merit Increase	Leaves of Absence	Holidays	Vacation	Retirement Plans	Percent State Paid
KS	1.5%	2.5% annually	Up to 2 days in a 7-day week, or as granted and applicable in Kansas Administrative Regulations	9, plus one discretionary	12-21, depending on years of service	State, SS and Deferred	4%
KY	NA	5% annual increment	12 (sick days) up to one year, medical and two years without pay	11.5	12 (7.5 hours per month)	State, SS and Deferred (Compensation)	18.66%
LA		4% on employee's anniversary date	FMLA available depending on situation, up to 12 weeks	8, but Governor may proclaim 3 additional	Approx. 8 hours/month up to 16 hours, depending on years of service	State, SS and Deferred	12.4%
ME	2%, thru collective bargaining agreements	4.5% approximately		12	8-16 hours/month, depending on years of service	State Plan only	
MD	Based on Governor's budget proposal with legislative approval	$300 award for outstanding rating	Variable, depending on reason (medical, military personal)	11, plus 6 personal leave days	10-25, depending on years of service	State, SS and Deferred	Variable, depending on plan in effect
MA	No Response						
MI	3%	None	13 (sick days)	13	13-33 depending on years of service	State, SS and Deferred	3-7% depending on available options
MN	Unable to respond at this time						
MS	Determined annually by the Legislature		12 (Major Medical)	10	18, including personal leaves	State and Deferred	None
MO	Directed by Governor as appropriated by Legislature	NA	15 (sick days)	13	15-21 depending on years of service	State, SS and Deferred	12.58%
MT	NA	NA		10	21	State SS and Deferred	
NE	2%	None	120, military; 12-30, sick	12	12-25 depending on years of service	State SS and Deferred	1.56%
NV	3%	5%	Up to one year, with approval of appointing authority	11	depending on years of service	State Plan only	10% on joint contribution plan; 18.75% on employer only plan; 14.75% on CO's if joint plan; 28.5% on CO's if employer-only plan
NH	2-5%, determined by the Legislature	1%	As needed	12	12-24 depending on years of service	State Plan and Deferred	5.52%
NJ	Dependent upon effective contract	Approximately 5% of 1st step of salary range	1/2 to 1 day up to 1 calendar year; 15 days per year thereafter	13	12-25 depending on years of service	Public Employee's Retirement System (PERS)	Joint pay
NM	None	3 5%	Up to one year without pay	10	10-20	State Plan and Deferred (CO's); State Plan, SS and Deferred (Others)	25.72% (CO's) and 16.59% (Others)

1999 FRINGE BENEFITS OFFERED IN ADULT CORRECTIONS, *continued*

	Cost of Living	Merit Increase	Leaves of Absence	Holidays	Vacation	Retirement Plans	Percent State Paid
NY	NA	NA	NA	12	13 plus 1 bonus for each year of service up to 7 years 20 thereafter	State Plan only; optional Deferred Compensation Plan	Varies
NC	2%, when funded by the Legislature	Legislature discretionary	Only with Division approval	11	12-25	State, SS and Deferred	8.5% of total
ND	$30/month across the board		Determined based on reason for absence	10.5	1-2 per month depending on years of service	State and SS, with Deferred as an option	5.12% (At this time, state also pays 4% employee's amount)
OH	3%	NA	Variable	10	10, after one year of service	State Plan only	13.3%
OK	NA	NA	10-25 depending on years of service	10	10-25 depending on service	State, SS and Deferred	12%
OR	3%, negotiated annually	4.75% 7-step range	8 hours/month (sick)	3	15-27 depending on years of service	State and SS, with Deferred as an option	Unknown
PA	Negotiated in collective bargaining process or awarded by Governor's office	Varies, granted on longevity, from 1-2.5% annually	Various (parental, sick, civil, bereavement, etc.)	11	7-26, determined by bargaining agreement	State, SS and Deferred	7.53% to age 50; 5.61% to age 60
RI	3%, 1998 contract	5-20% depending on years of service	15 days per calendar year	10	10-28 depending on years of service	State Plan only	
SC	2.5%	NA	NA	12, plus one in election year	15-30 depending on years of service	State, SS and Deferred	9.73%
SD	3%; plus 2.5% movement to job worth, if applicable	NA	15 with no maximum accrual	10	15-20 depending on years of service	State, SS and Deferred	8%
TN	Determined by salary administration policy	4.5% (Equity Increase) may be recommended by appointing authority	Subject to approval of appointing authority, on unpaid basis	11	12, increasing depending on years of service	State, SS and Deferred	100%
TX	Legislatively mandated	Legislatively mandated	At discretion of Executive Director	14 3	7-14 hours per month, depending on years of service	State, SS and Deferred	6%
UT	No Response						
VT	3% to 6-30-99	3-7% for continued outstanding performance		12, with two of them "floaters"	12 for new hires to 4 years	State Plan and Deferred	1 0%
VA	No Response						
WA	2%	NA	Up to 15 days without pay; variable thereafter	11	12-22, depending on years of service	State, SS and Deferred	7.5%
WV	$756 across the board by legislative action	5-10%	6 months medical, without pay	14	1 1/4-2 days per month, depending on experience	State Plan only	9.5%

	Cost of Living	Merit Increase	Leaves of Absence	Holidays	Vacation	Retirement Plans	Percent State Paid
WI	Grid basis, according to contract	3% for supervisors	6 months-3 years; more with approval	9 plus 3 personal	80-200 hours depending on length of service	State Plan and SS; Deferred is an option	18.4%-protective; 14.2%-general
WY	Legislatively mandated	Up to 7.5%, depending on available funds	Available, but discretionary	9	12-24 depending on years of service	State, SS and Deferred	11.25%
FBP	Unable to respond at this time						
MB	Negotiable	3.8% approximately	Approved on individual basis	11	3-6 weeks depending on years of service	State Plan only	50%
NB	.5-1%, via bargaining process	4.8-9%, depending on union/non-union class	5 days - 2 years, depending on reason	11	15-25 depending on years of service	State Plan only	50%
NS	2.2%	2.4%	18 for general illness	11	15-25 depending on years of service	State Plan and SS	Variable and based on years of service
ON	None since 1992	3%	Variable upon request and approval	11	15-30 depending on years of service	Provincial Canada Pension Plan and Old Age Security Plan	
SK	Unable to respond at this time						
YK	None	4% on anniversary date	6 days	12	$1\frac{2}{3} - 2\frac{11}{12}$ days depending on years of service	Public Service Super Annuation Plan	Varies, depending on years of service

Notes:
1. ARKANSAS: Governor optionally adds a day at Thanksgiving
2. HAWAII: Prior to 1985, employees could not opt for a contributory plan to retire at a higher rate.
3. TEXAS: Four of the days require skeleton crews and can be accrued and used as vacation time.

Types of Insurance Offered in Adult Corrections—1999

as of January 1999

	Types of Insurance by Agency	Percentage Paid by Employee	Percentage Paid
AL	Health; Life and Health/Disability are optional	$320/month	None for Health; dependent coverage offered at employee's expense
AK	No Response		
AZ	Health, Life, Long/Short-term Disability; Medical & Child Care Reimbursement; Vision; Dental	Based on plan code in effect, per region	Based on plan code in effect, per region
AR	Health; Life	$130.50 bi-weekly for Health	Varies by plan for both Health and Life
CA	Health; Life; Dental; Long-term Disability; Vision; Legal Services	Varies by bargaining unit and exclusions	Varies based on employee status
CO	No Response		
CT	Health/Dental; Life; Disability	Total for employee on Health/Dental; a portion for dependents	All elected coverage under Life and Disability
DE	Health; Dental; Life	Based on plan selected	Depends on plan selected
DC	No Response		
FL	Automobile; Disability; Legal; Life; Prepaid College; Accident/Disability; Cancer; Dental; Hospital Supplement; Tuition-free College Courses	100% state Health and state Life for superintendents; 80-85% for state Health and state Life for others	15-20% for state Health and state Life for general employees
GA	No Response		
HI	Comprehensive Health Fund and Life	100%	None
ID	Health; Vision, Dental: Life; Supplemental Life; Short-, Long-term Disability; Family Medical Leave Act (FMLA)	Up to $269.84/month for Health; Life; Disability; FMLA	Dental, available dependent coverage for Health; Supplemental Life
IL	Health (Indemnity, HMO, POS); Dental (Indemnity or Managed Care); Vision; Life	Depends on plan selected	Varies based on annual salary
IN	Health; Dental; Vision	Varies for Health; 100% for Dental and Vision for employee and dependents	Variable Health for both employee and dependents
IA	Variable	Depends on plan and collective bargaining agreement	Depends on plan and collective bargaining agreement
KS	Life; Disability; Health (varies by zip code)	Varies for Health	100% for Life and Disability
KY	Health (two plans depending on level); Life	Up to $207/month for Health	100% for Life and for all dependent coverage
LA	Health; Life; Dental, Accident; Cancer	50% for Health - up to $103/month single coverage; up to $203/month for family coverage	50% for Health; 100% for Life, Dental, Accident and Cancer
ME	Health; Dental; Basic Life; Deferred Compensation	$141.92 (combined for Health and Dental)	40% for family plan
MD	Variable Health; Dental; Prescriptions; Life; Vision	80% for Health	20% for Health; 100% for options
MA	No Response		
MI	Health; Life; Dental; Vision; Long-term Disability (rates for all insurance varies, depending on sick leave balances)	95%-Health; 100%-Life; 95%-Dental; 50%-Disability	5%-Health; 5%-Dental; 50%-Disability
MN	Unable to respond at this time		
MS	Health; Life; Dental; Cancer; Burial; Café	100% for Health; up to annual salary for Life	Additional Life up to double annual salary; 100% for Dental, Cancer, Burial and Café
MO	Health; Optional and Basic Life; Dental; Vision	$163-Health; $4.35-Basic Life	Any premium above State contribution
MT	Health (Blue Cross and HMO's); Vision	100% ($250/month) for basic plan	Vision and all family coverage
NE	Health; Vision; Dental; Life; Supplemental Life; Long-term Care	79% for Health	21% for Health; 100% for options
NV	Medical; Dental; Vision; Life	100%	100% for dependents
NH	Health; Dental; Life; Disability	100% for Medical and Dental; 85% for options	15% for options

	Types of Insurance by Agency	Percentage Paid by Employee	Percentage Paid
NJ	Health; Dental; Prescription Drugs; Vision; Deferred Compensation; Life; FMLA; Disability	Shared for all but Deferred	Shared for all but Deferred
NM	Health; Life; Dental; Vision; Legal	60-75%, depending on salary	25-40%, depending on salary; 100% for Legal
NY	Health (Blue Cross/Blue Shield, United Health Care, Value RX, HMO's); Dental; Vision (Council 82 members)	90% for individuals; 75% for family	10%; 25% for family
NC	Basic packages, with menu of HMO options	100%	100% for dependents
ND	Health; Life	100% for Health; $1,300 for Life	100% of any Supplemental Life
OH	Health; Dental; Vision	90%	10%
OK	Health; Dental; Life; Disability, plus comprehensive Health/Dental through network of HMO's. Optional coverage is available.	100% for employee and portion for dependents	Balance of dependents and 100% of options
OR	Health, Life; Dental; Short/Long-term Disability	Benefit Dollars program, depending on class of employment and AOCE or AFSCME category guidelines.	
PA	Group Life; Self-Insured Workers Compensation	100%	None
RI	Choice of seven plans	100%	None
SC	Basic plans	$2,160, per employee, per year, depending on the plan in effect	
SD	Health; Life; Vision; Dental; Major Injury; Disability	100% for Health and Life	100% of Vision, Dental, Major Injury, Disability and all dependent coverage
TN	Health (HMO's and POS); self-insured state plan	80%	20%
TX	Health; Dental; Term Life; Accidental Death/Dismemberment; Dependent Life; Long/Short-term Disability	100% by state for employee; 50% for dependents	Varies based on optional coverage in effect
UT	No Response		
VT	Health	80%	20%
VA	No Response		
WA	Health; Dental; Life; Disability	$341.75 flat rate	Difference, based on the plan
WV	PETA (Public Employees Insurance Agency); HMO's	Portion, depending on policy and employee wages in effect	
WI	Health; Life; Income Continuation; Accidental Death and Dismemberment (EPIC)	The lessor of 90% of standard plan or 105% of the lowest qualifying HMO in each county	Varies according to plan selected
WY	Health; Dental; Life	Maximum of $175/month for single/family coverage	Any amount over $175
FBP	Unable to respond at this time		
MB	Group (employee and dependents); Medical Extended; Dental; Vision	50%	50%
NB	Basic Life; Supplementary Life; Dependent Life; Long-term Disability; Accidental Death and Dismemberment; Health; Dental	100% for Basic and Supplemental Life, AD&D and Disability; 50% for Dependent Life and Dental; 75% for Health	50% for Dependent Life and Dental; 25% for Health
NF	Group Blue Cross; Dental; Long-term Disability; Dental	50% as negotiated per employee/employer contract	
NS	Life; Long-term Disability; Workers Compensation		
ON	Supplemental Health; Vision; Hearing; Dental; Life; Dependent Life/Supplemental Life	100% for Supplemental Health, Dental, Life (including dependents); 60% for Vision and Hearing	40% for Vision and Hearing
SK	Unable to participate at this time		
YK	Extended Health, including Vision; Dental; Long-term Disability; Death Benefits	80% for Extended Health; Up to $75/year per family Dental; Equal to 70% of monthly earnings for Disability; Up to two times adjusted annual earnings upon death	

Beginning Salaries of Probation and Parole Officers
County and Local Systems
As of February 1, 1998

	Responses/ Total Field	Under $13,000	$13,001– $20,000	$20,001– $25,000	$25,001– $30,000	$30,001– $35,000	$35,001– $40,000	$40,001– $45,000
AL	4/66			25%	50%	25%		
AK	*							
AZ	11/24			18%	82%			
AR	19/40	21%	63%	11%	5%			
CA	17/110			20%	20%	20%	20%	20%
CO	*							
CT	*							
DE	*							
DC	*							
FL	*							
GA	2/19			100%				
HI	*							
ID	3/40	18%	34%	66%				
IL	25/84		18%	68%	5%	9%		
IN	86/143		12%	55%	18%	12%	3%	
IA	*							
KS	8/8			50%	50%			
KY	*							
LA	2/6		50%	50%				
ME	*							
MD	*							
MA	*							
MI	80/97		3%	21%	28%	31%	14%	3%
MN	19/60			29%	59%	12%		
MS	*							
MO	11/19			100%				
MT	8/20		38%	25%	38%			
NE	*							
NV	8/11				25%	75%		
NH	*							
NJ	*							
NM	*							
NY	46/62		4%	25%	38%	21%	13%	
NC	*							
ND	*							
OH	83/132		17%	50%	33%			
OK	4/5			100%				
OR	35/101				50%	50%		
PA	77/102	3%	29%	52%	17%	2%		
RI	*							
SC	*							
SD	*							
TN	*							
TX	20/47		5%	53%	42%			
UT	*							
VT	*							
VA	*							
WA	46/72		6%	24%	24%	29%	6%	12%
WV	8/14		50%	40%	10%			
WI	5/47			60%	40%			
WY	3/5			66%	33%			

* Statewide systems

Probation/Parole Officers—
Minimum Educational Requirements
County and Local Systems

As of February 1, 1998

	Response/ Total Field	HS	ASSOC	BA	BA+Exp	MA	Other
AL	4/66			66%	34%		
AK	*						
AZ	11/24			100%			
AR	15/40	53%		33%	20%		
CA	40/110	7%	7%	67%	13%		7%
CO	*						
CT	*						
DE	*						
DC	*						
FL	*						
GA	2/19			50%	50%		
HI	*						
ID	3/40	33%			64%		
IL	52/84			88%	13%		
IN	86/143			97%	3%		
IA	*						
KS	8/8			100%			
KY	*						
LA	2/6			100%			
ME	*						
MD	*						
MA	*						
MI	76/97			57%	39%	4%	
MN	36/30			71%	29%		
MS	*						
MO	21/48			100%			
MT	12/20	8%		42%	42%	8%	
NE	*						
NV	8/11			50%	50%		
NH	*						
NJ	*						
NM	*						
NY	45/62			46%	54%		
NC	*						
ND	*						
OH	75/132	2%	31%	48%	10%		
OK	3/5			50%	50%		
OR	31/101			50%	50%		
PA	71/102			85%	11%		4%
RI	*						
SC	*						
SD	*						
TN	*						
TX				53%	42%		
UT	*						
VT	*						
VA	*						
WA	43/72		6%	59%	35%		
WV	12/32			92%	8%		
WI	2/47			50%	50%		
WY	2/5			50%	50%		

* Statewide systems

Mandated Training for Probation/Parole Officers and Child Care Workers
County and Local Systems
As of February 1, 1998

(Numbers reflect percent of respondents who answered affirmative out of total respondents answering question)

	HOURS REQUIRED FIRST YEAR				HOURS REQUIRED AFTER FIRST YEAR				Line Staff Used As Trainers (Percent)
	1–20 (Percent)	21–40 (Percent)	41–60 (Percent)	60+ (Percent)	1–20 (Percent)	21–40 (Percent)	41–60 (Percent)	60+ (Percent)	
AL		25		75		25	75		50
AK*									
AZ		50	10	40	100				100
AR		46	23	31		100			58
CA		8		92		100			75
CO*									
CT*									
DE*									
DC*									
FL*									
GA		50		50	50	50			50
HI*									
ID		100			100				100
IL	14	82		4	75	25			65
IN	82	15		3	85	15			26
IA*									
KS		13							50
KY*									
LA	50	50			50	50			10
ME*									
MD*									
MA*									
MI	43	14		43	33	17		50	33
MN	6	93			6	93			53
MS									
MO	20					20			60
MT	20	80			60	40			75
NE*									
NV		75		25		50	50		100
NH*									
NJ*									
NM*									
NY	5	50		45	5	82		14	75
NC*									
ND*									
OH	35	55	5	5	41	53		6	56
OK		100				100			66
OR		75		25		100			100
PA		90	6	4		98	2		58
RI*									
SC*									
SD*									
TN*									
TX		89		11		100			29
UT*									
VT*									
VA*									
WA	14	50		36	21	71		7	44
WV		90	10		22	67	11		83
WI		100			100				50
WY*									

* Statewide systems